CAMBRIDGE STUDIES IN EARLY MODERN HISTORY

Editors

J. H. ELLIOTT   H. G. KOENIGSBERGER

CAMBRIDGE STUDIES IN EARLY MODERN HISTORY

Edited by Professor J. H. Elliott, The Institute for Advanced Study, Princeton, and Professor H. G. Koenigsberger, King's College, London

The idea of an 'early modern' period of European history from the fifteenth to the late eighteenth century is now widely accepted among historians. The purpose of the Cambridge Studies in Early Modern History is to publish monographs and studies which will illuminate the character of the period as a whole, and in particular focus attention on a dominant theme within it, the interplay of continuity and change as they are represented by the continuity of medieval ideas, political and social organization, and by the impact of new ideas, new methods and new demands on the traditional structures.

The emperor and his chancellor

A study of the imperial chancellery
under Gattinara

JOHN M. HEADLEY

Professor of History,
University of North Carolina at Chapel Hill

CAMBRIDGE UNIVERSITY PRESS

Cambridge
London   New York   New Rochelle
Melbourne   Sydney

CAMBRIDGE UNIVERSITY PRESS
Cambridge, New York, Melbourne, Madrid, Cape Town, Singapore, São Paulo, Delhi

Cambridge University Press
The Edinburgh Building, Cambridge CB2 8RU, UK

Published in the United States of America by Cambridge University Press, New York

www.cambridge.org
Information on this title: www.cambridge.org/9780521244442

First published 1983
This digitally printed version 2008

A catalogue record for this publication is available from the British Library

Library of Congress Catalogue Card Number: 82-4525

ISBN 978-0-521-24444-2 hardback
ISBN 978-0-521-09019-3 paperback

TO COSMOS

Contents

Acknowledgments

Like so many contemporary students of the Renaissance I received at the inception of my research the encouragement and generous support of Paul Oskar Kristeller, who helped to identify and put me in contact with the relevant branch of the Gattinara family. In this respect I wish to thank those persons and members of the family, cited in the Introduction who were instrumental in the opening of the family archive. I am most grateful to my colleague and friend Ronald G. Witt of Duke University for reading the manuscript and for making helpful suggestions. And, while I assume full responsibility for any errors in the transcription of the documents appearing in the appendices, I gladly take this opportunity to recognize the aid of several colleagues whose expert opinion on some of the more difficult readings I occasionally consulted: Dr Laetitia Yeandle of the Folger Shakespeare Library; Professors Edward Montgomery and G. Mallary Masters and Dr William Ilgen of the University of North Carolina at Chapel Hill. Furthermore at a critical moment Dr Peter Marzahl of the University of Konstanz kindly provided me with a copy of that document which appears here as Appendix IV. To the directors and their staffs of the archives and libraries cited in this work, as well as to the European Law Division of the Library of Congress, the Humanities Room, Wilson Library, University of North Carolina and to Dr Carlo Revelli of the Bibliothece Civiche di Torino, I wish to acknowledge their indulgent assistance. I am indebted also to the John Simon Guggenheim Memorial Foundation for a year's grant in 1974, to the Folger Shakespeare Library for a term's fellowship in 1976, to the American Council of Learned Societies for a summer's grant in 1977 and for several instances of timely support from my own department and the Research Council of the University of North Carolina at Chapel Hill.

In having this work accepted for the Cambridge Studies in Early Modern History I was fortunate both to come under the scrutiny and to make the friendship of its distinguished editors. I particularly wish to thank Helmut

Acknowledgments

G. Koenigsberger for his careful efforts in the improvement of the manuscript.

Finally to my wife, who always sees the larger picture, I can but say that with the publication of this research the vibrant presence of Mercurino, who with her forebearance long dominated the household, now must come to rest, embalmed in print.

JMH
Chapel Hill, North Carolina

Abbreviations

ACA   Archivo de la Corona de Aragón – Barcelona
AGRB   Archives Générales du Royaume de Belgique – Brussels
AGS   Archivo General de Simancas
ASV   Archivio di Stato di Vercelli
BMB   Bibliothèque Municipale de Besançon
BNM   Biblioteca Nacional de Madrid
BRT   Biblioteca Reale di Torino
HHSA   Haus-, Hof- und Staatsarchiv – Vienna
RAH   Real Academia de la Historia – Madrid

Introduction

The historical endeavor often pursues a curious, apparently inexplicable path. Some subjects receive prompt, continuous, even inordinate attention; others, for lack of a sympathetic public, readily accessible source material or of proper conceptualization, remain buried, ignored indefinitely, perhaps forever. When there is a conjunction of all three impediments – the absence of an audience which has some sort of vested interest in the subject, the unavailability of important sources and the inability to fashion effective lenses to perceive the dimensions of the issues involved, then the historical exposition of the subject surely falters and is left unachieved. In the case of Charles V's Grand Chancellor all three of these factors have conjoined to obstruct the historical recovery of this major Renaissance figure. For only in these terms can we begin to understand why historians have ignored until the last few decades a man who appears to be one of the leading statesmen of early modern Europe and an outstanding architect of Habsburg hegemony.

Certainly since the seventeenth century Mercurino de Gattinara has not lacked biographical sketches that emphasized an aspect of his career or local studies made by a regional patriot or enthusiast.[1] Yet the decisive step

---

[1] The first study of Gattinara appears to have been a Kiel University dissertation of the eighteenth century, written by Philip Frederick Hane, which constitutes a part of his *Historia sacrorum* (Kiel, 1728) that was intended to serve as a highly schematized *Handbuch* for the systematic representation and study of Protestant church history. In accordance with the Melanchthonian tradition Gattinara was here presented as a would-be Protestant. I am indebted to Dr Birgitte Hvidt of Det Kgl. Bibliotek, Copenhagen, for a reproduction of its copy, that of Kiel University Library having been destroyed in the last war. The Munich University Library has a Leipzig, 1729 copy, 4° H. eccl. 1969 (2). In March and May 1753, M. de Courbezon read two papers to the Academy of Besançon on Gattinara (BMB, MS. 1102, II, fols. 402–31; and Fonds de l'Académie, MS. 5, fols. 131ᵛ–42). There followed Carlo Tenivelli's 'Vita di Mercurino da Gattinara', an unpublished manuscript composed in 1781 and read in the Accademia di Torino on 12 December 1782 (BRT, Misc. 114.6). The first real biography of Gattinara was that of Carlo Denina, *Elogio storico di Mercurino di Gattinara Gran Cancelliere dell'imperadore Carlo V e cardinale di S. Chiesa*, Piemontesi Illustri (Turin, 1783), III, which still has merit. Only in the nineteenth century did a number of limited studies of Gattinara begin to appear: M. Huart, *Le Cardinal Arborio de Gattinara Président du Parlement de Dole et chancellier de Charles-Quint* (Besançon, 1876); A. Le Glay, 'Etudes

Introduction

toward a more critical and comprehensive knowledge of the Piedmontese statesman occurred only with the archival investigations of Carlo Bornate at the beginning of the present century and his editing of Gattinara's autobiography together with some of his memoranda and correspondence.[2] Nevertheless, Bornate's achievement could well have remained unnoticed had it not been for the researches of Karl Brandi two decades later in preparing his great study of Charles V. Gattinara's published papers together with those Brandi himself found in the archives of Vienna had a decisive impact upon his understanding of the formative period in the emperor's reign.[3] From his pages, Gattinara emerges as the political educator of Charles and the man who provided the vision of and the justification for a world empire. Whatever attention Gattinara has received by historians is largely attributable to the researches of Brandi and the widespread recognition of his masterpiece.

The historiographical field broadened and produced a nationalist reaction in the case of the Spanish scholar Ramón Menéndez Pidal, who insisted on the Spanish rather than Italian origins for the idea of an empire standing for peace among Christians and war against the infidel; he asserted the concept of a *universitas christiana* as opposed to the apparently more aggressive *monarquía universal* of Gattinara.[4] Contemporaneous with Brandi's investigations were the researches of Fritz Walser in the archives of Simancas. His work culminated in the posthumously published study on the Spanish central administration in which the author saw Gattinara as responsible for the reorganization of the Iberian governments in the early 1520s.[5] A quite different aspect of Gattinara's far-ranging activity came into focus with Marcel Bataillon's *Érasme et l'Espagne*: Gattinara was

biographiques sur Mercurino Arborio di Gattinara', *Société Royale des Sciences...de Lille. Mémoires, 31* (1847), 183–260; Gaudenzio Claretta, 'Notizie per servire alla vita del Gran Cancelliere di Carlo V, Mercurino di Gattinara', *Memorie della Reale Accademia delle Scienze di Torino, 47* (1897), 67–147 and Gaudenzio Claretta 'Notice pour servir à la vie de Mercurin de Gattinara, Grand Chancelier de Charles-Quint d'après des documents originaux', *Mémoires et Documents Publiés par la Société Savoisienne d'Histoire et d'Archéologie*, 2nd Series, *12* (1898), 245–344. Both Le Glay and Claretta are important for the documents published therein. Although quite incomplete, the best bibliography for Gattinara can be found in Karl Brandi, *Kaiser Karl V*, II, *Quellen und Erörterungen* (Darmstadt, 1967), p. 43.

[2] Carlo Bornate (ed.), 'Historia vite et gestorum per dominum magnum cancellarium...con note, aggiunte e documenti', *Miscellanea di Storia Italiana, 48* (Turin, 1915) 233–568. (Hereafter this work will be cited as Bornate, 'Vita' or 'Doc.').

[3] Karl Brandi, *The Emperor Charles V*, tr. C. V. Wedgwood (London, 1954). The first German edition appeared in 1937.

[4] Ramón Menendez Pidal's article, 'La idea imperial de Carlos V', first appeared in the *Revista Cubana, 10* (1937) and has since seen several different versions. I am using here the Madrid 1955 edition published in conjunction with three other essays by the same author. See pp. 9–35, esp. 16–21.

[5] Fritz Walser, *Die spanischen Zentralbehörden und der Staatsrat Karls V* (Göttingen, 1959). Published posthumously, this work has been reorganized, supplemented and completed by Rainer Wohlfeil who in places is as much the author as Walser.

2

Introduction

seen as an avid correspondent and friend of Erasmus, providing crucial support within the government for the spread of Erasmian humanism in Spain.[6] Finally in a work of comparable scholarly stature M. Giménez Fernández revealed Gattinara as giving decisive and enthusiastic support to the efforts of Las Casas for reforming the administration of the Indies.[7]

Although the Grand Chancellor figures centrally in the respective studies of four major scholars of the early modern period, there has apparently been no attempt to present anything like a comprehensive view of Gattinara. The late recognition which he has achieved is itself a problem that cannot be satisfactorily explained simply by the considerable difficulty of the sources that are scattered from Uppsala to Seville, from London to Naples in Latin, French, Italian and Spanish. These technical problems are obviously not insurmountable. That the Gattinara family archive remained closed until this past year has certainly been a considerable deterrent for anyone attempting to understand the family background and early career of Gattinara, and for rooting him in his Piedmontese setting. Nevertheless, for purposes of a political biography, the Belgien section of the Haus-, Hof-und Staatsarchiv (HHSA) at Vienna offers the most important body of material supplemented by more memoranda, remonstrances and correspondence found at Brussels (AGRB), Simancas (AGS) and Madrid (RAH). Of notable significance is that fragment of Gattinara's own archive represented by the *Mazzo* Miscellanea politica del secolo XVI, in the Biblioteca Reale di Torino (BRT). For his earlier career prior to becoming Grand Chancellor in October 1518 are later sixteenth-century copies of valuable documents at the Bibliothèque Municipale de Besançon (BMB), supplemented by other materials at Turin which pertain to his work as President of Burgundy (Franche-Comté). A major collection of some 320 letters at the Archives du Nord (Lille), constituting the correspondence with Margaret of Austria in the period 1507–18, concerns his diplomatic activities for the dynasty, culminating in the settlement of Charles' succession to the Iberian kingdom, his mission to Spain (July 1510 to April 1511) and his stormy administration of the free county of Burgundy. Furthermore, a fair proportion of his papers have long been available in the great British publications of the calendars of state papers. Finally, on matters pertaining to Spanish colonization and the New World and American affairs, his signature, which appears on so many of the royal *cédulas* during these years, leaves a trail that must be traced through the Indiferente General section of the Archivo General de Indias.[8]

For understanding what has so long prevented a comprehensive study

[6] Marcel Bataillon, *Érasme et l'Espagne* (Paris, 1937), *passim*.
[7] Manuel Giménez Fernández, *Bartolomé de las Casas* (Seville, 1960), II, *passim*.
[8] Cf. *ibid.*, 282–3, 1245, 1254–72, 1280–6.

3

Introduction

of the Grand Chancellor, a more basic difficulty needs to be sought. To apprehend the world of Gattinara one needs those imperial and dynastic perspectives which Brandi himself elucidated and sought to maintain.[9] Indeed, a biographer of Gattinara would encounter the same problems confronting one of Charles V in attempting to free himself from national categories and attain a supranational perspective. More than anything else it would appear to be the propensity for understanding modern European history in national categories that has allowed this part Italian, part Burgundian but thoroughly Habsburg statesman to be overlooked. Given the Whig interpretation of history, by no means limited to British historiography, whereby the past is read in terms of the present to the detriment of the historical context, an intellectual barrier would prevent the recovery of such imperial perspectives. Particularly forbidding for the Italian historian is the emotional obstacle of dealing with the period of Spanish and Habsburg domination of the peninsula. Indeed, there is precious little in this dynastic servant – more responsible than any other single individual in the retinue of Charles V for laying the foundations of Habsburg hegemony, first in Italy and then in Europe – that would recommend him to the eye of an Italian patriot. One has only to wander through the city of Turin today to perceive something of this attitude: while Machiavelli receives a splendid avenue, Guicciardini a fine concourse and the cultural and political heroes of the Risorgimento and beyond are suitably commemorated, each with his corner plaque providing name, date and professional endeavor, for the unwary visitor who hastens to the outskirts of the city, naively expecting the Grand Chancellor to be similarly celebrated by that street designated with the family name, he will discover instead a pathetic alley, faceless, nameless, indifferent to the individual members of that family that had been so securely established by the great Mercurino. Turin, a city rich in monuments, lacks and is unlikely to have a monument to its past Habsburg affiliations.

In fairness to the ignoring of Gattinara by many modern Italian historians and historians of Italy and to the extreme difficulty they have had in coping with the historical realities represented by such a man, it is appropriate to consider the nationality of our subject in this most un-national age. The term 'Italianità' has been used to connote a feeling or awareness of belonging to a certain cultural group characterized by a common language, literature, set of customs and history.[10] Gattinara would only dimly qualify, if at all, as a champion of *Italianità*. In the first place, the lands of the Duke of Savoy were more under French than Italian cultural

---

[9] Cf. Brandi, *Emperor*, p. 91.
[10] Vincent Ilardi, 'Italianità' among some Italian intellectuals in the early sixteenth century', *Traditio*, *12* (1956), 342.

4

Introduction

influence at the beginning of the sixteenth century and Piedmont was a backwater of the Italian Renaissance. Gattinara's thought was not untouched by the values of humanism, as evinced in his definition of nobility, and he could allude to Sallust and the others; but his Latinity smacked more of the lawyer and of scholasticism than it did of classical influences and would cause the fastidious, condescending Erasmus to sniff ever so slightly.[11] Secondly, in accepting the presidency at Dole in 1508, he shortly afterwards bought the ill-starred Chevigny estate in Franche-Comté and became a Burgundian subject of Margaret. For not entirely political reasons he studiously affected after 1513 a Burgundian origin to his family.[12] The reacquisition of the duchy of Burgundy was long central to his plans and negotiations and he could even consider the exchange of Milan in order to obtain it.[13] His very devotion to the principles of honor and reputation, so central for understanding his unswerving loyalty to the Habsburg dynasty, suggests more the chivalric ethos of the Burgundian court than the culture of the Italian Renaissance with its emphasis upon *virtù*.[14] On the other hand, the remonstrance of September 1514 to the Emperor Maximilian reveals an intellectual entertainment of humanist notions of justice and nobility as they apply to the legal profession.[15] Yet at least down to the period of his chancellorship, when after 1524 the Erasmian influence becomes preeminent, Gattinara's personal deportment seems to have been shaped more by the Burgundian chivalric ethos than by the new currents of humanism. At no time does *Italianità* of any sort assert itself.

Notwithstanding these arguments, Gattinara's pronounced affection and concern for Italy are undeniable and exert a central influence upon his efforts to guide imperial policy. On more than one occasion, but particularly before embassies from Italy, he would identify himself assertively as an Italian.[16] The formidable witnesses of both Guicciardini and Contarini represent him as conscientiously seeking to ameliorate the condition of Italy

[11] See Gattinara's remonstrance to Margaret of Austria in Claretta, 'Notice', pp. 277–8. Cf. P. S. Allen *et al.*, eds., *Opus epistolarum Des. Erasmi Roterodami* (Oxford, 1906–58), IV, 479.

[12] Le Glay, 'Études', p. 197; Claretta, 'Notizie', pp. 71–4 *et passim*. Claretta seems to be alone in raising the problem of Gattinara's patriotism, which he associates with his property interests in Italy. For Gattinara's perpetuation of the myth of his Burgundian ancestry, see Bornate, 'Vita', p. 237 and the editor's footnote.

[13] See *Calendar of Letters, Despatches and State Papers relating to the Negotiations between England and Spain preserved in Archives of Simancas and elsewhere*, eds. G. A. Bergenroth, Pascual de Gayangos *et al.* (London, 1866), II, 630–8 for the emperor's instructions to De la Roche 14 May 1524 which bear the marks of Gattinara's presence. Cf. also Bornate, 'Doc.', p. 470 for Gattinara's consulta of September 1525.

[14] Walser, *Zentalbehörden*, p. 174.

[15] 'Remonstrances de Messire Mercurin de Gatinare [sic], Président de Bourgongne faictes a Maximilian I Empereur sur les traverses causées à sa personne et au Parlement par le Marschal de Bourgongne' (BMB, Collection Chifflet, CLXXXVII, fols. 116–34).

[16] *Calendar of State Papers and Manuscripts existing in the Archives and Collections of Venice*, ed. Rawdon Brown (London, 1869), III, no. 401.

5

in a period of Spanish domination.[17] The shrewd Venetian ambassador recognized him basically as Italian. But he then went on, somewhat uncharitably, to add that while Gattinara had no particular liking for Venice, he entertained a great affection for the Duke of Milan, who, apparently with the emperor's knowledge and at his goading, bestowed an estate on Gattinara from which the chancellor derived a yearly income of 6000 ducats.[18] In fact, Gattinara had definite landed interests in northern Italy and would later seek to consolidate his scattered fiefs into a single estate in the area of Masserano and Crevacuore.[19] Undoubtedly it is partly as a reaction to the devastation suffered in and around the *borgo* of Gattinara during the campaign of 1523 that the Grand Chancellor, never one to mince words, can in July 1525 speak so forcefully to Charles:

> For the abuses that your troops commit are indeed so abominable that Turks and infidels would not do them and instead of naming you liberator of Italy they will be able to say you have introduced the greatest and most excessive tyranny that ever was. For neither the Goths nor the Lombards nor Attila, who was named *flagellum dei*, who for a long time tyrannized Italy, ever committed such cruelties.[20]

The sack of Rome evoked no such passionate reaction on the part of this, at best, north Italian, preoccupied with the acquisition of the twin cities of Genoa and Milan in order that his master might possess the gateway to the peninsula and the bastions for his domination of Italy and thus of the world.[21] Instead there is the cool, calculated advice as to how the emperor should extricate himself from this new predicament.[22] Despite the enormous political and ideological import of Italy in Gattinara's thought and diplomacy, it has little bearing upon the question at issue – the degree and quality of national consciousness evident in his personal life – and need not be rehearsed here.

By the last quarter of the twentieth century the dissolution of the conceptual and emotional barriers obstructing any study of Gattinara is

---

[17] For Contarini see *Cal SP Ven.*, III, nos. 956, 1064; for Guicciardini see his *Storia d'Italia*, ed. Silvana Seidel Menchi (Turin, 1971), Bk XVI, Chap. 14.

[18] Eugenio Albèri, ed., *Relazioni degli ambasciatori veneti al senato* (Florence, 1840), II, 56: Contarini to the senate 16 Nov. 1525. Cf. Bornate, 'Doc.', pp. 446–7: Francesco Sforza to Gattinara, 24 April 1525; Claretta, 'Notizie', pp. 70–5.

[19] On this point see Claretta, 'Notizie', pp. 107–20, esp. p. 111. Cf. Gattinara's statement to the emperor in his remonstrance of 1522 in Claretta, 'Notice', p. 316.

[20] Cf. AGRB (PEA), 1471 (4), fols. [15–15ᵛ]/[20–20ᵛ]. The documents in the fourth folder of bundle 1471 are not numbered, but taking into account those documents preceding this very important remonstrance of Gattinara to the emperor, one arrives at a foliation that runs from 14 to 24ᵛ. Unfortunately this investigator found the order within this particular document disturbed. Consequently in referring to what will be called the Brussels remonstrance I will give the correct number of the folio first (i.e. [15–15ᵛ]) and the existing order, as of 1974, after it (i.e. [20–20ᵛ]).

[21] HHSA (Belgien), PC 68, fols. 22–22ᵛ. A partial transcript of this important memorandum appears in Ernest Gossart, *Espagnols et Flamands* (Brussels, 1910), pp. 250ff.

[22] Bornate, 'Vita', p. 348; HHSA (Belgien), PA 94, fols. 451–52ᵛ; cf. Brandi, *Quellen*, p. 185.

Introduction

made possible by developments within the historical profession. A less partisan attitude to the issues of the age, a greater comprehensiveness and sympathy for the context, an enhanced sensitivity to the past all afford the historian the possibility of reapproaching the problem of this part Piedmontese, part Burgundian Renaissance nobleman, this late medieval lawyer, imperial counsellor, dynastic servant, statesman, bureaucrat. Not two decades have passed since the eminent historian Giuseppe Galasso remarked, in surveying the historical research on Charles and his empire, that the real need is for studies of the men around the emperor and above all an updated biography of Gattinara. [23]

Since Galasso's trumpet call to the task, some progress has been made in examining aspects of Gattinara's career and thought. The first in the field was a Novarese scholar, Giovanni Barbero,[24] writing shortly after the 500th anniversary of Gattinara's birth, who noted the deafening silence with which that event was celebrated and attributed it to the belief that Gattinara appeared to be lacking in modernity and realism – what the American undergraduate would call 'relevance'. In his highly suggestive study he correctly observed that for Italy the political realities of this pre-national period moved around the poles of universalism and particularism, and the apparent anomaly of Gattinara with his imperial idealism was in fact all too pertinent and realistic to the Italy of the twenties and its future – far more relevant it might be added than the much acclaimed proto-national appeal of Machiavelli or the diplomatic adventurism of Guicciardini which led from the League of Cognac to the cataclysm of Rome's sack.

This transcendence of the national perspective and increased sensitivity to the polarity between the local or provincial and the universal or supranational both have their role in the work and world of Mercurino de Gattinara. And in our own time the recovery of this perspective would be promoted by regional and international interests that ultimately removed those barriers preventing the historical penetration to a hitherto obscured world. Briefly, we need to address the existence of these poles in Gattinara's political experience before turning to the reasons for the recent transformation of an otherwise indifferent or even hostile public and the opening of the last cache of archival material to investigation.

As President of Burgundy from 1508 to 1518 Gattinara assumed responsibility for the administration of Franche-Comté and the maintenance of justice throughout the province. Striving to reorganize and cleanse his

[23] Giuseppe Galasso, 'L'opera del Brandi e alcuni studi recenti su Carlo V', *Rivista Storica Italiana*, 74 (1962), 93–119. Since the time that the following section was written, a short biography of Gattinara has appeared, written by Franco Ferretti: *Mercurino di Gattinara, un Maestro di politica* (Gattinara, 1980), most valuable for his background and early years.
[24] Giovanni Barbero, 'Idealismo e realismo nella politica del Gattinara, Gran Cancelliere di Carlo V', *Bollettino Storico per la Provincia di Novara*, 58 (1967), 3–18.

7

Introduction

own parlement at Dole, he aroused local suspicions. In trying to enforce a rigorous justice upon a restless, intractable nobility, he incited a segment of that nobility to seek his removal, if not by death, by appealing first to the Emperor Maximilian in 1514 and then definitively to his daughter Margaret at Malines in 1516. Gattinara's actions during these years reveal the prejudices and self-esteem of the doctrinaire and of the contemporary legal profession, trained in Roman law and bent upon asserting *la chose publique* as well as affirming the preeminence of their office and their kind. At the time his fall from the presidency proved a bitter experience, but judged in terms of later decisions and admonitions as Grand Chancellor, the stormy experience in Franche-Comté imparted to Gattinara a healthy respect for the customs and institutions of individual provinces and territories.[25]

In the defense of his administration before the Emperor Maximilian, Gattinara adduced one issue that requires our attention here: when insisting upon the preeminence of the civil over the military he expresses some current attitudes concerning the office of chancellor and the magistracy in general. His argument moves in the context of the late Roman Empire and assumes the terminology of Roman law and its current interpreters who associated the *praefectus praetorio* with the contemporary chancellor and the *praefectus militum* with the office of constable. Despite the fact that both the post-Constantinian empire and the majority of sixteenth-century jurists gave precedence to the constable and the military officialdom, Gattinara urges the reverse: namely, that the chancellor and the civil officialdom have preeminence, for the praetorian prefect in his civil function is the *consiliarius principis*. Asserting that the *milites armati* are only serviceable to princes in time of war, while the *milites togati* are at all times necessary he continues:

The robed knights, however, are at all times able to counsel and be useful because of the legal science with which they are imbued [and] which has arisen for the sake of ruling, governing, defending the human race and for promoting the aids to a prosperous and upright life, without which no sovereign rule nor commonwealth is able to be... It is not to be doubted that the robed soldiery are to receive preeminence – at least the counsellors who are at the side of the prince and those who exercise the offices in the name of the prince [and] who are members and part of his very body.[26]

---

[25] For Gattinara's experience in Franche-Comté see the present author's 'The conflict between nobles and magistrates in Franche-Comté, 1508–1518', *Journal of Medieval and Renaissance Studies, 9* (1979), 49–80.

[26] 'Remonstrances de Messire Mercurin de Gatinare President de Bourgongne faictes à Maximilian I Empereur sur les traverses causées a sa personne et au Parlement par le Mareschal de Bourgongne', BMB, Collection Chifflet, CLXXXVII, fols. 116–34: 'D'aultant que milites armati non sunt apti in servicio principis nisi tempore belli, togati autem omni tempore consulere et prodesse

8

Introduction

It is important to recognize that Gattinara is here neither unique in his judgment nor simply being perverse. His representation to the emperor occurs within that very period lasting from 1488 to 1515 when in France the office of constable had been kept vacant. In fact to bolster his argument Gattinara cites the case of the recent constable, the Count of Saint-Pol, whom the parlement of Paris had tried, condemned and executed in 1475.[27] Writing in this same period which experienced the suspension of the constableship, perhaps indefinitely, Guillaume Budé and Nicolas de Bohier add their formidable authority to the current, if minority, opinion presented by Gattinara. In his *Annotationes in pandectas* Budé says:

Therefore in this assembly [of the Estates General] we have seen the *magister militum*, namely the Constable, as everywhere true legate of the prince in matters military to be seated in first place among the magistrates and next to him the Chancellor. But now the name of this magistrate seems to have been removed and the realm (*respublica*) has lacked a constable for a long time. Thus today the office of chancellor is the highest summit of dignities beyond which nothing may be hoped for a private, robed man – as if some sort of solstice for the aspiring mind, having authority over all affairs.[28]

Since he dedicated this publication of 1508 to the current chancellor, Jean de Ganay, Budé had more than one reason for rhapsodizing over the virtues of the chancellorship at this opportune moment.[29] Nevertheless, Nicolas de Bohier writing in 1512 also presents one of the most exalted conceptions of the chancellorship, providing us with a valuable description of its functions:

After the prince the chancellor is preeminent, and without his seal no patents of letters have any authenticity; under the prince he has the highest tribunal, and all magistrates are inferior to him; it is proper that he be at all times near the prince and that the chancellery be in the palace, for the lord chancellor must explain all letters and legations to the prince as well as patents of grace that by his discretion

possunt ob legalem scientiam qua imbuti sunt quae ad genus humanum regendum gubernandum, deffendendum, ac ad vitam vere, beateque agendam adiumenta extitit sine qua nullum imperium nulla res publica potest esse...'; fols. 119–119ᵛ: 'ne faict a doubter que togati sunt preferendi saltim les conseilleurs qui sunt ad latus principis et ceux qui exercent les offices au nom du prince qui sunt membra et pars corporis ipsius principis....'.

[27] Roger Doucet, *Les institutions de la France au XVIᵉ siecle* (Paris, 1948), I, 112–13, notes the vacancy of the constableship for this period. On Saint-Pol's trial see Commynes, *Memoires*, IV, 12; cf. 'Remonstrances', BMB, Collection Chifflet, CLXXXVII, fol. 123 although Gattinara does not mention him by name.

[28] 'In eo igitur concilio novimus magistrum militum, id est Constabularium, Principis ubique Legatum in re quidem militari, primo loco inter magistratus sedisse, proximeque eum Cancellarium. Sed illius iam magistratus nomen sublatum esse videtur, quo tamdiu respublica caruit. Itaque Cancellariatus summum est hodie honorum fastigium, ultra quod nihil sperare licet, homini quidem privato et togato, quasique quoddam summa quaeque ambientis animi solstitium.' G. *Budaei Operum Tomus III in quo Annotationes in Pandectas* (Basel, Nicolaus Episcopius, Jr, 1557), p. 109.

[29] David O. McNeil, *Guillaume Budé and Humanism in the Reign of Francis I* (Geneva, 1975), p. 15.

9

Introduction

and eminent knowledge of letters the prince may be guided; it is in this sense that 'omnia iura civilia in scrinio pectoris' is to be understood; as privy to the secrets of the prince, he is equivalent to an archduke or cardinal; he sits on the left side of the dais at public occasions involving the ruler, although Bohier in citing Peter of Belluga claims that in the kingdom of Aragon the chancellor sits on the right side of the prince immediately after the first born.[30]

Thus, when in mid-October 1518 Gattinara took the oath of offices as chancellor between the hands of young Charles at Saragossa, he and members of his profession had used the opportunity afforded by the suspension of the constableship to carry one step further the aspirations of the lawyers as a class to shape and direct the emerging monarchies of early modern Europe.

Among his most immediate tasks as Grand Chancellor, Gattinara sought to galvanize first the royal government and then the Castilian people for the vocation of empire. In the days following the news of Charles' election as emperor he proclaimed his master to be a new and greater Charlemagne who would revive and restore the hitherto faltering empire and bring peace and justice to the world. Subsequently as the court was making its all too hasty removal from Spain the chancellor participated in and possibly inspired an address placed in the mouth of young Charles which parallels part of the famous speech given by Bishop Mota to the cortes of Santiago. The manuscript for the published address is to be found among Gattinara's personal papers.[31] Although the celebrated words 'pene alio aurifero orbe', referring to America and added in the margin of the manuscript, are not in Gattinara's hand, as the official mouthpiece of the emperor elect, the chancellor would have had to participate both within the royal council and then in the chancellery in the composition of the address and assume responsibility for its publication at Rome by Jacobus Mazochius, at Augsburg and even a German version from the press of Martin Landsberg of Leipzig. *The Address of Charles, King of the Romans, to the Spanish Cortes, immediately before his Departure* reflects the difficulty of relating a theoretical claim to universal empire with the fact of a medley of disparate lands.

At last to me empire (*imperium*) has been conferred by the single consent of Germany with God, as I deem, willing and commanding. For truly he errs who reckons that by men or riches, by unlawful canvassing or stratagem the empire

---

[30] *De authoritate magni consilij et Parlamentorum Francorum Christianissimi regni tractatus* (Venice, 1575), fol. 8 (paraphrased here).

[31] For an analysis of the *mazzo* St. d'It. 75 (Miscellanea politica del secolo XVI), BRT and the manuscript for this address, fols. 569–70, see the present author's 'The Habsburg World Empire and the Revival of Ghibellinism', *Medieval and Renaissance Studies, 7*, ed. Siegfried Wenzel (Chapel Hill, 1978), pp. 120–1, fn. 28. It has been recently pointed out to me, however, by Professor Heinrich Lutz that my earlier suggested attribution of the MHAV device, appearing on the title page of the German version, to Michael Hillen of Antwerp properly pertains to the Leipzig printer Martin Landsberg.

of the entire world is able to fall to anyone's lot. For from God himself alone is empire. Nor have I undertaken that charge of such great measure for my own sake. For well was I able to be content with the Spanish Empire (*Hispano imperio*) with the Balearics and Sardinia, with the Sicilian kingdom, with a great part of Italy, Germany and France and with another, as I might say, gold bearing world...But here befalls a certain fatal necessity concerning matters which urges me to take sail. Furthermore decision must be taken out of proper respect for religion, whose enemy thus far has grown so that moreover neither the repose of the commonwealth, nor the dignity of Spain nor finally the welfare of my kingdoms are able to tolerate such a threat. All these are hardly able to exist or be maintained unless I shall link Spain with Germany and add the name of Caesar to Spanish king...[32]

The Santiago-Corunna manifesto suggests both the conceptual and the practical problems of squaring a dynastic assemblage of diverse territories with a soaring vision of universal empire. To assume, as some interpreters have, that Gattinara, being trained in Roman law, would necessarily seek to press an absolutist resolution upon the diversity of Habsburg real estate is to misconstrue Roman law as being univocal and to ignore that constitutional element which inheres to it as well as to the sixteenth-century conception of absolute monarchy.[33]

Gattinara's idea of universal empire would appear to owe as much to the Post-Glossators as it does to Dante. Students of Bartolus and Baldus, in their effort to define the origin of particularistic sovereignty and in some instances to establish that crowning anachronism of the national state in the late Middle Ages or early modern period, fail to recognize that both jurists were imperialists desirous of maintaining and preserving imperial authority in so far as it was at all possible. As direct heirs of Dante's jurist friend Cino da Pistoia, Bartolus and Baldus presumed the continuing authority of the emperor. While some jurists, especially north of the Alps, might deny the *de jure* as well as *de facto* authority of the emperor, the main strand of the *mos Italicus* recognized its reality in the sovereignty and universality of Roman law. Gattinara, who frequently quotes Bartolus and Baldus on controversial legal issues, can be identified with this tradition which at once sought to associate the broad legal authority of the emperor with an emerging world of crystallizing sovereign states. This universal framework of law entertained such concepts as *jus gentium* and *jus Italicum* which gave recognition to the customs and institutions of some territories and municipalities within the empire.[34] As a practical statesman, however,

[32] Charles V, Holy Roman Emperor, *Caroli Ro[manorum] Regis Recessuri Adlocutio in Conventu Hispaniarum* [Rome, Jacobus Mazochius, 1520], sigs. [A₁₁ᵛ–A₁₁₁].
[33] For example see Charles McIlwain, *Constitutionalism. Ancient and Modern* (Ithaca, 1947), esp. Chap. 3.
[34] On a constitutional rather than absolutist interpretation of the work of the Post-Glossators see Donald R. Kelley, 'Civil science in the Renaissance: jurisprudence Italian style', *Historical Journal*, 22 (1979), 790–3; M. H. Keen, 'The Political Thought of the Fourteenth-Century Civilians' in

Introduction

committed to the advancement of the house of Habsburg, Gattinara could not be satisfied merely with the *auctoritas* of his emperor. In his quest to restore the reality of the empire he must attend to the emperor's *potestas* conceived as a broad hegemony coordinated by such centralizing institutions as a Council of State and imperial chancellery, but admitting and working with the particular institutions and laws of disparate territories and kingdoms. In his *relazione* to the Venetian senate, Gasparo Contarini attributed to the chancellor a view of empire that was by no means unknown to the late Middle Ages: according to the Venetian aristocrat's understanding of Gattinara's purposes, the Romans, Cyrus and others who have produced something like universal monarchies have nevertheless not ruled all directly but have had other kings and other friendly republics that have favored them, enjoying their fraternity; this was the way the chancellor guided His Imperial Majesty.[35] Consequently *monarchia* neither connoted nor aspired to an uniformly organized empire but intended rather a looser hegemony which gave room to the local privileges, provincial customs and native institutions of the various lands.[36]

Our effort to conceptualize the historical problem of Gattinara's world has led to the recognition of a curious symbiosis between the particular and the general, the local and the universal to the displacement of territorial consolidation and national unity. Similarly, the transformation of public attitudes in our own time and the gaining of access to the last significant body of archival material reflects something of this same polarity.

The opening of the family archive, an event which would shatter the last of the three barriers to the historical recovery of the cardinal-chancellor, was preeminently the accomplishment of the young editor-in-chief of the *Bollettino Storico Vercellese*, Dr Prof. Luigi Avonto. Having been invited to give a lecture at Gattinara on the subject of the great Mercurino, Dr Avonto quickly recognized the value of calling attention to the founding member of the family fortunes and began to think in terms of some sort of conference and celebration that would honor the fast approaching 450th anniversary of Mercurino's death. Unfortunately, most persons whom he approached manifested ignorance or indifference and the idea seemed still-born. But with the fortuitous visit of the youngest of the three

Beryl Smalley, ed., *Trends in Medieval Political Thought* (Oxford, 1965), pp. 105–26. On Bartolus' appreciation of the emperor's power rather than the jurist's usual representation as expositor of particularistic sovereignty, see Jan Baszkiewicz, 'Quelques remarques sur la conception de Dominum mundi dans l'oeuvre de Bartolus', *Convegno commemorativo del VI centenario di Bartolo* (Perugia, 1959), pp. 9–25. For an example of Gattinara's repeated recourse to the two great jurists see his extensive memorandum of 1525 on the issue of Burgundy: Carlo Bornate, ed., 'Memoire du chancelier de Gattinara sur les droits de Charles-Quint au duché de Bourgogne', *Bulletin de la Commission Royale d'Histoire*, 67 (1907), 391–533, *passim*.

[35] Albèri, *Relazioni*, p. 59.   [36] Cf. Headley, 'Ghibellinism', pp. 109–10.

12

Introduction

daughters of the late marchese, Mercurino Francesco III, namely Signora Alexander Lenard from Brazil, Dr Avonto recognized her as one interested in promoting intellectual and cultural matters. Working in cooperation with the chief provincial archivist, Dr Maurizio Cassetti, he was able both to obtain the support of Signora Lenard for promoting an international conference in October 1980 and to initiate the steps within the family for the transfer of the family archive to the Vercelli State Archives. This task would have been impossible without the assent and cooperation of the Marchesa Teresa di Gattinara, her three daughters and the eldest grandson Count Ferrante Benvenuti Arborio di Gattinara, curator of the archive itself. Gradually, by force of their own personal momentum, Drs Avonto and Cassetti were able to transform the initial local inertia into enthusiastic involvement so that when October arrived the regional support for the conference, which contrasted with the apathy on the national level, was assured. At the same time Dr Avonto had been able to engage some interest and attention from the wider field of international scholarship. The general inattention on the national level only dissolved after the regional and international support for the event had become consolidated and the conference was actually in session.[37]

In conclusion, it should be noted that the present study has no pretensions to a biography. It began as an effort to understand the tensions between state secretaries and the Grand Chancellor within the context of the medieval institution of the chancellery. The tensions and conflict were shaped by access to and influence upon the young emperor as he groped to develop his own personal style of government. The study developed into a broader consideration of the imperial chancellery as an institution. The very personal administration of the chancellery was at all times affected by the relationship between chancellor and emperor and needs to be seen in that context.

For the sake of ready recognition and to avoid further confusion I have used throughout this book the form of the Grand Chancellor's name which has been traditionally used by most historians: Mercurino de Gattinara. However, he never appears to have employed this form. At least after 1509 he always signed himself Mercurin or Mercurinus de Gattinara. Occasionally, with intimate friends like Peter Martyr of Anghiera, he used the colloquial 'Gatinera'.[38] Perhaps this variety is what one would expect

---

[37] I have drawn here freely from two of my articles which at the time of writing this Introduction have still to appear in print: 1) 'Toward the historical recovery of Charles V's Grand Chancellor: problems, progress, prospects', *Atti del Convegno di Studi Storici su Mercurino Arborio di Gattinara nel 450° anniversario della morte*, ed. Luigi Avonto (Vercelli, 1981); and 2) 'Germany, the Empire and *Monarchia* in the thought and policy of Gattinara', *Das römisch-deutsche Reich im Politischen System Karls V*, Internationales Colloquium in München, 6–9 May 1981, to be edited and published by Heinrich Lutz.   [38] See Ferretti's article in *Atti*, p. 165.

Introduction

from a part Piedmontese, part Burgundian statesman serving the international monarchy of the Habsburgs.[39]

[39] Of the mangling of Gattinara's name there is a long and rich tradition which seems to begin with no less a person than Erasmus, who at first substitutes Guilielmus for Mercurinus (Allen, *Opus*, v, 59). It culminates with that paragon of accuracy in the western world, the papal chancellery, which addresses him on 29 January 1524 as Maturino de Gatinaria (AGS, Patr. Real, 62, no. 18), then on 7 June 1524 as Mercurio, to be perpetuated by the incomparable Sadoleto on 9 March 1525, although previously corrected on 28 September 1524, remangled on 3 April 1525 and 14 December 1525, only to be at last corrected in the Clementine chancellery, 2 March 1526. (AGS, Patr. Real, 60, nos. 109, 118, 115, 113, 117, 125, 126). The most hilarious distortion, probably a scribal error, appears in P. Mexía's 'Historia de Carlos Quinto', who renders the name as 'Marco Loveno Catinara, gran cançeller', (*Revue Hispanique*, 44 (1918), 391.) In the Italian translation of Antonio de Solis' *Istoria della conquista del Messico* (Venice, 1715), pp. 490–505, one reads of Mercurio de Catinara.

The administrative threshold

The sixteenth century has been recognized as being an age of lawyers, bringing a litigious dimension into daily life. From the perspective of the infant sovereign state the century can be viewed also as an age of secretaries, the mere clerks of an earlier period, who, as portals to the king's attention and bearers of his business, strained toward the defining of those later ministries and departments that have become such a dominant feature of modern existence. For among the innovators of the age – and there were others beside Martin Luther – is the striking presence of the state secretary – Francisco de los Cobos in Castile, Florimond Robertet in France, Thomas Cromwell in England.

All this is well known and need not engage the attention of the historian except perhaps for the parallelism of developments in western Europe during the first half of the century. What is less well recognized is that the emergence of these super-clerks, bearing with them the seeds of modern bureaucracy, occurs at the expense of a great medieval institution – the chancellorship. For if the century was good for secretaries, it was bad for chancellors. The fate of Wolsey and of More comes readily to mind, followed thereafter by the whirlwind of bureaucratic activity that marked the career of Cromwell. But the case of France, where the office of chancellor was as old as the monarchy itself and would only perish with that monarchy, presents a fairer test of the point being made here. In the history of the Grande Chancellerie, the century provides us with a paradox: for while the chancellor came to enjoy irremovability, surrounded himself with a burgeoning apparatus and achieved an ultimate exaltation, as seen in the careers of DuPrat, Olivier and L'Hôpital, nevertheless the office suffered a serious displacement and reduction of its sphere of activity. Indeed, with the emergence of *secrétaires d'État* and a new mode of validation or authentication, the signature now came to compete with the regime of the seal.[1] Very simply, more than any other process effecting change, the

---

[1] Hélène Michaud, *La grande chancellerie et les écritures royales au seizième siècle, 1515–89* (Paris, 1967), pp. 393–5, cf. also pp. 208, 242.

increasing political correspondence among European rulers burst through the mold of tradition and routine that characterized the medieval chancellery and promoted the secretary of state as the executive agent of a new type of government. If in England and in France the chancellor never lost his eminence, what has been authoritatively said about the English development applies in fair degree to the French: 'the chancellor had become so burdened with the routine duties of a judge that it was increasingly difficult for him to be an administrator and controller of policy'.[2]

In contrast to the apparent eminence attained by the French chancellor stands the significant case of the Neapolitan chancellorship at the beginning of the modern period. Indeed, the deliberate reduction of that office by Ferdinand the Catholic represents a portent of later developments within the Spanish *monarquía*. Looking back at mid-century to the first decade of the sixteenth century, the eminent Neapolitan jurist Marino Freccia noted a transformation which has since been largely ignored by historians. Freccia recognized that for Budé and others in France the chancellor was deemed the preeminent official of the monarchy, yet among the seven principal offices of the Neapolitan crown the chancellorship had become in fact the lowest. In keeping with a royal directive pertaining to the order of the Seven at public ceremonies, 8 April 1505, while the Grand Constable was situated immediately to the right of the king, the Grand Chancellor sat third from the left – the Grand Seneschal sitting directly at the feet of the king. For according to the intentions of that most calculating of European monarchs the real business of government had been delivered into the hands of a small group of *reggenti* and their secretaries collaborating with the prince or his viceroy.[3]

During the last decades of the fifteenth and the first decades of the sixteenth century the developments in many chancelleries assumed the form of a general European phenomenon. Most significantly the real weight of effective political matters shifted from the official chancellery, with its privileges, legitimations and safe conducts, its ennoblements, naturalizations and authorizations, to the political correspondence of the prince's secretariat.[4] Furthermore, there is a progressive differentiation of the properly judicial from the bureaucratic functions of the chancellery: in Germany the Reichskammergericht was constituted in 1495; in France the Grand Conseil (1497); in the Burgundian Netherlands the Grand Conseil at Malines (1504). Prior to these dates there existed for the lands a united chancellery constituted by a writing bureau or secretariat for the privy

[2] G. R. Elton, *The Tudor revolution in government* (Cambridge, 1962), pp. 301–2 *et passim*.
[3] Marino Freccia, *De subfeudis baronum & investituris feudorum quibus accesserunt nonnulli Tractatus aurei* (Naples, Matthias Cancer, 1554), fols. 30, 41ᵛ, cf. fol. 21ᵛ. See *infra*, Chap. 3, fn. 44.
[4] Andreas Walther, 'Kanzleiordnungen Maximilians I, Karls V und Ferdinands I', *Archiv für Urkundenforschung*, 2 (1909), 343.

The administrative threshold

council and including a judicial section. The process of separation or differentiation within the chancellery eventually produced two distinct chancelleries, but this process was gradual and imperfect, especially in the case of the empire.[5]

In order to appreciate the issues involved in the potential conflict between chancellor and secretaries at the beginning of the sixteenth century, a preliminary definition of the chancellorship is necessary. Before there was a chancellery there was that official who according to Roman imperial practice mediated between the emperor and the public by drafting the individual imperial pronouncements behind a lattice work (*cancelli*). While the *referendarius* exercised this function for the Merovingians and in the late Carolingian period one hears of a *summus cancellarius*, the office remained fairly modest and indistinct, dependent upon the royal chaplain and stemming out of the royal *capella*, the court chapel, its first officials in fact being chaplains. Not until the latter half of the twelfth century, when secular government began to be defined in western Europe, did the term *cancellaria* appear, suggesting thereby the distinctive importance of the secretarial function within the emerging administration of the secular authority.[6]

To a world in which literacy is narrowly limited, in which the administering of justice is the primary task of royal government and in which the king's will, grace and word need a preeminent and authentic mouthpiece, particularly for those dependent upon privileges and favors, the chancellorship offered itself as the natural office to assist the king. In France, after the suppression of the office of the constable in 1627, the chancellor was the first officer of the crown. As custodian and executor of the seals the chancellor was responsible for all the business of the king; through the operation of the chancellery all documents – treaties, warrants, letters of privilege – received authentication and legitimacy in the eyes of a largely illiterate society. Besides standing at the bureaucratic center of medieval government, the chancellor was the highest judge and responsible for the operation of the entire judicial system. Initially clerical and secretarial, and continuing to keep its administrative character, the office of chancellor became increasingly judicial. Furthermore, as the official voice of the ruler, the chancellor and chancellery possessed a unique opportunity for shaping a coherent program of royal propaganda as well as for later influencing the development of the national language. In the French tradition at least the chancellor presided over royal councils and was the spokesman of the crown before the Estates General. Two final points need

---

[5] *Ibid.*, 349–50.
[6] Hans-Walter Klewitz, 'Cancellaria: Ein Beitrag zur Geschichte des geistlichen Hofdienstes', *Deutsches Archiv für Geschichte des Mittelalters*, *1* (1937), 44–79.

The emperor and his chancellor

to be emphasized: at a time when a society of limited literacy expected all the actions of royal government to be authenticated by a readily recognizable seal, the chancellor formally controlled the various royal seals; and secondly the chancellor, as chief of the personnel of the chancellery, was the natural protector and guardian of the college of notaries and secretaries of the king.[7] In the words of one historian he was the father of the burgeoning officialdom soon to emerge.[8]

In the case of England and France the rise of state secretaries with the consequent displacement of the medieval chancellorship or the deterioration of some of its functions is a well-known story. It has not, however, been presented in the context of tensions developing within the chancellery. The case of 'Spain' – or more precisely the kingdoms of Castile and Aragon – is less well known and except for Keniston's treatment of the conflict between the secretary, Francisco de los Cobos, and the Grand Chancellor, Gattinara, one tends to assume that something roughly parallel occurred in the Iberian peninsula.[9]

Although Fritz Walser, in his magisterial study of the subject, attributes to Gattinara the overhauling and reorganization of the Spanish central administration during the 1520s, he has nothing specific to say about the true base for whatever power Gattinara wielded, the chancellery, except to assume that all business went through the chancellor's office,[10] and outstanding contemporary witnesses have only served to confirm this opinion. Nevertheless, buried in a footnote, he adumbrates a fact of late medieval political life which can well serve as the portal to the present inquiry into early modern administrative developments: the secretaries 'have intruded upon the inheritance of the medieval chancellor and notaries more strongly in Castile than in the other states'.[11] An examination of the conflict between Gattinara as Grand Chancellor and those first state

[7] Michaud, *Chancellerie*, pp. 47–8, 53. With particular reference to the Neapolitan Grand Chancellor's range of powers, Pietro Giannone, *Istoria civile del regno di Napoli* (The Hague, 1753), III, Bk XI, Chap. 6, p. 190 says: 'Il G. Cancelliero per la sopratendenza della giustizia, capo di tutti gli Ufficiali di pace, e Magistrato de' Magistrate, dipendendo da lui i Giustizieri, i Protonotarj, e tutti gli altri minori Cancellieri'. On language and the chancellery see John L. Fisher, 'Chancery and the emergence of standard written English in the fifteenth century', *Speculum,52* (1977), 870–99; also Hans Rothfels, 'Grundsätzliches zum Problem der Nationalität', *Historische Zeitschrift, 174* (1952), 339–58: 'Nichts ist dafür charakteristischer als die Tatsache, dass das Hauptvehikel moderner Nationalität, die nationale Hochsprache, so häufig durch die königlichen Kanzleien vorgeformt worden ist. In Spanien und Portugal ist das besonders deutlich; Selbst in Deutschland gilt es bis zu einem gewissen Grade von der böhmischen und der sächsischen Kanzlei' (p. 344).

[8] Andreas Walther, *Die burgundischen Zentralbehörden unter Maximilian I und Karl V* (Leipzig, 1909), p. 140.

[9] Hayward Keniston, *Francisco de los Cobos: Secretary of the Emperor Charles V* (Pittsburg, n.d.), pp. 31–2, 99–103.

[10] Walser, *Zentralbehördern*, pp. 243–6. For Gasparo Contarini's portrait of Gattinara see Alberi *Relazioni*, pp. 54–6. For Baldassare Castiglione's opinion see *infra*, Chap. 6, fn. 2.

[11] Walser, *Zentralbehörden*, pp. 62–3, fn. 108.

18

secretaries of early modern Europe, Francisco de los Cobos and Jean Lalemand, may serve to explicate this statement. Our inquiry will extend to a definition of the imperial chancellery in this period and a consideration of the tense relations between the emperor and his chancellor which affected the conduct of its business.

2

The emerging government of Charles V

On 15 October 1518, Mercurino Arborio de Gattinara knelt before Charles, King of Castile, shortly to become King of Aragon and emperor elect, and thereupon between the hands of the young Habsburg monarch took the oath of office as 'Grand Chancellor of all the realms and kingdoms of the king'.[1] In rising to his feet the new chancellor could hardly have surmised, beyond the obvious burdens and difficulties of trying to keep in harness so many diverse lands, the specific problems involved in trying to impose a Franco-Burgundian conception of the chancellorship upon a variety of realms each of whose chancelleries stood at a different stage of growth or decay. As former head of Margaret of Austria's privy council as well as President of Burgundy, i.e. the parlement at Dole, Gattinara had for the past ten years been thoroughly exposed to Franco-Burgundian administrative practices.[2] Furthermore, as a self-conscious disciple of Justinian and a renowned Turin lawyer for ten years prior to his service with the Habsburg dynasty, Gattinara had developed a driving mastery of detail, an eye for the practical issues in a situation, a promptness of thought, a mind that sought to shape, order, improve. With these qualities and experience he would now attack his formidable responsibilities.

As is evident from an examination of the remnants of his private archive at Turin, Gattinara invited memoranda from subordinates at the beginning of his chancellorship as a means of informing himself about the needs, problems and resources of the lands and institutions under his master's lordship. Among such papers dating from this period can be identified the *extraict* of Philippe Hanneton, *audiencier* of the Netherlands government, explaining at some length the office of chancellor.[3] As *audiencier*, which

[1] Brandi, p. 90.
[2] See the present writer's 'Conflict', pp. 49–80.
[3] BRT (Misc.), fols. 683–86ᵛ. In his first remonstrance addressed to the emperor, Gattinara mentions Hanneton, who sent the Summary to him, as having died. Cf. Claretta, 'Notice'. Doc. II, p. 312. As Hanneton died on 18 April 1522 (cf. Walser, *Zentralbehörden*, p. 20, fn. 82) and Hanneton in the Summary (cf. BRT (Misc.), fol. 685ᵛ) refers to Chièvres as Marquis of Arschot, and Charles only created this marquisate at Saragossa on 18 November 1518 (cf. Georges Dansaert, *Guillaume*

2
20

combined many of the qualities of a first secretary with those of a
vice-chancellor or protonotary, Hanneton was responsible for the reception,
the audience, of the secretaries and *maîtres des requêtes*, who brought to the
chancellery the particular decisions of the king or royal council that needed
to be judicially reviewed and sealed by the chancellor. The *audiencier*
presided over a second sort of audience concerned less with judicial than
with accounting matters and especially with those letters of privilege on
which a tax or fee was payable. Such letters were separated out and
delivered by the *audiencier* to those who had petitioned for them.[4] Thus
the *audiencier* was in an authoritative position to describe the organization
of the Burgundian chancellery together with the responsibilities and powers
of its chancellor. What does Hanneton have to say?

The chancellor of Burgundy ranks as the second person of the royal
household. He controls the seals of the prince for the dispatching of all that
has been determined in council. The chancellor is the head of the judicial
apparatus; he presides over all the councils of the prince, whether the latter
is present or absent, determines the agenda, elicits responses, pronounces
the conclusions and commands the secretaries in the expediting of letters
close and patent as well as of privileges. His purview includes not simply
justice but matters concerning war, finance and any matter of importance
so that nothing can be dispatched without his seal. The sealing of
documents is normally done at the house or lodging of the chancellor on
Wednesdays and Saturdays before the mid-day meal. With the advice of
the privy council, the chancellor is able to make all manner of ordinances
'quil treuve servir au bien du prince utilite et commodite de la chose
publicque'.[5] The secretaries are under strict obligation to dispatch letters
and the various sorts of charters of privilege only at the command of the
chancellor. A possible ground for later tension can be perceived in the
statement that the secretaries, in dispatching some directives commanded
by the prince or by the chancellor in the privy council, name the principal
members of the council present at the dispatch.[6] In the order of signature
and in matters of precedence the chancellor comes after the great prelates,
the princes of the blood and the Grand Chamberlain. In his legal review
and scrutiny of all directives from the prince, the chancellor can reject those
that reveal some incompatibility, but his remonstrance can be overriden
by the prince 'de sa puissance absolue'.[7] The chancellor is responsible for

de Croÿ-Chièvres (Paris, Courtrai, Brussels, 1942), p. 168), the Summary itself dates from the first
years of Gattinara's chancellorship, probably 1519. For a transcription of this document see App.
I.
[4] Michaud, *Chancellerie*, pp. 324–8, 335; Walther, *Zentralbehörden*, pp. 158–9; cf. Henri Pirenne,
Histoire de Belgique (Paris, 1922), II, 395–8 where Philip the Good's chancellor, Rolin, appears
as a veritable prime minister.   [5] BRT (Misc), fol. 684.
[6] *Ibid.*, fol. 685.   [7] *Ibid.*, fol. 685ᵛ.

maintaining good order among the ranks of servants in the royal household. Finally while he, the Grand Chamberlain and the Grand Master of the household take their respective oaths of office in the hands of the prince, all counsellors, masters of requests, secretaries, ushers and others associated with the council take theirs in the hands of the chancellor.[8]

Given the background as well as experience of the new Grand Chancellor and the strong possibility that he had solicited the memorandum by Hanneton, it may be safely presumed that Gattinara's views of the chancellery and chancellorship were shaped by the Franco-Burgundian tradition. To be noted in the development of this tradition both before 1518 and in the subsequent two centuries is the fact that the judicial, administrative and political functions of the chancellor were not splintered and divorced from one another but, if modified and curtailed, retained something of their essential coherence. Also striking is the close relationship between chancellery and privy council. With respect to regular business the two bodies were one using the same space, the same register and acts and supervised by the same official, the chancellor.[9] In contradistinction to the French experience, which manifested a more unitary secretarial organization, both the English and the Iberian developments in the late Middle Ages tended toward proliferation: a succession of seals from great, to privy or secret, to signet, each of which produced its own secretariat, none of which is to be conceived as a branch of the chancellery.[10] If we compare, however briefly, the Franco-Burgundian development with that of Castile's chancellery, some important differences become glaringly apparent. For apart from the personal differences, the historical contingencies and the disagreements over policy which would increase the tension between the Emperor Charles V and his chancellor, there existed deepseated, institutional developments that militated toward a rupture.

The Castilian development reveals no lack of precocity and sophistication but is early marked by a splintering of increasingly distinct functions which would prepare the ground for the inroads of the secretaries. Accompanying this splintering goes an apparent duplication of offices promoted by the itinerant character of late medieval monarchy. Common enough to all the kingdoms of Latin Christendom and continuing into the sixteenth century, this last feature, particularly evident in the case of Castile, was conducive to the relatively early formation of distinct administrative bodies. By the beginning of the thirteenth century the chancellor had emerged as the most important official at court after the royal chaplain for he must examine all

---

[8] *Ibid.*, fol. 686. See App. 1 for a transcription of Hanneton's Summary.
[9] Walther, *Zentralbehörden*, p. 102.
[10] T. F. Tout, *Chapters in the administrative history of medieval England*, 6 vols. (London, 1930, repr. 1967), v, 156–7.

documents before affixing the seal. By the end of the century, under Sancho IV (1283–96), there began to develop the distinction between the *chanciller mayor* and the *chanciller de la poridad*, the latter pertaining to a cameral secretariat attendant upon the king and separated from the general chancellery. With Henry II (1369–79) the *chanciller de la poridad* had also acquired the title of *chanciller mayor* and the functions of both began to crystallize. The *chanciller mayor* retained all the royal seals and dealt with documents concerning justice and grace. The *chanciller de la poridad* retained the secret seal and attended the prince. In the subsequent reign of John I (1379–90), the *chancillería* emerged as the highest tribunal of justice and came to be identified with the *audiencia* fixed at Valladolid. In September 1494 a second *chancillería* was created at Ciudad Real, soon after translated to Granada. At the same time the personnel of the chancellery proliferated. By the cortes of Segovia in 1390, John I designated a distinct *notario mayor* for Castile, Leon, Toledo and also for Andalusia to be later supplemented by one for Granada. Each *notario* had three *escribanos*. The *mayordomo mayor* and the appropriate *notario mayor* collaborated in the vital function of issuing letters of privilege. The chancellery also included a financial section run by *contadores mayores de hacienda* for drafting and sealing warrants directing disbursements from the royal treasury. A very important official was the *registrador mayor* responsible for keeping a record as an authentic test of what had been issued. As with the chancellorship, so the registry was divided, one remaining with the *audiencia*, the other attending the court. Completing the chancellery's personnel were the *secretarios*. Finally it needs to be observed, in order to appreciate the tenuous coherence of this complex institution, that by the end of the Middle Ages none of the high officials of the chancellery exercised his function personally but delegated it to a lieutenant. *Chanciller mayor* had become an honorific title.[11]

Such was the institution inherited by Ferdinand and Isabella. The heightened role of secretaries bespeaks the increase of executive action on the part of the royal pair. With Ferdinand came a veritable cloud of Aragonese secretaries some discharging business in both the Castilian and the Aragonese chancellery but all thriving and rich in a short time. Of these the greatest was Miguel Perez de Almazán who in his exclusive dedication to international affairs has been reputed the first secretary or minister of state which Spain, or for that matter Europe, had.[12] Indeed, since the middle of the fifteenth century secretaries had become increasingly

[11] I am here following the valuable research of M. S. Martín Postigo, *La cancillería castillana de los reyes católicos* (Valladolid, 1959), esp. pp. 146–50, 155–6, 163, 176–8, 265; and F. Arribas Arránz, 'Los registros de cancillería de Castilla', *Boletín de la Real Academia de Historia, 162* (1968), 182–3.
[12] José Antonio Escudero, *Los secretarios de estado y del despacho 1474–1724*, 4 vols. (Madrid, 1969), I, 15.

The emperor and his chancellor

involved in authenticating and expediting documents; the secretary's
practice of countersigning as a replacement to the chancellery's seal is first
evident in 1463, associated with the infante Don Alfonso whose registers
at his untimely death may have been passed on to his sister, Isabella. Given
the nomadic character and organization of the court, the personnel of the
chancellery accompanied the Catholic monarchs in their repeated dis-
placements. The clutch of secretaries became ever more evident and each
monarch moved about attended by his or her group. All the business of
government – royal letters, letters patent, royal decrees, missives emanating
from the royal will – were redacted by the secretaries. Each had his own
group of scribes who did the actual work of drafting the document under
the direction of the secretary, leaving blank place and date which the
secretary himself would fill in at the moment of obtaining the royal
signature.[13]

The evidence of diplomatics attests to the ramifying penetration of the
secretaries into the central administration. Two series in the section
designated 'Camara de Castilla' at Simancas are of particular interest, the
first pertaining to matters of grace and justice, the second constituting 376
registers from diverse offices relating to war, defense and the Moors. The
registration here indicates the simultaneous functioning of more than one
administrative organ, which, if it does not transcend the dispatching of
letters of confirmation and privileges by the *chanciller mayor*, reveals the
dispatch of the daily business of government according to the countersigning
of a secretary rather than by the traditional seal of the chancellery. In such
instances each court or administrative body was attended by one or more
secretaries, who by reason of their office had the task of registering the
documentation that they dispatched; for this task they held the corres-
ponding registry books whose titles read like a roll call of the great
Ferdinandine secretaries: 'From the office of Hernand Alvarez', '...Lope
Conchillos', '...Alvarez de Toledo', '...Fernando de Zafra'.[14]

In contradistinction to the Castilian development, the Aragonese chancellery at the end of the Middle Ages retained considerable coherence and
represented one of the finest expressions of this institution in Europe. What
is immediately striking in the case of Aragon is that the chancellor was a
high prelate limited to the ecclesiastical, while the vice-chancellor was a

[13] Martín Postigo, *Cancillería*, pp. 224–53; Arribas Arránz, 'Cancilleria', pp. 191–3.
[14] Arribas Arránz, 'Cancillería', pp. 189–98. Is it possible, however, that during the revolt of the
Comunidades the Junta through collective necessity reaffirmed the corporate effectiveness of the
chancellery in the brief period from September 1520 to April 1521? See F. Arribas Arránz, 'La
organización de la cancillería y el despacho de documentos durante las comunidades de Castilla',
Hispania: Revista Española de Historia, 10 (1950), 61–84, esp. 78–80. Although Joseph Perez
includes this article in the bibliography of his *La révolution des 'Comunidades' de Castille* (Bordeaux,
1970), he never treats the chancellery other than in its purely judicial form.

24

The emerging government of Charles V

canon concerned with lay matters and ever attendant upon the king. During the period 1387 to 1484 the vice-chancellorship became pluralized in response to the disparate realms of the Crown of Aragon, the chancellorship remaining united and general in its scope, all lands appertaining to the crown recognizing its occupant's authority. The vice-chancellor was not only the high notary of the kingdom and the highest administrator of justice but a counsellor of the king in all matters. The chief requirements of the office were that he be a native and trained in law. When Ferdinand created the Council of Aragon in 1494, the natural president for such a body was the vice-chancellor. The tradition of successive vice-chancellors, who were recommended to the presidency of the council by reason of their juristic background and obvious administrative preeminence, would not be disputed until the seventeenth century with the growing pressure of courtiers and noble place-seekers – the *capa y espada*. Significantly enough, the only irregularity in the sixteenth century occurred with Gattinara and his more famous subordinate Nicholas Perrenot, Lord of Granvelle.[15]

An ordinance of 15 April 1480 reorganized the chancellery and its archive to which deposits would be regularly made henceforth in ten year intervals.[16] Omitting the chancellor, vice-chancellor and *regentes*, the ordinance provides us with the chancellery's personnel and a sense of its complexity: the protonotary, his lieutenant, three secretaries, one archivist, twenty-one *escribanos de manament* expediting the dispatch of documents, twelve *escribanos de registro*, four sealers, four *peticionarii* or scribes placed at the disposition of the *audiencia*, one solicitor, one *calendos de cera*, one runner and three treasury scribes. Because the chancellor had long been removed from the chancellery and the energies of the vice-chancellor were largely consumed in administrative and judicial functions, the daily routine of the chancellery fell to the protonotary and shortly to his lieutenant who provided the effective direction of that institution's personnel. Over the course of the fifteenth century the secretaries grew relentlessly in numbers and importance. In vain did Alfonso V attempt by his *Pragmática Sanción* of 10 October 1451 to reduce the excessive number of secretaries and scribes. By the turn of the century the secretaries were in the habit of following the king, attending his person, ready to read the letters received and prepare replies through dispatch and copying. Fixed at twelve, the number of this swollen group hovered around sixteen.[17]

[15] J. Abadía Lalinde, 'El vicecanciller y la presidencia del Consejo de Aragon', *Anuario de Historia del Derecho Español, 35* (1965), 182, 186–7, 192–3, 201–8, 224–7.
[16] J. Ernesto Martínez Ferrando, 'Aportación de datos acerca del archivo real de Barcelona y de sus archiveros durante los reinados de Juan II y Fernando el Católico', *V Congreso de Historia de la Corona de Aragón* (Saragossa, 1961), pp. 87, 107.
[17] Francisco Sevillano Colom, 'La cancillería de Fernando el Católico' *V Congreso de Historia de la Corona de Aragón* (Saragossa, 1955), pp. 215–53, esp. pp. 220, 226, 231–9. See also the same

The emperor and his chancellor

Arriving in the Iberian peninsula toward the end of 1518, Gattinara could hardly flatter himself that he had been present at the creation – a creation that had taken place in Brussels during the years 1516 and 1517. Two who had, would considerably affect the career of the Piedmontese dynastic servant as Grand Chancellor: first Guillaume de Croy, Lord of Chièvres, Grand Chamberlain and tutor of the young Habsburg prince, an *alter rex* whose authority was so overweening that Gattinara must simply accommodate to this fact of life in the succeeding months; the other Francisco de los Cobos, a rising star, secretary for Castilian affairs, the recipient of an increasing number of royal favors, grants and powers, not least of which was his office as keeper of the patronage lists – a man to whom, because of his self-aggrandizement, mounting influence and especially his control of favors, Gattinara would never be able to reconcile himself. In the ensuing years the specific arena of the chancellor's Iberian activities – quite apart from his efforts to organize the motley Habsburg world empire and direct its foreign policy – would be Aragon, and this for several reasons: it was removed from the specifically Castilian activity of Cobos; it was through the Council of Aragon that Charles' Italian possessions and interests were administered and finally the Aragonese chancellery retained greater cohesion than that of Castile. The actual presence of Gattinara's exercise of the office of chancellor in Castile appears negligible. He had inherited here a honorific post and the documents attest that a secretary, Urbina, would sign 'pro chanciller'.[18]

Such was not to be the case with Aragon. During his second sojourn in the Iberian peninsula, Gattinara remained in the realms of the Crown of Aragon from his arrival at Saragossa to the departure of the court in February 1520 from Aragon, which constituted over four-fifths of his total time in Spain. From the available evidence it is apparent that he directed his considerable organizational talents to reordering for his master the administration of the diverse lands and kingdoms composing the Crown of Aragon. Indeed the fruit of his ruminations in this regard is represented by the great consulta of early 1520 that he urged upon Charles before the departure of the court for Castile and Corunna.[19] The consulta sets the tone and intent for his recommendations for reform in this first period of his chancellorship. There is discernible here a desire for rationalization and simplification of offices in the interests of thrift and efficiency. This theme is amplified in two memoranda pertaining to Neapolitan offices, and

author's 'Cancillerías de Fernando I de Antequera y de Alfonso V el Magnanimo', *Anuario de Historia del Derecho Español, 35* (1965), 169–216, esp. pp. 203–16 for a more detailed study of the personnel of the Aragonese chancellery.
[18] M. S. Martín Postigo, 'La cancillería castellana en la primera mitad del siglo XVI', *Hispania: Revista Española de Historia, 24* (1964), 527, 541, 548–51.
[19] Bornate, 'Doc.', pp. 414–22.

26

probably deriving from this period: the first calls for the abolition of superfluous and unnecessary offices, but only upon the death of their present incumbents – a point that Gattinara emphatically respects; the second treats those alienated from the crown but able to be reunited at the time of succession.[20] Although the emphasis in the consulta of early 1520 falls upon financial matters, with the creation of a sort of controller-general to keep track of revenues received, there is one aspect of this office which was fraught with significant implications. For Gattinara urges Charles to issue an ordinance declaring that no authorization, grants or favors be dispatched or sealed unless enregistered and signed by this controller, as was presently the case with Cobos in Castile; the office of this controller should be bestowed on some faithful secretary who would not be distracted by another task.[21] Beyond the obvious interest that this recommendation holds with regard to an incipient specialization of tasks and defining of functions, it would prove particularly ironic that Gattinara in this early period should urge the adoption in Aragon of an office whose model in Castile he would later attack incessantly. Even earlier and in a more sweeping recommendation Gattinara had urged as a general principle that individual secretaries should concentrate on specific tasks, distributed according to geographic rather than functional criteria. In his Barcelona consulta of 12 July 1519, a veritable *speculum principis*, he concluded by urging among other changes that the number of secretaries be restricted and that each might have assigned to him all the business of a particular land or realm and that there should be no trespassing upon the jurisdiction of another.[22]

Here is not the place to consider all Gattinara's tentative efforts of reform in the Crown of Aragon but only those that pertain to the chancellery and his relations to the secretaries. Among the papers present in that fragment of the chancellor's archive at Turin is one designated by a contemporary hand on the back of the last folio as 'las dudas de Soria'. It attests to being nothing less than an internal governmental reaction to the reforming efforts of Gattinara. Alonso de Soria, a former secretary of Ferdinand and now serving in the itinerant Council of Aragon,[23] addresses his criticisms to

[20] *Ibid.*, p. 421, fn. 1 gives simply the titles to the two memoranda which only became available with the recent opening of the family archive: ASV, (Gattinara) 8, nos. 2 and 3.
[21] Bornate, 'Doc.', p. 420.
[22] *Ibid.*, p. 414. Both the chancellery ordinance for Margaret of Austria, dated 17 December 1516 drawn up by Gattinara, and also the earlier ordinance of 1497 manifest an express interest in controlling and disciplining the secretaries. See the Apps. 3 and 4 of Walther, *Zentralbehörden*, pp. 198–203.
[23] Walser, *Zentralbehörden*, pp. 116, 156, 225. Alonso de Soria is not to be confused with Lope de Soria, imperial orator at Genoa during these same years. By the time of the Diet of Worms Alonso de Soria had become lieutenant of the protonotary in the Aragonese chancellery. See HHSA (Belgien), PA 91/2, fols. 101, 102[v].

'muy excelente senor' who, from the context, can only be Gattinara. The subject under discussion is an ordinance recently composed by the chancellor. Although the text of the ordinance remains unknown, its substance can be deduced from Soria's doubts raised by the ordinance, apparently invited by the chancellor and here presented in a substantial memorandum.[24] After treating the council's administration of high justice, its voting, the need to retain as in the past a Valencian lawyer on the council just as there are an Aragonese, a Sicilian, a Neapolitan and a Catalan each for his respective land, Soria comes down hard on the proposal to have a single secretary disposing of favors and graces. By the chancellor's own admission there is no business that needs so much to be free and yet by setting up *el secretario senor dela negociacion* a virtual tyranny may well develop. Instead this business ought to be free and able to be dispatched by any secretary or *escribano de mandamiento*; such was the practice prevailing in the chancellery in the past, particularly during the time of the Catholic king, who did not countenance one absolute secretary for a single type of business. To argue that dispatching by many hands would lead to confusion and contradiction overlooks the fact that all dispatches are enrolled in one register and authenticated by one seal. For Soria the implications of this particular reform would be to expel from office the chancellery's twenty-two scribes for the expediting of documents (*escribanos de mandamiento*) – many of them very good men of service.[25] The final and most extensive criticism of Gattinara's reforming measures concerns the implicit attack upon the office of protonotary as the proper official for supervising the maintenance of the registers and thus the whole traditional order and operation of the chancellery. By removing worthy register scribes from offices, which they should expect to hold for life, and by suppressing offices long established and clearly necessary to the proper functioning of the protonotary's responsibilities, the new ordinance would reduce the chancellery to total disorder.[26]

It would be rash on the basis of the fragmentary evidence available to claim that Gattinara was promoting an entire program of reform during these months in and near Barcelona. Nevertheless, some fairly distinct motifs emerge from the surviving documents that specifically bear upon our problem here. In his proposals to rationalize and order some of the administrative bodies there is discernible a desire to effect a specialization of functions. There is also evident a conflict between a desire to reduce expenses and an effort to preserve 'jobs'. The result, ironically enough,

[24] BRT (Misc.), fols. 384–8. [25] *Ibid.*, fols. 385–385ᵛ.

[26] *Ibid.*, fols. 386–386ᵛ. For a transcription of the relevant passages of 'Soria's Doubts' see App. II. A comparison of the lists of personnel for the chancellery of Aragon at the beginning and at the end of the twenties reveals no important changes. Cf. Walther, 'Kanzleiordnungen', Dok. 2 (a) and (b), pp. 383–7.

considering the chancellor's later complaints, was to accent and exalt the roles of some secretaries. The final outcome resembled nothing so much as Cobos' system of absolute control of graces and favors in Castile which here seemed to provide a sort of model for the specialization and promotion of certain secretaries in the Aragonese context. After 1522, and the return of Charles to Spain, the imposition of a Castilian model on the financial resources and officialdom of the Crown of Aragon cropped up repeatedly in the memoranda directed to the Grand Chancellor.[27] Nevertheless, whether influenced by his earlier sobering experience in Burgundy or persuaded by memoranda such as that of Soria, Gattinara remained cautious and conservative. Only in his desire to expand and redefine the responsibilities of some of the secretaries did he appear radical. In the consulta of 1520 he urges Charles to adhere most strictly to observing the laws and customs of the realms of Aragon.[28] It was an admonition that the young Habsburg would appropriate and impart to his son.[29]

With the election of Charles as Holy Roman Emperor and the departure of the court for Aachen and Worms, the Grand Chancellor came to be exposed to a new set of problems: what seals and titles might dignify the new Charlemagne? By what means might his will be expedited over so many diverse lands? What was to be the role of the Grand Chancellor in the Holy Roman Empire and his relation to its Archchancellor? Even before leaving Aragon, Gattinara had addressed himself to some of these problems. With his usual conceptual alacrity the chancellor composed at Barcelona, less than a week after receiving the news of the imperial election, that splendid consulta in which he elaborated for Charles the opportunities and responsibilities of universal empire.[30] At the end, when he is struggling with the problem of expediting the more routine matters of justice and with sparing the emperor elect's time from petty details, he advocates the use of a miniature seal or stamp, bearing the name of 'Charles' or 'E. empereur'. He recognizes the need to redefine titles and arms on seals and coins but defers this matter to a moment of leisure.[31]

Before the year had ended Gattinara was composing a new consulta which specifically treated that question of titles, arms and seals which only a chancellor was competent to determine. The entire memoire breathes the need for clarity in their usage. Evident throughout are his careful choice and distribution of titles and the positioning of shields: for example, that of Castile or Aragon is conjoined with rather than subordinated to the shield bearing the arms of the emperor, whereas in the seal for Flanders and Burgundy the arms of the emperor are placed above the arms of those lands,

[27] BRT (Misc.), fols. 489, 536, 571[v].
[28] Bornate, 'Doc.', p. 419.
[29] Walser, *Zentralbehörden*, pp. 85–6.
[30] Bornate, 'Doc.', pp. 405–13.
[31] *Ibid.*, pp. 412–13.

The emperor and his chancellor

and in each instance the assemblage of shields is subsumed under the all-hovering imperial crown.[32] Moving back and forth from one language to another he manifests a firm grasp of different usages and of their fundamental political and legal relationships.[33] In treating the seals of the empire at this time Gattinara recognizes the need for several: one pertaining to the German monarchy proper and dealing with its regular dispatches remained in the hands of the Archbishop of Mainz who was in fact the Archchancellor of the empire; the seal dealing with Italian matters was exercised by the Archbishop of Cologne; and that pertaining to the empire's French lands by the Archbishop of Trier. Besides resorting to this rather archaic, if not Ottonian, arrangement, Gattinara hastens to add that the seal of *l'empire universel* ought to be always near the emperor himself for sealing all the most important matters.[34]

The apparent complexity of this preliminary definition among the chancelleries derives from two basic problems: the potential incoherence tending to dualism within the constitution of the Holy Roman Empire, between Kaiser and Reich so that what was imperial pertained more often to the Reich than to the Kaiser, this prominence of the Reich or more precisely Reichstände, imperial estates, being evinced by the original and primary imperial chancellery functioning under the direction of the Archchancellor, the Archbishop of Mainz; and secondly the itinerant nature of medieval government which had the effect of necessarily duplicating institutions, the original juristic secretariat remaining fixed, and tending toward a sclerotic condition, while its more political copy thrived in attendance upon the ruler. The residential imperial chancellery at Mainz is thus removed from its source, the emperor, who has to develop his own German court chancellery. As the living member, this new institution has the opportunity of becoming dominant, for the life of a chancellery depends upon its relation to what it serves, just as in isolation, either by being removed from the emperor or from the empire, it becomes an absurdity. A final complexity to the German scene arose from the Habsburg need to administer their domainal lands. To meet this task there had developed an Austrian court chancellery quite apart from the two varieties of imperial chancellery. The Hofkanzlei would be attendant upon Charles' brother, Ferdinand.[35]

[32] Walther, 'Kanzleiordnungen', Dok. 1, p. 382.
[33] *Ibid.*, pp. 364–5.
[34] Walther, 'Kanzleiordnungen', Dok. 1, pp. 381–2.
[35] *Ibid.*, pp. 350–2. On the later relationship between the residential chancellery at Mainz and its judicial offspring, the imperial cameral tribunal, at Speyer see Jean Dumont, ed., *Corps universel diplomatique du droit des gens* (Amsterdam and The Hague, 1726–31/1739), IV/1, 58. On the identification of the term 'Reich' with the Reichstände by the end of the fifteenth century see Ernst Schubert, *König und Reich: Studien zur spätmittelalterlichen deutschen Verfassungsgeschichte* (Göttingen, 1979), p. 253.

The emerging government of Charles V

An obvious principle of sixteenth-century political life regardless of country becomes evident: political influence or political health is directly related to proximity to the prince. Even the all-powerful Wolsey at Calais in 1522 could be anxious about the secretary who stayed home, close to the person of the king, and handled the royal correspondence.[36] Protracted absence from the prince was only one of the many problems Gattinara had to contend with in the succeeding months. His successive ordinances for an imperial chancellery had to provide for a mobile secretariat that could remain in attendance upon the ruler. While recognizing the rights and jurisdictions of other chancelleries, he must throttle the emergence of any cameral type of government, constituted by a few secretaries in close association with the emperor, and by the superiority of his counsel make himself that person nearest to the ruler, following the death of Chièvres late in May 1521.

When Charles came into the empire for coronation as emperor elect, the relationship of the Mainz chancellery to the court chancellery had to be redefined. Ever since the end of the thirteenth century the German princes, in their desire to participate more prominently in the politics of the empire, had directed their efforts to the control of the imperial chancellery as one of the most important organs of monarchical administrative power. Successive archbishops of Mainz had claimed for their office of Archchancellor of the empire the right to name the imperial court-chancellor as their representative and even the right to determine the personnel of the emperor's chancellery. Rarely, however, did they actually realize their claim except in the federal reform movement of Berthold of Henneberg (1494–1502), and most recently in the period of dynastic uncertainty during the struggle between Francis I and Charles of Spain for the election to the imperial office. On 12 March 1519 Charles had confirmed the rights of Archbishop Albrecht of Mainz to control personally the chancellery and to appoint a deputy as imperial vice-chancellor. Under the new arrangement Nicolas Ziegler, previously first secretary of the Emperor Maximilian's chancellery, became the first imperial vice-chancellor. Thus when Charles and his Grand Chancellor came upon the scene, the long standing claims of Mainz and its present incumbent, Albrecht of Hohenzollern, had at last been realized.[37]

---

[36] Florence M. G. Higham, 'A note on the pre-Tudor secretary', A. G. Little and F. M. Powicke, eds., *Essays in medieval history presented to Thomas Frederick Tout* (Freeport, N.Y., 1967), pp. 364–6.

[37] On the history and broader context of the German imperial court-chancellery see Heinrich Kretschmayr, 'Das deutsche Reichsvicekanzleramt', *Archiv für österreichische Geschichte, 84* (1898), 381–501 and the more recent study by Lothar Gross, *Die Geschichte der deutschen Reichshofkanzlei von 1559 bis 1806* (Vienna, 1933), esp. pp. 1–4. The earlier and more extensive study by Gerhard Seeliger, *Erzkanzler und Reichskanzleien* (Innsbrück, 1889) still has value.

They were to be of momentary duration. Political reality conforms to power, not right, and power stemmed in the new age from the immediate milieu of the prince. On 25 January 1521, the Archchancellor and Grand Chancellor met to define their roles in an order confirmed six days later by the emperor. According to this agreement it was ruled that when the Archchancellor was absent from court, the exercise of the chancellor's rights passed to the Grand Chancellor.[38] The new determination had the effect of removing the earlier recognition granted Mainz who now operated in a much more limited capacity except in times of actual attendance upon the imperial court. Consequently Gattinara, while privy to the formulation of the Edict of Worms against Luther, did not formally preside over its expedition in the imperial chancellery. In fact on the morning of May 26, when the papal nuncio Aleander ran to the Grand Chancellor for his signature to the edict, he thereby indicated his own uncertainty as to the appropriate source for authentication. On finding Gattinara confined to his quarters with the gout, Aleander turned to his replacement, Mota, Bishop of Palencia, and only then went to the proper authority in this instance – the Archbishop of Mainz.[39]

When the emperor left German soil, Gattinara took possession of the chancellery administration by issuing at Ghent on 1 January 1522 what would be the first of his ordinances organizing and ruling the imperial court chancellery.[40] Its details cannot concern us here and can be deferred for later comparison with the Valladolid ordinance of 1524. Only the most outstanding features detain us at this point. By this ordinance Gattinara apparently sought to amalgamate the Austrian chancellery with the imperial court chancellery. To this end he appointed two vice-chancellors – John Hannart, former *audiencier* in the Brussels chancellery, to deal with Austrian business, and Nicolas Ziegler to handle German imperial business. The chancellery's personnel indicated a multi-national, polyglot background: of the three permanent secretaries Jean Lalemand was Burgundian, Maximilian Transylvanus, German and Philip de Nicola, Aragonese; of the seven permanent scribes all but Alfonso de Valdés were German; the offices of registrar, contrarelator and taxer were all filled by Germans, but the receiver of the fees paid by petitioners was a Vercellese relative of Gattinara's. Of the five registers, constituting in effect five divisions within

---

[38] Walter, 'Kanzleiordnungen', pp. 367–8.
[39] Paul Kalkoff, *Die Depeschen des Nuntius Aleander vom Wormser Reichstage 1521* (Halle a.s., 1897), p. 249, cf. pp. 241, 247. Cf. also *Deutsche Reichstagsakten unter Kaiser Karl V*, eds., Jüngere Reihe, A. Wrede *et al.*, (Gotha, 1893) II, 460–3 for the signing and publication of the Edict of Worms. While Ziegler countersigned the German version for the empire, Hannart countersigned the Latin one for the hereditary lands. On Gattinara's general support of Aleander's draft of the mandate see Petrus Balan, ed., *Monumenta reformationis Lutheranae 1521–25* (Ratisbon, 1884), p. 205.
[40] Walther, 'Kanzleiordnungen', p. 368.

The emerging government of Charles V

the chancellery, the first used Latin and German and was intended to deal with all things pertaining to his imperial majesty, namely business of state (*negocia status*); the second, German, and pertained to the empire proper; the third, Latin, and also dealt with the empire, but with particular reference to Italian matters; the fourth, Austrian matters; and the fifth, petitions. When in the light of the significant number of extra-German personnel in the chancellery one ponders the potential universality of the first register and the ambiguous scope of the third register, the impression is gained that Gattinara had in mind at this time something more than the mobile chancellery of the Holy Roman Empire and perhaps one that pointed to a Habsburg *empire universel*. Certainly on paper the presence of German business looms as being unmistakably paramount, but the fact that with all his linguistic ability Gattinara never apparently mastered German necessitated a distinct division within the secretariat headed by Hannart, who after 1524 departed Spain and no longer functioned as a vice-chancellor. His duties were promptly assumed by Balthasar Merklin, Provost of Waldkirch, who was not appointed to the vice-chancellorship until early in 1527. Thus, while the imperial chancellery lacked a head to its German division during this period of over two years, the Hispanic element came to prevail in the chancellery, as can be traced in the career of Alfonso de Valdés.[41]

The Ghent ordinance disguises a difficulty which was not apparently recognized at the time. Or is the ordinance to be interpreted as an effort on Gattinara's part to counter the rising influence of the secretaries and bring them under the control of a strict chancellery discipline? Such a view would seem to be belied by the fact that in looking back upon the course of events in the summer of 1525 the Grand Chancellor dated his difficulties as beginning only after the return to Spain in the summer of 1522.[42] Nevertheless, the problem of the chancellor with the secretaries had an earlier origin.

Following the death of Chièvres, Gattinara had emerged as the most forceful personality among the counsellors of the young emperor and the shaper of his foreign policy. The attitudes supporting the Francophile treaty of Noyon fell into desuetude, hostilities broke out between Charles and Francis during the months succeeding Worms and Gattinara moved toward an alliance with the pope.[43] In the emerging realignment the position of

[41] Cf. Walther, 'Kanzleiordnungen', Dok. 3, pp. 387–92. On Waldkirch's assumption of all the paperwork pertaining to German affairs and the empire see also *Acta Tomiciana, eds. W. Ketrzyński and Z. Celichowski* (Posnan, 1852–60, 1876–1915), VII, 129, VIII, 344. (Hereafter cited as AT.)

[42] Cf. AGRB (PEA), 1471 (4), fol. [19ᵛ]/[24ᵛ].

[43] Kalkoff, *Depeschen*, p. 115; Garrett Mattingly, 'Eustache Chapuys and Spanish diplomacy in England (1488–1536). A study in the development of resident embassies' (unpublished Harvard dissertation, February, 1935), p. 433; *Cal. SP Spain*, II, 372–6, 473–559 *passim*; Francesco Nitti,

33

England was crucial. In 1521 she was hardly prepared to participate in a war against France, particularly when many English counsellors received pensions from France. Wolsey sought to give the appearance of composing the differences between Charles and Francis, while gaining time to negotiate with Charles for a joint invasion of France.[44] Thus came into being the autumn conference at Calais, the meeting of chancellors, Du Prat for Francis I, Wolsey for Henry VIII and Gattinara with a large delegation for Charles V. Chancellors Du Prat and Gattinara arrived, prepared to concede nothing. Cardinal Wolsey seemed genuinely desirous of bringing about an accord between the two contestants, if only to enhance his own reputation and confirm the value of pageant politics. Nevertheless, his ultimate intentions were directed elsewhere – toward Bruges where resided the imperial court.[45]

The negotiations of the Calais conference, one of the most spectacular acts of diplomatic futility in early modern European history, do not concern us here. From the perspective of administrative history what interests us is the new situation created by the enforced absence of the emperor's supreme bureaucrat from the arena of political power, the imperial court at Bruges and Brussels from late July to early December 1521.[46] Gattinara appears to have been aware of the political and administrative dangers arising from his not being attendant upon his master. Indeed, while proceeding to his diplomatic assignment, he composed at Dunkirk on 30 July a memorandum for Charles, debating the relative advantages of peace or war but also conveying some uneasiness as to the possible vacuum created by his absence.[47] Well might the Grand Chancellor be anxious, for unlike Du Prat and Wolsey he did not carry with him the seals of office.[48] If the communications between Calais and Brussels are read with an eye to administrative minutiae, an important development is discernible. After the first month during which Gattinara paid a visit to the imperial court Charles reveals initially a great need for his chancellor. On 3 September he asks for Gattinara's express advice on letters come from Rome and Naples and he sends a letter from the hand of a secretary asking

Leone X e la sua politica (Florence, 1892), pp. 403–4. I wish to thank Mrs Garrett Mattingly for her gracious permission to consult her husband's dissertation.

[44] Mattingly, 'Chapuys', p. 429.

[45] For a recent treatment of the negotiations at Calais and what William Dunham has referred to as 'pageant politics', see Joycelyne G. Russell, 'The search for universal peace: the conference at Calais and Bruges in 1521', *Bulletin of the Institute of Historical Research, 44* (1971), 162–93.

[46] Cf. *Aktenstücke und Briefe zur Geschichte Kaiser Karl V*, ed. Karl Lanz (Vienna, 1853), p. 1/2, 476.

[47] *Aktenstücke*, pp. 231–3; cf. also *Letters and Papers, Foreign and Domestic, on the Reign of Henry VIII*, eds. J. S. Brewer, James Gairdner and R. H. Browdie (London, 1862–1932) 3/2, no. 1446.

[48] For Du Prat see *Journal de Jean Barrillon, Secrétaire du Chancelier Du Prat 1515–1521*, ed. Pierre de Vaissière (Paris, 1897–9), II, 203; for Wolsey see Elton, *Tudor revolution*, p. 53.

for its return. On the same day Charles writes to Wolsey complaining that since their departure for Calais some important matters which are not able to be properly dispatched without the presence of his Grand Chancellor remain unexpedited and that other pieces are in Gattinara's hands. He asks that the cardinal be willing to send back 'mon chancelier' and retain the other ambassadors of the imperial delegation.[49] Two days later he reiterates this plea saying that he has greater need for him than ever.[50] While Gattinara pressed for his own departure, Wolsey argued strenuously against it. After having shortly before refuted Du Prat point by point and left Francis' chancellor with a bad headache, Gattinara disclaimed his abilities, urging that his associates were better jurists, had a better sense of historical precedents and that his own absence did great damage to the emperor's affairs.[51] But to the members of his delegation and to the English cardinal his departure would mean the breakdown of the conference.[52] Convinced by Wolsey, Charles on 11 September wrote that although he wanted his chancellor with him, it was best that he remain at Calais. There was no other remedy. The emperor's letters of mid-September to Gattinara breathed a gratitude and confidence in him which was not to recur during the course of the decade.[53]

The later development in this massive Calais–Brussels correspondence suggests a growing independence on Charles' part and the initial development of his own style of rule, a style that might be designated as cameral. True, Charles does not fail to express a very real appreciation for the defensive action that his highly sensitive agent is waging; the emperor urges his chancellor to press the ancient quarrels of the Austro-Burgundian dynasty as only he knows how.[54] He hungers for the aged, experienced statesman's advice and invokes him to write often.[55] He manifests still some anxiety and dependence upon Gattinara for maintaining the bond with Wolsey.[56] Yet concurrently emerge issues promotive of disagreement, where the chancellor indicates a reluctance to sign, particularly in matters pertaining to appointments, and the emperor must simply impose his will.[57] Of the secretaries attendant upon Charles at this time and with whom Gattinara increasingly had to deal the names of Urries, García and Lalemand appear.[58] Don Ugo de Urries and Pedro García were both associated with the council and chancellery of Aragon.[59] Jean Lalemand, former clerk of the parlement of Dole, at every step a *créature* of Gattinara's

[49] *Aktenstücke*, p. 282.
[50] *Letters and Papers*, 3/2, no. 1546.
[51] *Aktenstücke*, p. 294, cf. pp. 285–9.
[52] *Ibid.*, pp. 303, 310.
[53] *Ibid.*, pp. 312–13, 323.
[54] *Ibid.*, pp. 323, 336.
[55] *Ibid.*, p. 325.
[56] *Ibid.*, p. 330.
[57] *Ibid.*, pp. 321, 399.
[58] *Ibid.*, pp. 315, 321–5, 399.
[59] Cf. Walther, 'Kanzleiordnungen', p. 384; Walser, *Zentralbehörden*, pp. 64, 129, 156, 225.

and dependent upon the Grand Chancellor for his advancement, had been made one of the three permanent secretaries of the imperial chancellery[60] and would soon enjoy a meteoric rise. Writing to Charles on 7 October concerning the irregularities of Diego de Mendoza in Catalonia and the need to replace him as viceroy with the Archbishop of Taragona, Gattinara gives vent to his growing anxiety and dissatisfaction. Advising his master not to lend credence to the opinions of Hannart, the vice-chancellor or Urries he continues:

According to my perception there are some aggressive spirits dispatching many things arbitrarily and without considering the issue. Thus in my belief many things are dispatched under the table without coming to my notice nor to that of another who might take them seriously. I have promptly written you that it may please you to establish M. de Palence [Mota] for signing in my stead. And it seems to me that you ought to continue during my absence to instruct all the secretaries that whatever letters they bring to you for signing should be seen and marked either by the said lord of Palence or by myself. I hope that you will concur and [that] matters will be dispatched more advisedly, for when dispatches are signed by your majesty without my signature there follows one of two sorts of mischief: either they are dispatched thus so that I remain uninformed and am unable to respond; or if they are brought to me for signing before first obtaining your endorsement, should I refuse to sign them, I would incur dislike. I thereby produce misunderstanding and irritation, while appearing to diminish your authority by refusing the dispatches which should be subscribed by your hand.[61]

Perhaps the chancellor could have subscribed to the observation of the Archduchess Margaret, rendered one month later: 'our emperor has a head like any other, subject to contrary winds applied to his ear, that sometimes are able to cause him to waver'.[62]

By 4 December Gattinara had rejoined the emperor at Oudenarde and took in hand the mounting correspondence with Henry VIII.[63] But the inroads made by the secretaries into the dispatching of business can be measured by the augmented role of Jean Lalemand, who in the preparation of the treaty of Windsor played a part second only to his master, the Grand Chancellor.[64] The rapid rise of Lalemand during these months can only be understood as taking place with the connivance and support of the Grand Chancellor. For not only did this bright, ambitious secretary appear a supple, facile instrument to the emperor in the implementing of his own policy, but he rapidly became the chief aid and, ironically, the occasional confidant of the ageing chancellor, overly burdened with responsibilities and wracked by repeated attacks of gout. Moreover, to appreciate what was

[60] Walther, 'Kanzleiordnungen', Dok. 3, p. 388.   [61] *Aktenstücke*, p. 387.
[62] *Ibid.*, p. 442.   [63] *Ibid.*, p. 476.
[64] Alonso de Santa Cruz, *Crónica del Emperador Carlos V*, La Real Academia de la Historia, 5 vols. (Madrid, 1920–5), I, 516; BRT (Misc.), fols. 526–27ᵛ.

happening during these early years of Charles' reign and in order to understand the gradual displacement of the chancellorship by the increasing use of secretaries, it is not enough to attend to the different stages and developments of respective chancelleries; both the personalities and interests of the major protagonists and the way in which they perceive each other must be taken into account.

Gattinara was the most untypical of Renaissance statesman or courtiers, violating all the sterotypes. Promptness of thought, an upright, even austere mentality, a burning devotion to the dynasty, an awesome capacity for work all recommended him as a servant of the Habsburgs. Yet his sense of personal honor which allowed him to be distant with his equals and proud with his masters gave him, as the Archduchess Margaret could well attest, an independence of mind that could be wearing on a superior. Behind an apparently jovial demeanor evident in his cordial treatment of foreign dignitaries and his huge efforts to be pleasing to them, the chancellor nourished a clear sense both of what was his due and how the imperial government should be run. Irrepressible in expressing his views, he could prove obdurate, impolitic, easily nettled. Age and illness accentuated these last qualities and drove an inevitable wedge between him and the young monarch whom he wished not only to serve but to educate and enhance to the role of a world emperor.

To the youthful emperor, struggling toward independence of mind and action, the unwearied attentions, directives, admonitions of his great servant, who was so experienced in diplomacy and administration, so unstinting in the business of government, were at first awesome and reassuring. But soon they had the accumulated effect of being slightly wearisome and an inherent check upon Charles' own development. Not that the reserved, dignified Habsburg expressed himself on the subject. We need to intuit from the situation in which he found himself and from the pronounced silences and failures to respond to his chancellor. In the first place the appointment of this elderly demon for work to the office of Grand Chancellor had been imposed upon Charles, by his aunt, the Archduchess Margaret, and his grandfather the Emperor Maximilian. The repeated use of the consulta or extensive memorandum whereby the old dynastic servant sought to instruct and guide his young lord reveals less a direct influence on Charles than a source of irritation. Judged by the silences and absences, the delayed or never attained audiences about which Gattinara complains,[65] the emperor early wearied of the deluge of didacticism, instruction and admonition from a man whose services were otherwise too precious for the dynasty to dismiss. Not that the chancellor lacked important influence upon the reluctant pupil, but it was often oblique and transmuted. After

[65] Bornate, 'Doc.', p. 415; Claretta, 'Notice', pp. 312–13.

37

The emperor and his chancellor

Chièvres' death, in May 1521, the emperor struggled during the next decade to define his own outlook upon the world, his own work habits, his own methods of government.[66]

The emerging personal government of Charles has been happily, if ponderously, identified as a *Kabinettsregierung* whereby the established offices and channels of government are circumvented and the ruler works closely and directly with a few trusted servants.[67] One of these agents, the affable hard-working Francisco de los Cobos, has become well known to history. With one hand on the emperor's pulse and the other in the public till, Cobos expected little other than a constant flow of favors from his master and undoubtedly proved an enormous relief to Charles from the demanding, difficult personality of his chancellor. The Castilian secretary's Aragonese counterpart was Jean Lalemand, a Burgundian, who owed his advancement to the chancellor and made the most of his master's need for able assistance with the paper work.[68] Despite the existence of sufficient material to constitute a fair sized political biography, Lalemand has been overlooked by historians and has to the knowledge of this author never received the extensive treatment that his work and role warrant. For, with the possible exception of Ferdinand's secretary Almazán, Lalemand can be identified as the first state secretary in early modern Europe. His rapid rise to imperial favor in some ways outpaced that of Cobos. Before the imperial court reached Worms he had been made controller-general for the Crown of Aragon, a post which allowed him to supervise the chancelleries of Aragon and Naples and intervene in treasury matters occasionally to his own personal aggrandizement.[69] While his master was absent at Calais, Lalemand rose in imperial favor by serving as principal expediter of foreign correspondence pertaining to England and the Netherlands, both inside and outside of the chancellery. After the treaty of Windsor and the return to Spain, this section of the chancellery's business fell to him, although his work was reviewed by Gattinara and personally supervised by the emperor, who took a direct hand in the Netherlands correspondence.[70] Charming and bright, dispatching mounds of work with amazing alacrity, Lalemand appeared ever more indispensable to both Charles and Gattinara. Martin de Salinas, the Infante Ferdinand's representative at the imperial court, early recognized Lalemand as most desirous of the archduke's favors and henceforth worth cultivating. To secure his further advancement the Burgundian secretary married the daughter of Philippe Hanneton (12 June

---

[66] Cf. Walser, *Zentralbehörden*, pp. 166–70, which presents the best analysis available on Gattinara and his relationship to the emperor.
[67] *Ibid.*, p. 28.   [68] Keniston, *Cobos*, p. 75.
[69] HHSA (Belgien), PA 91/2, fols. 1, 123–34.
[70] HHSA (Belgien), PA 13/3, fols. 1–104, PA 17/2, fol. 294.

1524) and soon after became Lord of Bouclans.[71] Comparable to Cobos in so many respects, Lalemand nevertheless lacked the discretion of the Castilian secretary. By using his position to advance his own interests, often in a ruthless manner that bestirred distrust and jealousy among those who could do him harm, and by his tampering with and even counterfeiting public documents – always a real danger from those in or near the chancellery – this facile Burgundian secretary would eventually be responsible for his own downfall.[72]

[71] A. Rodríguez Villa, ed., 'El emperador Carlos V y su corte. Cartas de D. Martin de Salinas', *Boletín de la Real Academia de la Historia*, *43* (1903), 84, 164–5, 178, 180.

[72] Alfred Spont, *De cancellariae regum Franciae officiariis et emolumento 1440–1523* (Besançon, 1894), pp. 25–6 presents a document, *Contra empiricos*, dated 14 December 1485, directed against the swarms of forgers hovering around the chancellery.

3

The conflict between chancellor and
emperor

If during the Calais conference the seeds of future administrative friction
and dislocation were sown, the bitter first fruit became evident to Gattinara
himself with the return of the emperor to Spain in July 1522. According
to a hitherto overlooked memorandum, part consulta, part remonstrance,
that Gattinara composed probably in July of 1525, which will be designated
here as the Brussels remonstrance, the chancellor dated the beginning of
his ordeal from these months subsequent to Charles' reappearance in the
peninsula. Although the remonstrance attributes to the gout a protracted
illness in the late autumn, Salinas speaks of a pain in Gattinara's side
accompanied by a severe coughing that kept the chancellor incapacitated
for forty days. In fact it was feared that he would die and even though his
recovery relieved the minds of many at court, Salinas observed that such
an illness for a man of his age did not augur well. Wracked anew by the
gout, forced to try to keep up with the roving court of his master as it moved
from Valladolid to Burgos and later to Pamplona and Vitoria,[1] Gattinara
sensed his authority as chancellor being circumvented and his influence
with the emperor waning. Added to his extreme physical discomfort and
his growing fear as to the reduction of his office and role in the Habsburg
administration was the increasing anxiety caused by his mounting debts
and Charles' failure to pay a salary that was one year in arrears. The
physical, political and financial factors combined to produce that petulance

[1] AGRB (PEA), 1471 (4), fols. [19ᵛ-20]/[24-24ᵛ]. Cf. *supra*, Introduction, fn. 20. See App. III for
a transcription of the relevant passages. To my knowledge the only other scholar who has noted
the existence of this very important document is Hayward Keniston, who nevertheless confuses
it with the earlier remonstrance in Claretta, 'Notice', pp. 309-24, a confusion which he further
compounds by identifying this last document in French with the remonstrance addressed to the
Archduchess Margaret which was translated into Italian. Cf. Claretta, 'Notice', pp. 324-32.
Although the later Brussels remonstrance will occasionally draw upon materials and language
presented earlier in the Claretta 'Remonstrance', the two are quite different works, which forces
one to conclude that Keniston never read the AGRB manuscript. Cf. Keniston, *Cobos*, p. 397,
fn. 7. On the movement and location of the imperial court cf. Jean de Vandenesse, *Journal des
voyages de Charles-Quint de 1514 à 1551*, II, Collection des voyages des souverains des Pays-Bas, ed.
[L.P.] Gachard (Brussels, 1874), pp. 33-6. On Salinas' remarks see Rodríguez Villa, 'Cartas de
Salinas', *43*, 56-8.

40

discoverable in the first of several remonstrances which Gattinara in succeeding years would direct to his master. Their tone was hardly designed to improve relations between the emperor and his chancellor.

Gattinara's first remonstance can be dated as having been composed sometime in the late spring or early summer of 1523.[2] Here he pungently represents himself as one who is ignored by the emperor or kept waiting one or two hours for an audience with him, while his master receives nonentities, dispenses trivia and thus reduces his chancellor to a 'tavern sign'.[3] Set in the context of his overall service to Charles and the mounting disappointment and frustration that he experiences, the remonstrance largely pertains, however, to his personal finances and his inadequate remuneration. Precious as these financial details may be to a biographer, they do not concern us here. In passing, however, one may note that Gattinara claims as his greatest single expense the maintenance of a table to which he invited with some degree of regularity members of the diplomatic circle at court, royal counsellors and visiting dignitaries. Only toward the end of the remonstrance does he address himself to the political aspect of his disenchantment. As a bridge between the financial and political motifs he observes rather interestingly and with some justification that the chancellors of England and of France enjoy a remuneration quadruple that of their Burgundian imperial counterpart – but Gattinara hastens to claim as his not entirely undesired recompense that he has quadruple their work.[4] In concluding, Gattinara asks that the emperor either reaffirm and reestablish the powers of his chancellorship or dismiss him from office that he might retire to a much desired rest on his Italian estates.[5]

In this instance the chancellor's request for the reassertion of his office, as he conceived its powers to be, bears repetition here:

I beg you Sire, very humbly that your good pleasure may be to let me know if my service is agreeable to you or not. And if it is agreeable that you give such evidence of it by external acts that all others may know it, by daily granting to me agreeable audiences in order that I might be able to communicate, treat and conclude the affairs of my charge, as my predecessors in this office have been accustomed, without suffering others to occupy the preeminent aspects of my office; and that all decisions pertaining to favors, graces, appointments to and distribution of offices be done in my presence and that it not be in the power of the secretary nor any other to tell or declare them to the parties involved without [consulting]

---

[2] Although when the remonstrance refers to the present pope as one who along with Chièvres and others received a distribution of money from Charles at Barcelona (1519–20), Claretta unaccountably identifies him with Clement VII, the reference can only be to Adrian VI, who as Cardinal of Tortosa was present at Charles' court at this time. Furthermore, Gattinara speaks twice of having been in the office of chancellor for four and one half years, which counting from his installation on 15 October 1518 would suggest April 1523. Cf. Claretta 'Notice', pp. 318–20.

[3] *Ibid.*, pp. 312–13.

[4] *Ibid.*, p. 322, cf. p. 315.   [5] *Ibid.*, pp. 323–4, cf. p. 309.

me and by my mouth; and to provide that when I, just as my predesessors have been accustomed, may summon a council in my apartments or at court or before the Grand Chamberlain or in another place as designated – be [such council] for the Indies, or petitions or other particular matters of your affairs as need may occur – that they be obliged to come, under penalty of losing their wages, except if they have the legitimate excuse of illness, or that Your Majesty has commanded some other task for them and that they be required [thus] to inform the usher who would summon them.[6]

Before leaving the consideration of this remonstrance we need to emphasize at once the difficulty and importance of its dating. Its early twentieth-century editor did not even commit himself to a year but implied some time in the period between the beginning of Clement VII's pontificate (November 1523) and the coronation of Charles V (February 1530). Keniston justifiably placed it in 1526 at a time when the strained relationship between the emperor and his chancellor is a known fact. Walser, without sensing the problem, placed its composition some time after the death of Philip Hanneton and before the news of the death of Adrian VI (November 1522 to November 1523). In the opinion of the present writer Walser is correct, the time being about April 1523,[7] although it might seem surprising that the relationship between emperor and chancellor had deteriorated so rapidly. In this respect the Brussels remonstrance of 1525 resolves the problem by making it clear that the tension between the two was already considerable immediately after the return of the court to Spain.

Despite the burden of this deteriorating relationship, the growing pressure of penury and the frequent pain produced by the gout, the period 1523 to 1525 marks the height of Gattinara's creative efforts in the proliferation of those councils which would constitute the reorganization of the Spanish central administration.[8] More than any other person Gattinara was responsible for this governmental overhaul and the directing force of his mind is evident in a circular memorandum that he sent out to the emperor and his own fellow councillors at the very end of 1523 for their reactions and contributions. Gattinara designated the topics for consideration, set forth the issues involved with each and by his interjections or conclusions maintained his control of the discussion. Of the seven topics treated – fear of God; selection of personnel; order of consultation; finance; subjects' love; reputation; the securing of Italy – only the third is immediately relevant to the administrative issue at hand.

By *ordre de conseil* the chancellor seeks to discover means of expediting

---

[6] *Ibid.*, pp. 323–4.

[7] On the question of the document's dating see Keniston, *Cobos*, p. 106; Walser, *Zentralbehörden*, p. 164; and *supra*, fn. 2.

[8] This achievement has been magnificently presented by Walser, *Zentralbehörden*, pp. 199–228.

The conflict between chancellor and emperor

the dispatch of the emperor's business all in an effort to realize greater rapidity and order in the decision-making process. Disturbed by the way in which his master loses time and holds the couriers waiting, while dispatching trivia, Gattinara asks for the introduction of the French practice of using a cachet for expediting all unimportant business, leaving the emperor's time free for dispatching the important matters of state, war, finance, favors and graces. The use of the cachet would provide security against fraud, spare the emperor and accelerate affairs. Gattinara offers the alternative of a secretary's signature, but if the cachet is used a person should be assigned to guard and use it under the control of the chancellor.[9]

Fearful that his master's time would be consumed among the very diversity of councils, that efforts overlapped so that important matters became buried and that the councils spent their time in consultation rather than execution, Gattinara urged as his second recommendation the establishment of an overall Council of State. In order that it might possess this general superintendence and that the more important councils might participate in its activities, councillors from finance, war and the Indies would serve on this council and the consultas from their councils would first be submitted to the Council of State. Thereby Charles, *sans rompre la teste*, might quickly be exposed to pressing matters of importance. In lending his enthusiastic support to this proposal, the Grand Master, Gorrevod, observed that both France and England had something comparable for the dispatching of important business which would here augur well for the conduct of affairs.[10]

In order to realize the effectiveness of the new Council of State, Gattinara proposed that an able secretary be appointed to manage the business of the council, expedite its decisions and maintain its agenda. As an outline of the responsibilities exercised by those supervisory secretaries, one of whom came to be attached to each of the many councils and served as the real agent of their operation, Gattinara's words here are worth repeating:

He alone will have charge of redacting in writing every day what will be done and concluded in your Council of State – all the deliberations and resolutions with the commissions and provisions for executing them and the names of the persons to

---

[9] The manuscript of this important consulta, HHSA (Belgien), PC 68, fols. 3–30, is available in two published versions: the first, somewhat abbreviated but more readily available redaction, by Ernest Gossart in the appendix to his *Espagnols*, pp. 236–58; and Karl Brandi's complete redaction, 'Aus den Kabinettsakten des Kaiser', Berichte und Studien zur Geschichte Karls V, XIX, *Nachrichten von der Akademie der Wissenschaften zu Göttingen*, Philologisch-Historische Klasse (1941), pp. 181–222. It should be noted that only with the opening of the Gattinara family archives in 1980 did the original consulta, covering eight folio sides in the chancellor's own hand, come to light (ASV, 7/8). To produce the circular consulta of HHSA (Belgien), PC 68, fols. 3–30, Gattinara simply had a chancellery scribe copy out the entirety of the original in consecutive passages, leaving sufficient space for the reactions of the imperial councillors, his colleagues. I am grateful to Drs Maurizio Cassetti and Luigi Avonto for freely providing me with a xerox copy of this consulta.   [10] Brandi, 'Kabinettsakten', pp. 194–7.

43

whom will be given the responsibility for their execution and that at the beginning of each council meeting the first order of business will be to have the relation and information of what has been executed and of what remains to be completed from the preceding decisions in order that the task of the council may be known and that faults may be remedied so that nothing is neglected or overlooked.[11]

After the four councillors consulted rendered their prompt support Gattinara, as was to be expected, recommended his most valuable secretary Jean Lalemand for the position. Among his other responsibilities he would keep the register for the council.[12] By thus providing a vital institutional basis for the secretaries within their respective collegiate contexts, Gattinara ironically contributed to that development of the imperial government in a direction other than what he had envisaged.

Desirous of making more effective the instrument of the new council, Gattinara laid out in an incisive consulta of mid-September 1524 a tighter pattern of work for his fellow councillors and more specifically a reordering of the finances, the military and the offices of the imperial household. The consulta reflects the principles controlling Gattinara's reorganization of the central government at this time: first a definition of tasks and a distribution of the members of the emerging Council of State to address those tasks; secondly a heightened professionalism evinced by the express effort to equip these task forces with the best legal and technical assistants available; thirdly, a confluence of several bodies of ordered information and counsel whereby the various dossiers might be reduced to one – 'all in a single volume, well organized according to the rubrics of each office' – which could be readily reviewed and acted upon by the emperor. Here also we find the chancellor resuming his previous effort, attempted in Aragon and Naples, to trim bureaucratic fat by cutting down on superfluous personnel from counsellors and secretaries to chamberlains and concierges who swelled the numbers of an officialdom already out of control. For his attack upon the supernumeraries populating the councils and the offices of justice, Gattinara sought the assistance of possibly the most gifted political and legal mind in Castile, Galíndez de Carvajal. And yet despite the transcendent principles of regularity, uniformity and simplification operative in and shining through this most suggestive document of early modern administration the two chief secretaries mentioned therein, Lalemand and Cobos, would by their close association with the emperor help to move the processes of government in a different direction. While certainly the most articulate of all Charles' counsellors, Gattinara was not thereby the more successful in achieving his goals. For in its effort to coordinate the various

[11] *Ibid.*, pp. 197–8.
[12] *Ibid.*, p. 198.

collegiate bodies and their functions, the Council of State never received the support that it deserved and soon withered.[13] The reform of the central government, initiated after Charles' return to the peninsula, had the effect not only of distinguishing and differentiating a number of councils but also of enhancing the authority of individual secretaries as the effective agents of these councils. As Salinas perceived the main outlines beginning to emerge from this reform, Cobos controlled all business for Castile, Urries for Aragon, Pedro García for Naples, Soria for Rome and Coacola for war, along with the special positions occupied by Lalemand and Hannart. Twenty months later he could report on their development: as secretary of the Council of State Lalemand had charge of the essentials and was very favored by Charles; Cobos for his part had charge of the Estado of Castile; the other secretaries were of no account, for in these two Estados consisted the Estado of His Majesty. As secretary to the Council of State, Lalemand in time would acquire the title of *el primero secretario*, first secretary.[14]

Whatever improvements emerged from the reorganization of the central administration during these months, the picture of the chancellor that obtains in this same period is one of a man overwhelmed with responsibilities. On the morning of Christmas eve 1523 he writes from Pamplona to the Archduchess Margaret in order to explain a lapse in the correspondence which had occasioned a misunderstanding. Because he has been relying on M. de la Roche, none of the dispatches in question have gone through his own hands or under his seal. And why was such a delegation of work necessary? Here the chancellor launches into the insupportable burden of responsibilities that he has shouldered since his arrival in Spain: his attendance upon affairs of state, the consultas for all the councils of the kingdoms of Castile, Aragon, Naples and also the Indies together with his assembling, presiding over and addressing the cortes have all constrained him to allow this delegation of responsibility so that he might spare himself. As Salinas apprised his master, all business ultimately went through the chancellor's hands.[15]

The chancellor became ever more dependent upon Lalemand both for expediting the business of the chancellery and also for gaining the attention

---

[13] HHSA (Belgien), DD 231, fols. 360–360ᵛ. I wish to thank Dr Peter Marzahl of the University of Constance for drawing my attention to this document and kindly providing me with a xerox copy. See its transcription in App. IV. For an analysis of the Council of State and its aborted development see Walser, *Zentralbehörden*, pp. 205, 231–66.
[14] Rodríguez Villa, 'Cartas de Salinas', *43*, 55–6, 84, 194. For a late example of Lalemand's title of first secretary see the dispatch of Miguel Mai, imperial ambassador at Rome, to him, dated 15 Nov. 1528: HHSA (Belgien), PA 95, fol. 308.
[15] HHSA (Belgien), PA 13 (alt 14)/2, fol. 294; Rodríguez Villa, 'Cartas de Salinas', p. 58.

of the emperor. Indeed it appears that whether out of Gattinara's inability
to keep up with the movements and changes of location of his master or
for some undisclosed reason the two were separated at times by a
considerable distance. As Lalemand remained in attendance upon the
emperor, the chancellor began to become dangerously dependent upon his
secretary. Driven by financial need, he appealed to Lalemand during the
middle of the autumn of 1524 on two separate matters to intervene in his
behalf with the emperor. The first instance concerned his desire to be made
a cardinal, which he had earlier refused at a time when the Archbishop of
Capua was in Spain on a special mission from the pope. The second
involved the emperor's license for Gattinara to undertake the sale of the
office of chancellor of Naples for 10,000 ducats.[16] Ultimately successful in
this last, he would nevertheless have to wait five years for the hat. As a
lay chancellor for almost the entirety of his tenure, Gattinara lacked the
necessary perquisites enjoyed by a Du Prat or a Wolsey – those ecclesiastical
emoluments that made possible the effective operation of the office and
whose absence so seriously hampered his own political activity. And as other
chancellors such as Wolsey had come to recognize, physical distance from
the source of power and the attendance of another upon the prince could
only weaken one's own position. Well might the Grand Chancellor have
cause to brood on the apparently more fortunate condition of his great
contemporary counterparts.[17]

   The culmination of our inquiry into the displacement of the chancellorship by the secretaries and the crisis of the relationship between the
emperor and his chancellor coalesce in the stormy events at Toledo in early
July 1525 as described by diplomatic correspondents and as set forth by
the protagonists. Three weeks beforehand, Gattinara's old friend Peter
Martyr of Anghiera indicated that a storm was brewing but confidently
remarked that the indispensable chancellor would be able to defend his
office against the intrusions of aggressive secretaries. On the eighth of that
month Tunstal, Richard Wingfield and Sampson, reporting to Wolsey,
observed that the chancellor had lately abstained from exercising his office
on account of certain Spanish secretaries that had 'usurped upon it' but
the matter was now settled.[18] A dispatch of the Venetian ambassadors,
Navagero, Contarini and Priuli to the Serenissima dated 6 July confirms
the facts that Gattinara sought to retire because of the usurpation of his

[16] HHSA (Belgien), PA 91/4, fols. 249ᵛ, 351–2 [or 318, 320]. The foliation here has been altered,
producing some uncertainty.
[17] For such comparisons with Wolsey and Du Prat by Gattinara see Claretta, 'Notice', p. 312.
[18] *Letters and Papers*, 4/1, no. 1483. On Martyr's observation see his letter to the Archbishop of
Cosenza, Toledo 13 June 1525, in Martyr's correspondence, *Opus epistolarum Petri Martyris
Mediolanensis...*(Alcalá, 1530), p. 399, no. 814.

The conflict between chancellor and emperor

office by secretaries. Three days later the Venetian embassy followed up their brief statement with a fuller report that warrants quoting.

Toledo, 9 July 1525: – Returning now to the matter of the Magnificent Grand Chancellor about whom we gave notice to the Council of Ten, because then it was very secret, but now quite public and resolved, we may impart it fully to Your Serenity. – His Magnificence accordingly on seeing how much his jurisdiction had been usurped by others, complained about it to His Imperial Majesty.in the presence of the Count of Nassau, the Governor of Bresse [Gorrevod] and Monseigneur de Beaurain. His Imperial Majesty replied to him that he ought to put in writing all these complaints and send it to him. This his Magnificence accomplished. After another day with the council attending and even all the Spanish, that is the Comendador mayor [Cobos] and Don Hugo de Moncada being present to witness, his Imperial Majesty caused to be read both the proposal of this Magnificent Chancellor and his own reply. This last stated that these laws of Spain, wherein for him his chancellorship was founded, had not been in use for many years and [were not] after all what they thus appeared to him to be. This [reply] was taken so ill by the Magnificent Chancellor that he, in the presence of all requested permission to retire [from court and the imperial service] which his Imperial Majesty very promptly granted him rather than denied. The following day, his Imperial Majesty, having repented his decision, sent the governor of Bresse to his house to make him understand how much he [the emperor] was displeased with the words that had followed and how he had desired that the proposal and response might have been burned, but that he invited from him another memorial as to what he requested so that he [the emperor] would understand him. Then he would have [the governor] beg [the chancellor] to continue at this court of Castile and to consult with the council in the palace. The chancellor sent him the memorial but did not want to remain at court nor to go to the palace before it had been dispatched. Nevertheless the first day was not to be repeated, as we report above. Yesterday then the bishop of Osma [Loaysa], confessor of Caesar, was to dine with His Majesty along with others sent by his Imperial Majesty so that they might conduct his Magnificence to the palace, where, when we understood and it was publicly divulged throughout the court, assembled by His Imperial Majesty, he was embraced most lovingly and treated with the most honorable and loving words able to be desired. After having seen all the council, His Majesty in the presence of all still said the most complimentary words concerning this Magnificent Chancellor, promising to grant him such a favor that all the world would know how much he loved him and how greatly he considered himself to be obligated to him. Thus we hope his Magnificence has been restored to greater reputation than ever and today the count of Nassau and the most Illustrious Viceroy [Lannoy] have gone to convey his Magnificence home where they have dined together.[19]

---

[19] The two letters are published in the first appendix of Hermann Baumgarten, *Geschichte Karls V* (Stuttgart, 1885–92), II/2, 707–8.

The emperor and his chancellor

Fortunately for our understanding of the decay of the chancellorship both of these memorials mentioned in the letter of the Venetian ambassadors are identifiable and available. Superficially, it would appear that the first of these is presented in the articles published by Herman Vander Linden in *Bulletin de la Commission Royale d'Histoire*[20] because of the marginal response of the emperor to each of Gattinara's complaints. But the preface to these same articles makes clear that they have been preceded by another memorial, that his retirement has been revoked and that the Grand Master Gorrevod is serving as conciliator, all of which corresponds with the Venetian report.[21] The first memorial can be identified with what we have called here the Brussels remonstrance.[22] Written in a tight, controlled secretary hand on both sides of eleven folio sheets, the remonstrance can be dated from internal evidence as having originated at this time.[23] The evenness of the prose would suggest less a draft than a copy. The memorial is composed in a number of fairly distinct parts, for the work seems to have been initially conceived to meet the imperial demands for putting in writing 'tutte queste sue querele,[24] but by the time that Gattinara had reached his third complaint, which his own hand would appear to have so designated in the margin, the format has assumed the basic features reminiscent of the earlier remonstrance of 1523: presentation of the three motives which caused him to accept the insupportable charge of Grand Chancellor. Whereas in the earlier instance he had claimed service to God and the public good of Christendom, increase of his own honor and reputation and giving order to his master's affairs, offices and estates, he now lists the desire for

[20] Cf. Herman Vander Linden, 'Articles soumis à Charles-Quint par son chancelier Gattinara concernant l'office de la chancellerie en 1528', *Bulletin de la Commission Royale d'Histoire*, 100 (1936), 267–74. Vander Linden's introductory remarks indicate that 1528 is a misprint for what he considers to be 1526 (cf. p. 265). Otherwise his is an accurate transcription of AGRB (PEA), 1471 (4), fols. 9–10ᵛ.

[21] Cf. Vander Linden, 'Articles', p. 267.

[22] *Supra*, Introduction, fn. 20. See also *supra*, fn. 1.

[23] The only statement in the remonstrance that might appear to date it a few months later is the reference to the providing for '*lestat et offices de la maison de limperatrice/et reyne votre compagne*': AGRB (PEA), 1471 (4) fol. [15ᵛ]/[20ᵛ]. Yet the entire passage, pertaining to Charles' departure for Italy, is to be understood in a prospective sense, and the imminence of Charles' marriage to Isabella of Portugal was evident among all at court well before July 1525 and indeed had virtually been imposed upon Charles by the cortes of Toledo (1525). Cf. *Cortes de los antiguos reinos de León y de Castilla*, La Real Academia de la Historia (Madrid, 1882), IV, 405. On 25 June 1525 Charles informed his brother of his resolve to marry Isabella of Portugal. See Wilhelm Bauer, ed., *Die Korrespondenz Ferdinands I* (Vienna, 1912–38), I, 308. On 3 April 1525 Salinas (Rodríguez Villa 'Cartas de Salinas', *43*, 407) had reported that Charles' decision had been made to marry Isabella, and as early as 10–27 March 1525 in his Madrid consulta. Gattinara was figuring the marriage into his calculations for prying the emperor loose from Spain to go to Italy. See Karl Brandi, 'Nach Pavia. Pescara und die italienischen Staaten, Sommer und Herbst 1525', Berichte und Studien zur Geschichte Karls V, XVII, *Nachrichten von der Gesellschaft der Wissenschaften zu Göttingen*, Philologisch-Historische Klasse (1939), p. 207.

[24] Baumgarten, *Geschichte*, II/2, 708.

honor, hope of remuneration and service to God.[25] The pressure of his own financial indebtedness and the need to frame specific complaints help to explain the weight given here to the issue of his own remuneration. Unfortunately the composition breaks off toward what would appear to be the end of his exposition of this issue. Thus, we are deprived of the treatment of his intention of serving God which, given earlier versions of the same basic topic, could well have proved valuable for his conception of empire and Christendom. Did time prevent him from completing his proposed exposition? More probably the remaining folios have been lost. Nevertheless, by far the most important section pertains to his honor, for it opens up the subject of the current functioning as well as the presumed rights of the chancellorship. Finally, the document as a whole has in many ways greater value for the biographer than Gattinara's more formal, self-conscious autobiography not only because of its providing precious links in his career but also because of its very directness and urgency. Only the light the Brussels remonstrance can cast upon the administrative issue and upon the relationship between the emperor and his chancellor interests us.

The dangers of the retrospective judgment, namely of the telescoping and of attributing to an earlier period, here 1522–3, the features of one's present condition, are greatly reduced in the interpretation of this document by the confluence and enfolding of times: the time represented by the April 1523 consulta/remonstrance provides a base supporting and confirming the more attenuated triangle of time evident in the Brussels remonstrance. Within this triangle of perceived time the forum of court and chancellery, the protagonists of emperor, chancellor and principal secretaries and the deepening tensions of disagreement have persisted.

By his opening remarks Gattinara indicates that the Brussels remonstrance addresses itself to the complaints which the emperor, on 4 July 1525, requested him to set forth; the chancellor welcomes the opportunity to present them in written form rather than orally and have as his audience the assemblage of counsellors.[26] Having established this point he proceeds to a constant theme throughout this and other remonstrances: the provision of graces and favours and their regulation according to the Aristotelian notion of a distributive justice whereby each receives in keeping with his merits and service. Preferment must occur in accordance with impartiality and disinterestedness rather than feeding the passions and interests of friends and relations. To proceed otherwise in violation of distributive

---

[25] AGRB (PEA), 1471 (4), fols. [16–16ᵛ]/[21–21ᵛ]; cf. Claretta, 'Notice', pp. 309–10. It is this sort of passage that may have misled Keniston into thinking that the Brussels manuscript was the same as the remonstrance published by Claretta.
[26] AGRB (PEA), 1471 (4), fol. [14].

justice would vitiate the subjects' love of their prince and allow good servants to fall into despair.[27] Digressing somewhat, Gattinara waxes hot against those bad ministers who delude the emperor and prevent him from going to Italy to correct the excesses of his soldiery:

> For the abuses that your troops commit are indeed so abominable that Turks and infidels would not do them and instead of naming you liberator of Italy they will be able to say you have introduced the greatest and most excessive tyranny that ever was, for neither the Goths nor the Lambards nor Attila, who was named *flagellum dei*, who for a long time tyrannized Italy, ever committed such cruelties.[28]

Small wonder that even Charles, who more than most rulers readily tolerated frank criticism, should on the following day urge that the remonstrance be burned.[29]

By honor Gattinara means the dignity of the office of Grand Chancellor. The authority and preeminence of this office has been illegally transgressed by subordinates who, he complains, instead of receiving orders come to tell him what ought to be dispatched. These inferior persons consult what the chancellor should properly consult and make reports and proposals which he ought to perform. Thus by an inversion of roles – *en retournant ce dessoubz dessus* – servants become masters in violation of what all previous chancellors have been accustomed to experience. As one of the principal ministers, an instrument of and participant in God's grace, and that minister who most often forms the opinion of the rest, he cannot afford to be crippled in the exercise of his office by a serious diminution of its authority. If he could be convinced that by this *desauctorisacion* the emperor's affairs might benefit, he would gladly welcome such deprivation and shame. More specifically this infringement upon his authority takes the form of some bold persons dispatching things at will without consultation and without his signature. In usurping his authority they seek to use its powers for their own aggrandizement: each becomes the master, each misleads innocent persons into believing that their cases are grave only to have them afterwards evaporate. In revealing a veritable paradise for graft and personal profit, Gattinara puts his finger on that feature of early modern bureaucracy that would particularly bedevil the Spanish civil service down to the twentieth century and contribute to vitiating the formal centralization of powers. By internal exactions and graft not only the secretaries but their clerks enrich themselves and pursue expedients without the emperor knowing about it. By selling safeconducts, legitimations, pardons and graces the secretary fattens at the emperor's expense. By conveying the impression

---

[27] *Ibid.*, fol. [14ᵛ].
[28] *Ibid.*, fols. [15–15ᵛ]/[20–20ᵛ].
[29] Cf. Bornate, 'Vita', p. 324 for a blander but equally moving indictment of what the imperial troops had done in Italy.

that those who dispatch favors are the same as those who grant them, the secretary makes himself absolute lord with his arbitrary and unique signature. Unwilling to have anything dispatched by means of a single signature, Gattinara urges a higher review and consultation.[30]

Arriving at the heart of his argument the chancellor avers that those who resist the imposition of order within the chancellery allege three positions against him:

The first, that the Catholic monarchs never had a chancellor in Spain but rather dispatched all through their secretaries and that this office is not necessary; second, that if Your Majesty would grant me authority such as my office requires, one would be able to say that I want to govern you, which would be badly received in Spain and elsewhere; third, that not having the distinctive powers of my office in the affairs of Spain and your departure for Italy being imminent, I ought to be patient now as before, having my hands full enough with affairs of state without occupying myself with more.[31]

Turning to the first of these accusations, Gattinara claims that the Catholic monarchs always had under another title an authorized person who performed the functions of a chancellor and whom all feared, esteemed and had recourse. Should the emperor find it in his interest to suppress the office as well as the title of chancellor, he, Gattinara, would have no cause to complain. But to maintain the title without its powers is a travesty. He continues:

The laws of Spain resolve the issue to the contrary. Accordingly my predecessor [Jean Le Sauvage] exercised it and I also before leaving this realm and after the return up to the time of my illness at Palencia and Valladolid. So much the more I would be able to use it now, since by the [action of the] cortes, without my asking for it, all offices and dignities have been opened to me, as a native of the kingdom, which is itself sufficient indication that I am pleasing to them in this office and am not poorly esteemed; neither have I nor would I transgress their laws by the exercise of my office.[32]

To the second accusation, he denies ever having wanted to govern the emperor; such an eventuality would be disastrous for his affairs. Yet he goes on to define an apportionment of work and responsibility whereby, while the chancellors of kingdoms have the task of dispatching all important

[30] AGRB (PEA), 1471 (4), fols. [16ᵛ–18]/[21ᵛ–23.] For the similarity between the end of this passage and Valdés' later portrait of the prototypal secretary see Alfonso de Valdés, *Diálogo de Mercurio y Caron*, ed. Jose F. Montesinos (Madrid, 1971), pp. 104–9.
[31] AGRB (PEA), 1471 (4), fols. [18–18ᵛ]/[23–23ᵛ].
[32] *Ibid.*, fol. [18ᵛ]/[23ᵛ]. On the unique acceptance of the naturalization of Gattinara for holding Spanish offices, first by the cortes of Toledo, 1 June–26 August 1525, and later by the cortes of Madrid in 1528, see *Cortes*, IV, 405, 453–4. For a recent valuable assessment of the cortes of 1525, see Charles David Hendricks, 'Charles V and the cortes of Castile: politics in Renaissance Spain' (unpublished dissertation, Cornell University, 1976), Chap. 6, esp. pp. 180, 210, 212.

business, kings and princes are always free to dispose at their pleasure of all offices, benefices and graces. Then redirecting the accusation toward his opponent he states:

One ought to say that you perform the dispatch of your affairs through the advice and council of your chancellor, and the entire kingdom will far prefer it to saying that in the ignorance of the chancellor and without his knowing how to speak about it, you conclude what belongs to his charge with a secretary who, as they say, commands the entire kingdom and induces you to do what he wants. If one is not able to have favors, nor offices, nor benefices except by his hands so that he holds them all bound and obligated and he knows well how to profit from them, having sole charge of everything which all the other secretaries are accustomed to have and exercising through himself and by his clerks five or six incompatible offices against the disposition of what you have accorded in the past cortes and what they ask now to be observed and executed, you, by not observing nor remedying it, are not able to apologize for Spain being divided into two factions, one being a single secretary who does all...and those of the other who will always be malcontent...[representing] the greater part of the realm.[33]

To the third objection he observes that as with his predecessor Jean Le Sauvage, prior to his leaving Spain in 1520, nothing was dispatched by a secretary without first being signed by him. But following the court's return to Castile in 1522 and since his having been overtaken with the gout at Palencia and Valladolid, matters have been altered and put on another track. From Burgos to Pamplona and then on to Vitoria, though punished continually by his malady, Gattinara sought a rectification of the present procedure. Obtaining a promise at Burgos, he found, nevertheless, that matters remained the same. Once having recovered from his own infirmities he now found that the emperor had fallen dangerously ill with quartan fever. Unable to obtain redress, he sought by the end of 1524 only to be allowed to retire to his estates and await the emperor's coming to Italy. Individual instances of secret commissions and even an oral provision to a benefice by the emperor without his being consulted drove him to the height of aggravation. If he could not enjoy his office according to the laws of Spain, he should be dismissed but not be allowed to suffer further humiliation.[34]

   Stripped of its details, Gattinara's memorial of 5 July 1525 constituted a massive attack against those secretaries who had been making inroads upon his jurisdiction as chancellor. Both the Venetian and the English ambassadorial reports make this abundantly clear. Although Cobos is never mentioned, it would have been evident to all that he was intended whenever reference was made to 'the secretary'. Was Lalemand included among these roving, rapacious secretaries? It was still too early for the chancellor to rid

[33] AGRB (PEA), 1471 (4), fols. [19–19ᵛ]/[24–24ᵛ].
[34] *Ibid.*, fols., [19ᵛ]/[24ᵛ], [20–20ᵛ]/[15–15ᵛ], [21ᵛ]/[16ᵛ].

himself of his illusions concerning his *créature* and invaluable assistant, his ostensible friend and presently his confidant. Nevertheless, to some observers Lalemand had by now definitely displaced Gattinara in the service of the emperor.[35] Behind his attack, serving as the support to his entire argument, was an understanding of the chancellery's development in 'Spain' which rested more on wish and fiction than on fact. He states and twice reiterates that the authority of the chancellorship is established by the laws of Spain. True, Gattinara could point to his immediate predecessor, Jean Le Sauvage, who seemed to enjoy or thought that he had enjoyed the full preeminence of a Burgundian Grand Chancellor translated to Spanish soil. But Sauvage's tenure and sojourn in the peninsula were too brief – barely a year – to serve as a test, and furthermore came at a time when the Flemings were riding high, playing fast and furiously. Projected back to the reign of Ferdinand and Isabella, the chancellor's vision corresponded even less to reality in this proto-secretarial age. Presumably by 'Spain' he intended Castile, but even in the case of Aragon it was the vice-chancellor rather than the chancellor who exercised real authority. Thus with good reason did the emperor on the following day fasten upon this point in his reply and deny that the laws of Spain provided currently for the authoritative office of chancellor.[36]

In the second memorial, invited by the emperor's efforts at a rapprochement evinced in the sending of Gorrevod, Gattinara returned to the charge. The ten articles with their introduction and conclusion addressed to the Grand Master constitutes a remarkable document, revealing the deep-seated institutional as well as personal tensions existing between the emperor and his chancellor. In the very first article he calls for the public reassertion of the full authority and rights of Grand Chancellor according to the laws and customs of each one of Charles' realms and lands. To this request, phrased more like a demand, the emperor through the Grand Master Gorrevod replies in the margin that the authority and predominance of the grand chancellorship pertains only to the Burgundian inheritance and does not apply in Aragon and Castile as the chancellor believes. In the second article Gattinara seeks the subordination and disciplining of the secretaries. His words reveal a deteriorating situation, the veritable hemorrhaging of the medieval chancellery:

That all the secretaries of the court be subordinated and obedient to the [office of chancellor] and do not meddle with proposals in the council, nor report anything, nor present nor read memorials to the council without orders from me as chancellor and that these secretaries do not dispatch nor cause to sign by His Majesty any letters whatsoever of state or of grace, if these letters have not been so ordered

[35] Rodríguez Villa, 'Cartas de Salinas', *43*, 407.
[36] Cf. Baumgarten, *Geschichte*, II/2, 708.

by His Majesty or by me in his name and that they first be seen and signed by me and that to this effect His Majesty does not conclude nor command to dispatch anything whatsoever of state or of grace when I am not present...[37]

In general Charles acceded to this demand but in recognizing the review by, and the seal of, the chancellor he shifted effective control to the president of the council from which the order emanated, thus affirming the new conciliar central administration that was so much the creation of his chancellor.[38] Charles flatly rejected as an unwarranted innovation the chancellor's effort to regularize and control all official communications with ambassadors and viceroys whereby all packets were to be delivered into his hands by the Master of the Post and in turn sent forth by the same official.[39] Furthermore, he refused the request that the chancellor have the right to review all the work of the Cámera de Castilla dealing with provisions, graces and favors, and likewise in Aragon intervene in these same matters hitherto committed to the vice-chancellor and the Council of Justice.[40] Charles found as irrelevant to the chancellor's office that a ban be placed upon plurality of offices practiced by counsellors and secretaries. Calling upon the observance of the law accorded at the cortes of Valladolid (1523) and reaffirmed at that of Toledo (1525), Gattinara had urged that none should enjoy a salary or emolument from an office that he did not directly exercise.[41] Here his blow was directed not only against Cobos and his ilk but also against the practice of using substitutes which had long existed in the Castilian chancellorship itself.[42] The last four articles are of a largely personal nature, only the eighth being pertinent to the frayed relationship between emperor and chancellor: he asked that he might have regular access to the person of the emperor for consultation and audience. Other evidence suggests that such ease of communication, expectable for a chancellor, had not been enjoyed since the return to Spain.[43]

This tense, angry exchange between the two protagonists is revealing. Beyond the obvious effort on Gattinara's part to extend the prerogatives and powers of the Burgundian chancellorship to their Spanish counterparts and to check, order and discipline the secretaries, there is the firm response on the young emperor's part to resist precisely this inflation of authority attempted by his great minister. Here Charles was on surer ground than his chancellor, for he could recognize and take into account the development of the secretaries under Ferdinand and Isabella. As he thus secured one further stone in the structure of his absolute power, he could afford to

---

[37] Vander Linden, 'Articles', p. 268.
[38] *Ibid.*
[39] *Ibid.*, p. 269.
[40] *Ibid.*, pp. 269–71 (Articles 4 and 6).
[41] *Ibid.*, p. 270. Cf. *Cortes*, p. 396, no. 90.
[42] Cf. Martín Postigo, *Cancillería*, pp. 265–6.
[43] Vander Linden, 'Articles', p. 272. Cf. Claretta, 'Notice', pp. 312–13.

mollify his sensitive, easily nettled chancellor. While Gattinara for his part might claim a personal triumph on 8 July amidst the imperial display of love and confidence bestowed upon him before the court, time would soon reveal that his situation had not changed at all and that the old problems persisted.

In the annals of political relationships there are few examples of such open confrontation between prince and minister which can parallel Gattinara's refusal to affix the seals to the treaty of Madrid. Neither Talleyrand's endurance of Napoleon's denunciation of his treasonous activities in 1809 nor Ludendorff's ultimatum to the Kaiser in 1917 conveys the same sense of challenging obduracy and defiance which Charles V's Grand Chancellor displayed in January 1526. The events that led up to this encounter derived from the embarrassments associated with the imperial victory at Pavia early in 1525. What to do with the captured French king and with a momentarily suppliant Italy became pressing issues when, to the consternation of both Charles and his chancellor, Francis I and his captor Lannoy, the viceroy of Naples, arrived in Spain on 17 June 1526. In the ensuing struggle between Lannoy and Gattinara over the treatment of Italy and more specifically the question of Milan – whether Francesco Sforza should be invested with the duchy or it be seized by the emperor as the generals urged – Gattinara, despite all his juristic and political knowledge, was at a distinct disadvantage. For Lannoy was a childhood chum of the emperor, a great Burgundian noble belonging to what was becoming the most august political club in Europe – the Order of the Golden Fleece. Ultimately it would be the chivalric argument rather than the voice of political discretion and far-sightedness that would carry the day with Charles of Habsburg.

The humanist Andrea Navagero, Contarini's successor as Venetian ambassador at the imperial court, early noted a discrepancy between the positions taken by the emperor and his chancellor. Although Gattinara sought to conceal the difficulty by insinuating that Navagero probably misunderstood the broad words of the emperor who, according to his chancellor, occasionally talked somewhat confusedly, Navagero deduced that the mind of the emperor on the vital question of Milan differed from that of the Grand Chancellor. Suffering from gout at home where Navagero visited him, Gattinara bombarded his master with statements that to depend on French promises would be ruinous. To the Venetian at this time, Gattinara appeared as *buonissimo italiano* and as one greatly fearing that from the union and peace with France much damage would come to Italy. That the ailing Gattinara should have been compelled, unwillingly, to let Lalemand draw up the heads of the later treaty of Madrid suggests that he was losing his long battle during the autumn of 1525 to convince the emperor that the Italian potentates rather than the King of France would prove better allies. In the midst of these negotiations Gattinara had difficulty in suppressing what was becoming an irrepressible urge to remove himself entirely from political affairs.[44]

Rather than pursuing these negotiations, we may avail ourselves of another shrewd Italian's account of the polarization of views within the emperor's council as how best to settle with Francis I and Italy. What Francesco Guicciardini presents in Book XVI of the *Storia d'Italia* as a single dramatic confrontation in the emperor's council between the viceroy Lannoy and Gattinara can, in the light of the Florentine historians's use of set speeches, be understood as a compression and clarifying of issues and events that may well have consumed several months in the latter part of 1525. Perhaps the crisis came in early December for, according to Navagero's letter of the tenth, gout had compelled the chancellor to withdraw from the arena, leaving the way clear to the viceroy and his party.[45] Whatever the particular set of circumstances, Gattinara vehemently urged the emperor to build upon the friendship of the Italian states, not seek to possess Milan but rather take Burgundy which was more justifiably his and not pursue the uncertain, indeed impossible, friendship of France's king. Lannoy, on the contrary, while advancing the generals' conviction that Milan must be possessed, argued that an alliance with the French was to be preferred to one with the Italians, 'our natural and eternal enemies', for one could put more confidence in the pledge of such a king than in the unnatural covetousness of priests and the suspicious baseness of merchants.[46] Reminded of his dignity, the emperor saw fit to reach an agreement with the King of France rather than pardon the Duke of Milan. Thus, when it came to affixing the seals to the treaty of Madrid on 14 January 1526 Gattinara adamantly refused, exceeding thereby the authority of his office. For, according to the Hanneton summary, the chancellor can object and have notice provided that he has remonstrated, yet ultimately he must accede to the *puissance absolue* of the prince.[47] But Gattinara, despite the justifiable indignation of the emperor, did not accede, claiming

---

[44] Emmanuele Antonio Cicogna, *Delle inscrizioni veneziane* (Venice, 1824–53, repr. 1969), VI, 182–5. This work includes sections from Navagero's correspondence and other valuable source material.

[45] Bornate, 'Doc.', pp. 478–9.

[46] Francesco Guicciardini, *Storia d'Italia*, Bk XVI, Chap. 14, pp. 1675–85; cf. Bornate, 'Doc.', p. 481.

[47] BRT (Misc.), fol. 685ᵛ; cf. Michaud, *Chancellerie*, p. 45. When in 1561 chancellor L'Hôpital, on first refusing to confirm the powers of the papal legate Hippolyte d'Este, later complied under royal command, he wrote under the seal *me non consentiente*. One may query whether Gattinara's action was contagious within the Habsburg system. For on 27 June 1528 the chancellor of Brabant refused to affix the seals to a new tax. His refusal provoked Charles' spirited aunt, Margaret of Austria, to affix them herself. For an Italian translation of the document see Antonio Marongiu, *Lo stato moderno: documenti e testimonianze del secolo XVI* (Rome, 1973), pp. 90–1.

that the authority with which he was invested ought not to be employed by him in such a dangerous and pernicious affair. Charles, while having the seals affixed, was heard to mutter that this was the last time that he would ever have a chancellor.[48]

The disagreement over the treaty of Madrid represented a new climax in the strained relations between the emperor and his chancellor. The papal nuncio Castiglione had noted the mounting displeasure of the chancellor during the immediately preceding weeks, and his inability to dissimulate it. When Gattinara asked Charles for permission to leave, Charles replied that he could go as far as Seville where the latter intended to remove the court and that the chancellor's attendance was necessary.[49] Gattinara acceded. But the nuncio went on to observe that from these demonstrations a fair amount of indignation is generated in the mind of the emperor and from indignation are borne bitter words and from these even greater indignation. On the day of the treaty's sealing Gattinara had repeatedly refused, claiming his unwillingness to violate his office. When the emperor apparently sought to obtain his consent by dangling the much-desired cardinalate before his eyes, he indicated that he was not to be so bought. And when Charles consoled himself with the thought that Gattinara would be the last chancellor he would ever have, the aged minister, as usual with the last word, reiterated the view already presented in the preceding July that the emperor should not await his death but have him serve either in the entirety of the office, or part of it, or reassign it now to whomever he pleased. Thus matters stood – or were allowed to drift along. The emperor confided that he knew very well he had not given the chancellor the *mercedes* that he deserved, but that he would. According to Castiglione, although it was not evident, some anger remained. At least in his eyes the Grand Chancellor ran his office in the succeeding weeks with the same authority as before, publicly expressing his belief that the King of France would not keep his promise.[50]

It was the opinion of Navagero that Gattinara somewhat removed himself from the normal course of affairs during the succeeding months.[51] The English ambassador Robert Wingfield writing to Wolsey observed that it was the viceroy as the 'imp' of Lord Chièvres and not Gattinara who had 'brewed the drink'.[52] In the quaffing which ensued, it soon became painfully apparent that the chivalric trust in Francis' word was without foundation. Nevertheless, the dawning realization as to the accuracy of the

[48] Guicciardini, *Storia d'Italia*, Bk XVI, Chap. 15, p. 1690; cf. Navagero in Bornate, 'Doc.', pp. 478–9 and P. A. Serassi, ed., *Lettere del conte Baldassare Castiglione* (Padua, 1769/71), II, 31.
[49] Cf. Bornate, 'Doc.', p. 483.
[50] Serassi, *Lettere di Castiglione*, II, 30–1; cf. Rodríguez Villa, 'Cartas de Salinas', *43*, 471.
[51] Cicogna, *Inscrizioni*, p. 188; Bornate, 'Doc.', pp. 482–3.
[52] *Letters and Papers*, 4/1, no. 2053.

chancellor's predictions hardly served to improve Gattinara's relationship with the emperor.[53] Expressing his own no small surprise, Castiglione observed later in the summer that the viceroy returned from France to be welcomed by the caresses and trust of his master, as if to stifle the mounting opinion against him.[54] Although Lalemand, along with Hugo de Moncada and the viceroy, had been among the three principal brewers and even signatories of the Madrid treaty, the difference over policy and the evidently enhanced role and authority of Lalemand do not appear to have introduced any animosity or strain in the chancellor's relation to the emerging state secretary. Is it possible, however, that Gattinara felt compelled to disguise his feelings in this regard because he considered Lalemand to be his best means of access to the emperor? Loaysa, the emperor's confessor and president of the Council of the Indies, might be a suitable channel for his friend Gattinara on matters of policy, but could the chancellor have recourse to him on matters of reimbursement and pay? Pressed ever further by his debts, Gattinara found himself in a humiliating position with respect to both of them. Catching the emperor on 17 June just before his departure for the hunt, Gattinara urged upon him a supplication which he had earlier entrusted to Lalemand, who had apparently done nothing to advance his master's cause.[55] Yet several weeks later he turned once more to Lalemand, vowing that he would never irritate the emperor again with his petty affairs: here he explains the necessary break up of his household for lack of pay and his plans for a three months' sojourn in Italy to rectify his affairs.[56] From this same period he again writes to Lalemand, expressing the fond desire that he might be able to serve His Majesty *gayement* all his remaining days and not be worn down by worry over his personnal affairs.[57] Little wonder that to the attentive eyes of Salinas, Lalemand now surpassed Gattinara in the service of the emperor.[58] Was Gattinara so blind, guileless or immune to jealously as to be unaffected by his dangerously increasing dependence on Lalemand? Surely he could not fail to perceive the augmented role of the secretary.

At this moment the irruption of the diplomatic crisis engendered by the League of Cognac had the effect of giving new prominence to the abilities of the chancellor and the functions of the chancellery.

[53] Bornate, 'Doc.', pp. 482–3, 487.
[55] AGRB (PEA), 1471 (4), fol. 1.
[57] HHSA (Belgien), PA 18 (alt 21)/2, fol. 257.
[58] Rodríguez Villa, 'Cartas de Salias', *43*, 407.
[54] Serassi, *Lettere di Castiglione*, II, 62.
[56] *Ibid.*, fol. 8.

58

The imperial chancellery

It would seem appropriate at this juncture to ask whether there ever was an imperial chancellery under Gattinara that attempted to function not simply for the Holy Roman Empire but for the entire Habsburg *monarchia*. What constitutes evidence? Ordinances, although they can provide valuable information as to the intended, ideal organization of the chancellery, do not by themselves suffice to prove the existence of an imperial secretariat that embraced both the empire proper and all the dynastic lands. The use of a seal conveying the idea of just such a larger conception of empire certainly makes its reality more tangible. Here we need to remind ourselves that Gattinara had early devised just such a seal of *empire universel*.[1] A further aid in trying to embody this elusive institution is the development of its personnel, together with the tasks performed and the ideas entertained by individual members of its staff. Another valuable type of evidence, only recently made available by the opening of the Gattinara family archive, is the series of tax receipts providing a breakdown of the emoluments derived from the individual territorial seals. Ultimately, the most satisfactory evidence can be provided by series of registers that chart the continuous activity and operation of the chancellery. In this last respect, however, the investigator is thwarted by the decimated condition of the Estado section at the archives of Simancas for this early period. The reasons for this regrettable fact are disputed but certainly one of them which cannot be left out of account is the increasing prominence of individual secretaries who, from the context of the chancellery, aspire to greater proximity to the prince, thereby transforming their office, straining the regular processes of this splendid medieval institution and promoting their own independence. In this regard Alfonso de Valdés as well as Lalemand are culpable in contributing to the dispersion of what a later age could dimly begin to recognize as state papers. For each secretary of any prominence by the beginning of the sixteenth century could be expected to have his own

[1] Walther, 'Kanzleiordnungen', p. 382.

archive.[2] And even in the late twentieth century the question of personal or public ownership of a great civil servant's papers remains obscure despite a far clearer definition of the state than Gattinara's age could ever know; by the very nature of administrative practice the question of ownership becomes almost inevitably a contested matter.

Nevertheless, what properly distinguishes a chancellery is the presence of a series of registers containing copies or recordings of all documents expedited by that secretariat. It is the remarkable continuity of such a series of register books from James I to Philip V at the Archivo de la Corona de Aragón which makes that archive one of the greatest for the study of the Middle Ages, and so valuable for conveying the rhythms in the operation of that most sophisticated of late medieval institutions – the Aragonese-Catalan chancellery. Likewise, the apparent absence of such a series for the imperial court chancellery under Gattinara helps to explain why this institution has been so long ignored and indeed even argues for its non-existence. Nevertheless, a few distinctions as well as qualifications need to be interjected. There exist a continuous series of registers for the Aragonese and for the German imperial chancellery, both of which institutions Gattinara's chancellery impinged upon, participated in and to some extent assimilated. In each case, however, the series pertains to the more formal and routine documentation constituted by the issue of privileges, legitimations and patents. We are reminded that the output of a chancellery basically assumes a dual form: letters patent and letters close or missives. By the very nature of the chancellery's operation, the former would enjoy the security of the institution's regular processes, while the latter would be vulnerable to the increasing independence and aspirations of the emerging state secretaries. If Gattinara's chancellery is therefore only partially discernible in the less revealing Aragonese and German registers that survive, it is necessary to determine the operation of the imperial court chancellery through the functions of its personnel and to elaborate this picture by examining the relations of this institution with those at Barcelona, at Mainz and at Naples.

On 26 August 1524 Gattinara at Valladolid brought forth another ordinance defining the order of the imperial chancellery. Except for changes in personnel, the differences between this and the earlier Ghent ordinance of 1 January 1522 would appear at first glance to be minimal, the later ordinance adhering to the organization and language of its predecessor. Nevertheless, important differences do exist. In the first place the Ghent

---

[2] See the case of Florimond Robertet in Michaud, *Chancellerie*, pp. 370–1. Although the separate bureaux of the great secretaries of the chancellery, each with his detachment of scribes (cf. pp. 290–3), may not be repeated in the case of the imperial chancellery under Gattinara, there is much in what Michaud depicts which seems reasonably applicable to it.

The imperial chancellery

ordinance is enacted with the subscription of the emperor and under his seal; the Valladolid ordinance seems much more of a personal matter between Gattinara and his secretary Valdés – a staking out, as if to preserve a political barony: it is enacted under the seal of Gattinara.[3] Secondly, the Ghent ordinance is a more careful and sophisticated statement for the operation of a chancellery. Here, the process for expediting privileges is carefully laid out: from the chancellor's reception of the emperor's schedule bearing the names of those who are to receive graces, to the execution of these mandates, their registration, their review by the chancellor, followed by his signature, and finally that of the emperor. This greater attention to detail is quite absent in the Valladolid ordinance which finds complete registration unnecessary for many types of concession and calls instead for the simple entry of a brief summary.[4] The later ordinance devotes much more attention to the distribution of receipts from taxation among the personnel of the chancellery. Furthermore, while the Ghent ordinance distinguishes between the use of the pendant seal with a stamp for letters patent and the use of the seal of the secret, together with its careful custody, for letters close or missives, the Valladolid ordinance makes no mention of the secret but groups together the expedition of letters patent and close together. On the basis of the limited evidence it is impossible to determine whether these changes are the result of the greater pressure of business, the increasing regime of the signature, the growth of secretarial independence or all of these combined.[5]

A more subtle and significant difference exists between the two documents. It has been observed that while the earlier pertained to the empire and the traditionally domainal lands of the Habsburgs, the later one refers only to matters bearing upon the empire – or so it would appear.[6] The existence of four registers, formerly five, define the four basic divisions or sections of the chancellery: business of state, *negocia status*, and other matters of particular importance to the emperor; business concerning the empire written in Latin; business written in German; and the reception of requests and the granting of favors and privileges. Much depends upon what precisely is to be understood by the first division. What is the meaning of *status* and, for that matter, Estado? During these years, and particularly under the direction of the chancellor, it was coming to signify foreign affairs, which in turn threw into relief Habsburg imperial interests conceived as

[3] Walther, 'Kanzleiordnungen', pp. 391–2; the manuscript of the 1524 original with the seal in fairly good condition is to be found in the Salazar Colección (A) at the Real Academia de la Historia *legajo* 32, fols. 105–7. On account of its greater accessibility we shall refer here to Adolf Hasenclever's publication of the document ('Eine Kanzleiordnung Gattinaras vom Jahre 1524') in the *Archiv für Urkundenforschung*, 7 (1921), 47–52.

[4] Walther, 'Kanzleiordnungen', p. 390; Hasenclever, 'Kanzleiordnung', p. 50.

[5] Walther, *ibid.*, p. 390; Hasenclever, *ibid.*, p. 51. [6] Hasenclever, *ibid.*, p. 47.

a totality in association with the person of Charles as distinct from the rest of the world.[7] Furthermore, if we compare the first three of these divisions in the 1524 ordinance with the first four of 1522 a difference is discernible. Although in 1522 the first is also described in terms of *omnes res tangentes suam Caesarem Majestatem, hoc est negocia status*, this division is principally distinguished by its handling of the relevant paperwork in the Latin and German languages. Likewise, the three subsequent divisions are either linguistically or geographically defined. By 1524 this linguistic distinction for the first section has been dropped; it is simply designated as *rerum status et negociorum particularium Caes. M^{tis}.* Had a more functional conception of this section come to replace the purely lingusitic and geographical? Unfortunately that very section pertaining to the *negocia status* which would tell us most as to the scope and emerging definition of the imperial chancellery under Gattinara's direction has been lost. What survives in the register books constitutes the less political materials relating to the routine granting of arms, titles, nobility, safe conducts, legitimations, *primarias preces* stemming from the other sections of the chancellery.[8]

Between 1522 and 1524 a few important changes had occurred in the personnel of the chancellery. In the Valladoid ordinance the names of the two vice-chancellors, Ziegler for the empire, who remained in actual fact in Germany, and Hannart, who was at the time representing the emperor in the empire, have disappeared, and although the Provost Waldkirch is mentioned both as taxer and as responsible for the German paperwork, it is not until the beginning of 1527 that he succeeds to the vice-chancellorship. The permanent secretaries are Lalemand, who also holds the position of contrarelator-general in the Aragonese chancellery, Philip de Nicola, a Spaniard, and the two Germans Wolfgang Prantner and Alexander Schweis, or Schwais. The five permanent scribes with one possible exception are all German. Perhaps the most striking change here is the promotion of Alfonso de Valdés from one of the regular scribes in 1522 to contrarelator and registrar. As contrarelator, or controller-general, Valdés displaced Dr Prantner who had been provisionally appointed to this post in 1522. The controller-general performed many of the functions of superintendence and review expected of an *audiencier* or protonotary in a chancellery lacking both such offices. It is questionable whether Valdés could determine the legality or suitability of a petition but as the second major responsibility of an *audiencier* he apparently reviewed and recorded the tax. That a Castilian

---

[7] Cf. Walser, *Zentralbehörden*, pp. 234–8.
[8] Hasenclever, 'Kanzleiordnung', p. 50; cf. Walther, 'Kanzleiordnungen', p. 388. For the remaining registry of the imperial chancellery see *Die Reichsregisterbücher Kaiser Karls V*, ed. Lothar Gross (Vienna, Leipzig, 1913/1930), pp. viff.

should succeed to a post traditionally conceived as properly pertaining to a German and to a Germanic understanding of the empire is suggestive both for the Castilian reshaping of the chancellery and of the nature of empire. In being made the new registrar, Valdés displaced Alexander Schweis from this provisional appointment of 1522. As keeper of the four registers, Valdés was able to reinforce his role of apparent superintendence within the chancellery and at the same time achieve close cooperation with the chancellor. Since Valdés could not read German the Valladolid ordinance provided that he should be aided in this regard by the scribe Joannes Fabri de Obernburg – an official of later distinction.[9]

In the two ordinances Gattinara lays bare the entire structure and operation of the chancellery, the hierarchy of scribes, secretaries, registrar, taxator, contrarelator and vice-chancellor, their remuneration, the forms used and the obedience enforced. The oath of offices is taken between the hands of the chancellor. The medieval character of the chancellery is further evident in the fact that the cabinets and cases containing the papers, registers and formularies, all of which being in the charge of Alfonso de Valdés, must be ready to be disassembled at the next inn or house near the person of the emperor – in keeping with the ambulatory character of government. Gattinara sees this mobile character of the chancellery as having its origins in Roman imperial practice.[10] Amidst the various officials of the chancellery we miss the presence of anyone comparable to the French chancellery's *chauffe-cire* or *cirier*. Some of the functions of the former had been combined with those already held by Valdés under Gattinara's direct supervision. As for the preparation of wax for the purposes of sealing, its use is evident from the lists of material expenses for the chancellery that have survived.[11]

The last section pertaining to the granting of favors and privileges, a practice which dates back to the time of the ancient Roman Empire, was of particular sensitivity and importance not only because it provided the staff with its pay but because of its larger social and political implications. In the registration of these instruments Gattinara attempted to break with the tradition established by the Archchancellor Berthold of Mainz in 1497 and base each registration upon the original rather than upon the draft, but comparison and a study of omissions in the registered documents reveal that according to actual practice the tradition of registration from the draft

---

[9] Hasenclever, 'Kanzleiordnung', p. 50. On the office of *audiencier* see Michaud, pp. 62–8, 324–8.

[10] Hasenclever, 'Kanzleiordnung', p. 49. On this point see A. H. M. Jones, *The Roman Empire* (Norman, Oklahoma [1964]), I, 366–7.

[11] AGS, Estado, 1553, no. 451. In the 31 December 1521 list of personnel for the chancellery of Aragon at Worms, a wax warmer is included. Cf. HHSA (Belgien), PA 91/3, fols. 101–101ᵛ. See *infra*, fns. 17 and 40.

persisted.[12] Gattinara sought to secure direct personal supervision and control over the issuing of privileges and letters patent for ennoblement, tax relief, concession of arms, palatines and the like. He complains that the pressure and importunity of those seeking these favors both for themselves and their kin have become intolerable and cheapened the former dignity or honor. The chancellery was not the sole sector of government through which Gattinara sought to restrict a patronage that all too often brought incompetents to office.[13]

The accrediting of a plenipotentiary placed a sudden strain on the chancellery and reveals it in action. When Beaurain was sent to Bourbon in Italy in late 1523, Gattinara drafted a memorandum which commanded among other things that he should be equipped with letters of credence: twelve in Latin were to be produced by Nicola; three in French by Lalemand; five in Spanish by Soria and ten more in Spanish by García.[14] In an instruction to the chancellery's staff which can be dated as occurring in the second week of November 1526 and which sought to support the special envoy Cesare Farramosca to the pope, Gattinara makes the following assignments: twelve distinct items in Latin for Valdés to execute, some of them, such as a response to the pope consoling him for Colonna's raid on Rome and a similar letter to the College of Cardinals, requiring considerable finesse; six of a more routine nature in Castilian to be executed by García and seven for Lalemand to execute in Castilian or French.[15] These directives are quite revealing. In the first place they clearly indicate that Lalemand, as late as Gattinara's departure for Italy, is very much a part of the chancellery and is expected to assist in its functions. Secondly, both he and Valdés are apparently granted considerable latitude in composing important communications even while subject to the formulae and formularies of the chancellery and under the supervision and review of the chancellor. Finally, it should be observed that Philip de Nicola, Pedro García and Alonso Soria are all very familiar faces in the Aragonese chancellery; even Lalemand ever since the summer of 1520 functioned as controller-general within this body. Thus, have we in both instances a directive to the Aragonese rather than to the imperial chancellery?

[12] For an analysis of the practice of registration in the imperial chancellery see *Reichsregisterbücher*, pp. xix–xxi.
[13] Hasenclever, 'Kanzleiordnung', pp. 51–2; on Gattinara's earlier treatment of this subject see Bornate, 'Doc.', pp. 421–2; on the previous operation of imperial chancelleries in this regard see Harry Bresslau, *Handbuch der Urkundenlehre für Deutschland und Italien* (Leipzig, 1912–15), I, 69–70, II, 1ff. Gattinara's ordinance for the chancellery in 1524 was later translated into Spanish and published in the mid-seventeenth century. Cf. Don Francisco Diego de Sayas Rabanera y Ortubia, *Anales de Aragón desde el año de MDXX del nacimiento de nuestro redemptor hasta el de MDXXV* (Saragossa, 1666), pp. 710–11.
[14] HHSA (Belgien), PA 13 (alt 14) I, fols. 153ᵛ–154.
[15] AGS, Estado, 1554, no. 497 (printed in *Cal. SP Spain*, III/1, 997–9).

The imperial chancellery

Several circumstances dictated the strong interconnections and occasional melding of the two chancelleries. In the first place Gattinara's own expertise and preeminent interest were Italian affairs and until the creation of the Council of Italy in 1558, the administration of Spain's interests in the Italian sphere leaned heavily upon the existing Aragonese-Neapolitan machinery. Concomitantly, despite the tangle of traditional *fueros* that had to be respected, there was a drive within the imperial government to make the Council of Aragon, and with it the chancellery, conform as closely as possible to imperial interests, and reduce the Crown of Aragon to an auxiliary role in the interests of the *monarchia*.[16] By an ordinance of 20 April 1522 issued at Brussels, Gattinara as president of the Council of Aragon was expected to assume the functions of the vice-chancellor whenever free from other obligations according to an arrangement that had some features reminiscent of the Worms accord of 1521 with the imperial Archchancellor. Although the incumbent Antonio Agustin continued undisturbed as vice-chancellor down to his death on 30 March 1523, he acted as Gattinara's deputy. Physical and material factors also dictated something approaching a coalescence of the two chancelleries. The Aragonese chancellery accompanied the emperor in his peregrinations. Furthermore, as Valdés was charged with the care of the Aragonese registers, the identical location of the cases and boxes of the two chancelleries, Aragonese and imperial, appears most likely.[17] Little wonder that a secretary like Nicola could be interchangeable, without creating any strain, and operate in both chancelleries, for the two were at times and in some instances, particularly in Italian affairs, actually one chancellery.

A survey of the Aragonese registers for this period bears out some of these features. Although the present state of the archives cannot be taken as a perfect representation of the materials deposited there during the early sixteenth century, the beauty of the Archivo de la Corona de Aragón is that its registers reveal a documentary continuity comparable to the Rolls Series. It must be admitted that Gattinara never personally appears as functioning within the context of a discrete Aragonese chancellery; where his name occurs, it is as subject rather than agent of the expedition. On privileges, a subordinate signs for him, similar to Urbina or Horbina in the Castilian context. In the section 'Curiae', which most closely corresponds to that

16 On this last point see Walser, *Zentralbehörden*, pp. 225–6.
17 Sayas Rabanera, *Anales*, pp. 435–51, esp. pp. 443–7. Cf. Walser, *Zentralbehörden*, p. 59, fn. 96; Santa Cruz, *Crónica*, II, 77. We have the list of personnel with respective salaries for the chancellery of Aragon attendant upon Charles V at Worms, 31 December 1521, signed by Alonso Soria and expedited by Lalemand: Michael Velasquez Climent is protonotary and Franciscus Carbonell, archivist; Soria, lieutenant of the protonotary; ten scribes for expediting (*scribe mandati*); two sealers; four counsellors (*peticionerii*); one solicitor; six registral scribes; one wax warmer; and one secretarial messenger. HHSA (Belgien), PA 91/3, fols. 101–101ᵛ. For similar lists from the same period see Walther, 'Kanzleiordnungen', pp. 383–7.

65

of Simancas' 'Estado' section, the remains are meagre indeed, with the vast majority of documentation stemming from 1519 when young Charles and his court were dallying in Barcelona; there is a brief flurry of activity in 1525 and 1526, and then a resumption in 1529 when the court returns to Barcelona.[18] As might be expected, that section which reflects the greatest regularity pertains to the expediting of privileges where Lalemand functions faithfully as contrarelator-general from 9 July 1520 to his fall in December 1528.[19] By January 1530, at Bologna Valdés has become preeminently responsible for the drafting and expediting of the royal mandates for these privileges and will continue to perform this particular function down to his death in 1532.[20] This extra-Aragonese presence of personnel belonging to the imperial chancellery in what would be considered the heart of the Aragonese chancellery is not limited to Valdés but includes John Hannart who operates steadily throughout the first stay of Charles in Spain, 1517–20.[21] Also not surprising is Cobos' presence which occurs with almost equal frequency.

The physical location of the two chancelleries in the same place and the apparent interchangeability of personnel would together argue for a more inclusive understanding of the imperial court chancellery. As with the registers, formularies and cases pertaining to the Reich, those pertaining to the Crown of Aragon were expected to remain in the domicile of the chancellor under the direct custody of Valdés.[22] From the point of view of the personnel and the actual performance of Charles V's central administration, its division by Karl Brandi into three parts – the main Burgundian core, the Spanish cabinet chancellery and the Reichskanzlei – appears too discrete. Certainly such formidable secretaries as Lalemand and Valdés violate any clear institutional division and the complementary responsibilities of the imperial and the Aragonese chancelleries in Italy argue for a more expanded or interconnecting, if not inclusive, jurisdiction for the former chancellery at this time.[23]

The relation of the imperial court chancellery to the imperial chancellery at Mainz is a matter subject to far less conjecture as it pertains generally to a long-standing traditional relationship and is specifically defined by a

[18] ACA (Curiae), 3896–7.
[19] The earliest privilege that I have discovered bearing the signature of Lalemand is Brussels 9 July 1520 shortly after his installation as the new contrarelator for the Aragonese chancellery. ACA (Privilegiorum), 3932, fol. CCLXI. The foliation is erratic in many of the registers inspected.
[20] ACA (Privilegiorum), 3938–40, wherein his signature is continuous.
[21] ACA (Curiae), 3896–7, (Diversorum), 3881–4, (Partium), 3954.
[22] Sayas Rabanera, *Anales*, pp. 710–11.
[23] Brandi bases his tripartite division on the work of Walser. See Karl Brandi, 'Die Überlieferung der Akten Karls V im Haus-, Hof-und Staatsarchiv Wien', Berichte und Studien zur Geschichte Karls V, V, *Nachrichten von der Gesellschaft der Wissenschaften zu Göttingen, Philologisch-Historische Klasse* (Berlin, 1932) pp. 18–51.

The imperial chancellery

number of agreements between Archbishop Albrecht and Gattinara. The first of these Worms accords dates from 10 January 1521. In groping its way through the thickets of minor difficulties besetting the relations between Archchancellor and Grand Chancellor, the earlier document seems more protective of Mainz's interests: all emoluments from the granting of privileges pertain throughout Germany to the Archchancellor; whatever enjoyed by the Grand Chancellor must be without prejudice to the interests of the Archchancellor; but to prevent altercations the Archchancellor will take one quarter of receipts remaining from the chancellery's taxes after expenses and the payment of the staff and he expects his counterpart when in charge to do likewise. In the penultimate article it is stated that all the seals of the Empire remain with the Archchancellor so long as he is in the court of the emperor, but if absent they are to be held by the Grand Chancellor *quia sic jussit Caesarea ipsa Majestas.* Finally, it is recognized that all these arrangements hold good only while the emperor is in Germany. The two chancellors, in affixing their signatures to the documents, personally pledged their adherence to its articles.[24]

Yet something seemed to be lacking – perhaps clarity and specificity. For the ultimate accord of 25 January 1521 begins with the definitive formula that the Archchancellor has superiority and full superintendence of the imperial chancellery throughout Germany and to him are reserved the seal and the secret 'but if he should depart from the imperial court or be occupied elsewhere with other matters' he is to surrender the seals to the Grand Chancellor according to the compact made with him and by the emperor's command.[25] The Worms accord then proceeds to detail the functions and functionaries of the chancellery. A number of features are worth noting: all officials swear fidelity to the emperor between the hands of the Archchancellor, thereby suggesting his control over appointments; the scribes of the registers (*registratores*) and those of expedition (*scriptores*) are expected to abide together in one house designated by the Archchancellor; the taxer, receiver (of the taxes) and controller-general work closely together serving as a check upon each other; the Latin registry is to be maintained in duplicate, one for the Grand Chancellor and the other for Mainz. The role of the *consiliarii* is particularly worthy of note. The earlier accord of 10 January had recognized them as being an integral part of the chancellery's staff.[26] It is specified that in order to avoid even the suspicion of purloining, the secretaries are to compose nothing unless it shall have been decreed thereupon by the counsellors and a written request presented; only by the will of the emperor or by either one of the chancellors can this process be circumvented. Furthermore, all letters and petitions are to be

[24] AGS, Estado, 1553, no. 453, fols. 1–2ᵛ.   [25] *Ibid.*, no. 454, fol. 1.
[26] *Ibid.*, no. 453, fol. 2.

presented to the counsellors and reviewed by them before being submitted to the Archchancellor.[27]

The critical role exercised by these *consiliarii* compels us to ask who they were. It would appear that they performed a function very similar to the contemporary *maîtres des requêtes* who, as the essential intermediaries between the King of France's council and his chancellery, were to constitute for over two centuries the very nerves and sinews of the central government. The fact that such counsellors do not figure in either one of Gattinara's ordinances raises some questions as to the function of the imperial chancellery in Charles' government. Does their absence argue for the greater isolation or proximity of the chancellery to the Council of State as compared with the Frence model? And if isolation, the isolation of what function within the multiple operations of the chancellery? Again any conclusions are conjectural, but it would seem that both answers are possible given the emerging role of the state secretaries. On the one hand a person like Cobos or Lalemand diverted an enormous amount of business into the immediate milieu of the prince, thereby leaving the chancellery as a sort of fifth wheel with respect to many of its more political and diplomatic functions. On the other hand Lalemand, and less so Hannart or later Valdés, enjoyed a twofold role serving both as immediate personal secretary to the emperor and as prime functionary within the operation of the chancellery. Not only his proximity to the emperor but also his office as secretary to the Council of State permitted Lalemand to serve as a major conduit between council and chancellery and thereby obviate the need for counsellors. At the same time, however, it permitted a dangerous accumulation of power. Yet on balance Gattinara's failure to include *consiliarii* in his understanding of the imperial court chancellery would suggest both its rather tenuous nature and the developments gestating within the central government at this time.

As a consequence of the Worms accord the resident (Mainz) and the imperial court chancelleries were expected to remain in contact with each other, exchanging information and a record of actions taken.[28] In his letter of 30 May 1522 from Nuremberg, Albert of Mainz recognized the reception of a schedule of privileges sent from the court chancellery and in turn forwarded to Spain some annotated petitions. While exhorting Gattinara to live up to the agreement, Albert expressed anxiety that some claims granted to petitioners had already been anticipated or engaged. Unable to find in his files the letters specifying the pensions for Hannart and the treasurer Villinger, the archbishop asked Gattinara to send copies.[29] Albrecht was not the only one in Germany to be apprehensive concerning the shift in the center of imperial administraion to Spain. In the eyes of

[27] *Ibid.*, no. 454, fols. 1–3.   [28] *Ibid.*, nos. 548–50.   [29] *Ibid.*, no. 449.

68

The imperial chancellery

the electors, writing to the emperor from Nuremberg three months earlier, the ordinances of Worms had become unstuck and needed to be reaffirmed, particularly as they pertained to the imperial cameral tribunal and the executive council.[30] Henceforth the correspondence between the two chancelleries from the German end was carried on, as might be expected, by the vice-chancellor, Nicholas Ziegler. In mid-May of 1523 he attempted to regularize the traffic in the meeting and the granting of petitions by proffering Gattinara seven different categories for them. While awaiting Gattinara's reactions to his suggested ordering of petitions and their expedition, he asks that copies of some privileges be transmitted in order to complete his files. On the other hand, to Gattinara's long-standing request that the Reichsregiment and the Reichskammergericht send copies of all transactions between the emperor and the imperial estates, he promises to renew his repeated requests to those bodies.[31] The problem lingered on, for when Ziegler, in writing almost a year later, sent new schedules of petitioners, he dwelt on the difficulties of transmitting the requested documents which would soon be on their way to Spain.[32] The communications between widely separated organs of imperial government left much to be desired.

In the apportionment of the revenue received from the chancellery's taxes, Gattinara's share shows a steady increase as traced from the Worms accord of January 1521, through the Ghent ordinance exactly a year later to the Valladolid ordinance of August 1524. According to the Ghent ordinance Gattinara is to receive one third of the tax, another third is to be taken by the vice-chancellor and the rest apportioned among the secretaries. In 1524, expenses having been deducted, the chancellor is to receive one half, the four secretaries one quarter plus one sixth of the remaining quarter; what is left is to be divided among taxator (Waldkirch), registrar (Valdés) and receiver. In a schedule of receipts and their distribution, which can be dated as deriving from late 1522, the following sums are apportioned from a net income of 495 reales:

Gattinara	192
Vice-Chancellor Ziegler	76
Vice-Chancellor Hannart	76
Secretary Lalemand	33
Secretary Maximilianus Transylvanus	33
Secretary Nicola	33
Registrar Alexander [Schweis]	26
Receiver Hieronymus [Ranzo]	26

The chancellor was already well on the way to his moiety.[33]

30 *Ibid.*, 635, no. 40.   31 *Ibid.*, 1553, nos. 565–6.   32 *Ibid.*, no. 495.
33 *Ibid.*, no. 551; Walther, 'Kanzleiordnungen', p. 389; and Hasenclever, 'Kanzleiordnung', p. 51.

69

Indeed, the records of the receipt of emoluments from the various seals provide the best clues as to the interlocking character of the Caroline chancelleries during the regime of Gattinara. In this respect the recent opening of the family archives affords access to valuable documents pertaining to the several chancelleries' finances, thereby suggesting the relations among them and the multiple roles of key members of their personnel. These reports, usually drawn up by the official receiver of the chancellery, give information on the income and sometimes its sources, expenses such as wax and other materials used, and the sum remaining for distribution among the chief officers of the chancellery. This last sort of information is particularly valuable for determining the members of Gattinara's staff at any one time. For example, the account of the receiver for the imperial chancellery, Jean de Grey, for the period from 12 May 1524 to the end of the year – reckoned apparently as 31 December – indicated a revenue of over 840 Rhenish florins of which 3 florins 18 Flemish gros are from the chancellery of Flanders; from this amount, after deducting expenses leaving 803 florins, the Grand Chancellor *iuxta ordinationem* gets his *medietas*; of the other half, one quarter of the whole and one sixth of that quarter are to be divided among the four secretaries, Lalemand, Nicola, Schweis and now Dr Prantner who has replaced Transylvanus, each receiving thereby 58 florins, 7 Flemish gros; of the remainder Waldkirch as taxator, Alfonso de Valdés as registrar and contrarelator and Jean de Grey as receiver each get 55 florins 18 Flemish gros.[34] The proportions in the distributions among the members of the staff remain constant in all these reports until the autumn of 1529, the Grand Chancellor receiving his half, the four secretaries each receiving the same sum and the three individual officers each obtaining a slightly smaller sum. Thus it is only important to note here significant alterations among the personnel and indications as to the relations between the chancelleries.

For the same year, 1524, what is designated as 'Computum cancellarie Imperialis' refers as much to the Mainz as to the court chancellery, for we learn that the sum of 300 florins represents receipts from the tax on *primarias preces* sent by Ziegler for distribution, along with expenses

---

[34] ASV, 8/5, Computum cancellarie imperialis (CCI), De Grey, May through December 1524. Since the folios are not numbered, all references will be to the particular account – CCI for the imperial chancellery, N for Naples – distinguished as far as possible by the name of the receiver or the secretary, and the date. Concerning the date on which the year was reckoned as beginning, although the financial accounts would suggest 1 January, the year began on 25 December for the Aragonese chancellery. See *Regesto della cancelleria aragonese di Napoli*, ed. Jole Mazzoleni (Naples, 1951), p. xiv. On money in general at this time and the denominations of the Rhenish florin in particular see John H. Munro, 'Money and coinage in the age of Erasmus', *The correspondence of Erasmus* (Toronto, 1974), I, 322–3, 347.

The imperial chancellery

incurred by the Mainz chancellery.[35] In its account for 1 January to 30 April 1526, the receipts from imperial letters amount to 599 florins 4 Flemish gros but after the deduction of expenses only 416 florins 4 Flemish gros remain for distribution. It is on this occasion that Valdés' name appears for the first time among the four secretaries, replacing that of Nicola, and yet the adroit Castilian manages to retain henceforth his other offices as receiver and contrarelator.[36] Of considerable interest as indicative of significant changes within the composition of the chancellery is the account for September 1529 rendered at Piacenza. The following are the recipients of the sum of 2334 florins representing the tax on letters expedited 1 June through 31 August 1529, less expenses:

Grand Chancellor	1167 florins	20 Flemish gros
Vice-Chancellor [Waldkirch]	330	40
Secr. Schweis	166	60
Secr. Valdés	166	60
Receiver & sealer [Ranzo]	166	60
Contrarelator & registrator [Valdés]	166	60
Cornelius Scepperus	166	60[37]

Several points are worth noting here: Waldkirch is at the time in the empire, deeply involved in negotiations with the Franconian knights[38] and thus of no effective use for the daily operation of the chancellery. Subsequent to the fall of Lalemand and the departure of Dr Prantner, Schweis and Valdés remain as the only secretaries of experience and standing. With the absence of the vice-chancellor and the imperial approach to Germany the position of Schweis was certainly enhanced. To him fell now the burden of dealing with the Protestant delegation sent to Piacenza and it is hardly surprising that the Nürnberg council would refer to him as *oberstem secretirier*.[39] Regarding Valdés, his own preeminence among the staff of the chancellery was by this time secure and becomes manifest in the account for 1 January through 5 June 1530, the date of Gattinara's death, where one finds among such chancellery expenses as red wax and board and keep at Bologna, Mantua and Trent an apparently new salary for Valdés *pro administratione Cancellarie* to be perpetuated after Gattinara's death at least until the end of the year.[40] With respect to those individual officials benefiting from the

[35] ASV, 8/5, CCI, De Grey, 1524.
[36] ASV, 8/5, CCI, De Grey, January through April, 1526.
[37] ASV, 8/5, CCI, Valdés, June through August 1529.
[38] *Deutsche Reichstagsakten*, VII/1, 881–7.
[39] *Deutsche Reichstagsakten*, VIII/1, 609.
[40] ASV, 8/5, CCI, Valdés, 1 January to 5 June 1530; *ibid.*, June through December 1530.

emoluments, they now receive for the first time the same amount as the secretaries. The appearance of Cornelius Scepperus' name in this single instance on the list of those receiving fees is at first puzzling but also suggestive. As former vice-chancellor of Denmark and more recently as a distinguished imperial envoy, Scepperus would seem to hold a position considerably beneath his talents and dignity. Yet as Gattinara's confidant and close friend in the last three years of the chancellor's life, Scepperus more probably represents a case, sixteenth-century style, of a person being placed on the government payroll with little more than nominal duties as a means of helping to ease his temporary financial needs. In fact one is struck by the very personal character of the chancellery – a sort of extension of Gattinara's household by the time of his death.

By the very nature of this documentation one gains the impression that Gattinara's chancellery was simply the financial receptacle for emoluments derived from work in the chancelleries of other lands pertaining to the Habsburg *monarchia*. We shall have occasion to remind ourselves that it never lost its functional character. Nevertheless, along with the receipts obtained from the Mainz chancellery there are included on two occasions from Flanders the insignificant sum of 3 florins for the latter part of 1524 and 7 florins 12 Flemish gros for the first half of 1525.[41] A far more significant case of a contributing chancellery is the exercise of the Castilian seal by Gattinara's functionary Horbina. According to an earlier arrangement the chancellor ascribed these more personal receipts to members of his family, his son-in-law Alessandro di Lingnana and the husband of his niece, Stupnix. Thus, in the account covering the period April 1523 to March 1527, Lingnana received 1200 ducats, Stupnix 233, the grandson of Gattinara 199 and the remaining 366 to be given to the *mayordomo*.[42] On two separate listings, receipts from the chancellery of Austria, namely that associated with Ferdinand, are mentioned without any detailed breakdown. In both instances the year is uncertain. On the verso of a list of receipts from the seal of Castile, Gattinara jots down – presumably as pertaining to personal income for an undesignated period – the totals, in ducats, from the various chancelleries:

Naples	88	Empire	249
Austria	98	Flanders	39
Empire	69		

[41] ASV, 8/5, CCI, De Grey, May through December, 1524; *ibid.*, January through May 1525.
[42] ASV, 8/5, Castile, Horbina, April 1523 to March 1527. In the expedition of privileges the *mayordomo* held a position next to that of the chancellor. Cf. Martín Postigo, *Cancillería*, p. 246. Gattinara's accounts indicate that he paid his functionary within the Castilian chancellery, Horbina, something like a salary. ASV, 8/5, CCI and N, Ranzo, [?] to end of March, 1524.

The imperial chancellery

A second list of receipts from the seals:

Castile	93 ducats	
Empire	175 ducats	
Austria	96 ducats	8 reales
Flanders	23 ducats	37 reales
Naples (for 8 months)	88 ducats[43]	

While the receipts from the Austrian and the Flemish chancelleries are each mentioned only twice without any elaboration and do not appear to have played any permanent role in the operation and expectations of Gattinara's chancellery, the role of Naples was another matter entirely and requires separate consideration.

To understand Gattinara's relationship to the Neapolitan chancellery it is necessary to appreciate the veritable administrative revolution which had been released by Ferdinand the Catholic and which was gradually being consummated during the first decade of Charles V's reign.[44] Except for

---

[43] ASV, 8/5, Collective, Ranzo, 1527 [?].

[44] The following two paragraphs are based principally upon the classic work of Giannone, *Istoria*, III, 536–50, and to some extent upon Giuseppe Coniglio, *Il regno di Napoli al tempo di Carlo V* (Naples, 1951), pp. 3–5 and Narciso Nada, *Stato e società nel regno di Napoli dalla dominazione spagnuola all'unità d'Italia* (Turin, 1972), pp. 37–9. Among the documents included in the Miscellanea politica del secolo XVI (BRT St. d'Ital. 75), fol. 273, representing part of Gattinara's personal file, is a mandate from Charles to his chancellor which is interesting in several respects: preeminently it reveals the readjusting of Neapolitan offices and especially the Seven so as to be associated with the viceroy or the most immediate, trusted friends of the king, namely Lannoy who would in 1522 succeed to the office of viceroy of Naples; secondly it suggests that the office of Neapolitan Grand Chancellor is already secure and provided for; finally it presents us with a clear case of the current practice of *ampliacion* as the right of inheritance.
'El Rey
Nuestro gran chanciller Nos havemos dado licencia al illustre mussiur de xiebres nuestro prima para que pueda renunciar sus officios denuestro Capitan general de la mar y denuestro grande almirante de napoles enpersona del illustre don Ramon de Cardona nuestro visorey del Reyno de napoles. Y tambien havemos hecho merced al Spectable Charles dela noy [Lannoy] nuestro gran Cavallerizo de uno delos siete officios principales de nuestro Reyno de napoles exceptados los officios de gran chanciller logothete y prothonotario y porque nuestra voluntad es que esto haya effecto porinde nos vos encargamos y mandamos que senaleys y despacheys los privilegios delos dichos officios de nuestro Capitan general de la mar y de nuestro grande almirante de napoles enpersona del dicho don Ramon de cardona para si durante su vida y con ampliacion para un hijo o heredero suyo/ y tambien la espetativa del dicho officio delos siete que primero vacare enpersona del dicho nuestro gran cavallerizo exceptados della los dichos officios denuestro gran chanciller y de logothete y prothonotario que assi procede de nuestra determinada voluntad. Datum en molin de rey a xxvii de otubre anno de mil quinientos y deznueve.
Yo El Rey
Garcia Secretario'
Concerning the Ferdinandine reduction of the Neapolitan chancellorship at this time, Marino Freccia, upon whom Giannone draws heavily for his understanding of the seven principal offices of the crown, perceived a significant transformation: 'hodie autem in multis diminuta est authoritas ac quasi deleta, non enim in Cancellaria libelli leguntur coram Cancellario, & cum assistentia iudicum & aliorum officialium, neque certi dies assignantur, prout antiquitus Lunae, uidelicet,

73

the ultimate establishment of the Council of Italy in 1558, this reorganization of the government of Naples would effectively achieve its definitive form by the time the heavy hand of the great viceroy Don Pedro de Toledo settled upon Il Regno in 1532. Two reasons had motivated El Católico to undertake the revamping of the kingdom's central administration. When he embarked from Barcelona 4 September 1506 for Italy, Ferdinand, suspicious of Gonzalo de Córdoba, who had won Naples for him, and alarmed by the latter's cavalier independence, had boldly determined to sack the Great Captain. The centerpiece in the succeeding governmental overhaul was the new Collateral Council constituted by two jurists, known henceforth as *reggenti*, imported from Aragon along with a secretary. Born out of Ferdinand's distrust of his viceroy, the Collateral Council was indeed appropriately named, for it was designed to attend the viceroy and serve as a check upon his actions. It rapidly developed as the major organ of the entire administration, its competence being political, financial, judicial and jurisdictional. Significantly it replaced the old chancellery, which was now dependent upon it for the drawing up and expedition of state documents. The council busied itself in all affairs, acted as a council of state and assumed the regency at the death or absence of the viceroy. To meet these multiple obligations a third *reggente* was added at the beginning of Charles' rule in the person of the eminent native jurist Sigismondo Loffredo. This last proved so useful in advising Charles that he was called to Germany and attended the movements of the court for three years. In meeting the very real need of the central imperial government for advice pertaining to Italy, Loffredo and his successors represented the seed that would mature into the Council of Italy with Charles' son. In 1519 the young Habsburg monarch provided the Collateral Council with a replacement for Loffredo and in the next few years the council was successively augmented to five members: two Italian and three Spanish, plus a secretary.

If Ferdinand's strained relations with Gonzalo had impelled him to introduce the new council, a second reason militating toward such an action and providing a dynamic to the creation of a new sort of administration was the simple fact that the King of Naples henceforth would reside no longer in Naples but somewhere in Spain. Thus, what Alfonso the Magnanimous had never thought of doing after the final conquest in 1443,

Mercurij, & Veneris, non etiam de literis decernit, tam gratiae referendae, quam iustitiae, nec illas lacerat, si uideantur iniustae reijcit uel expungit, sed a diuo catholico Rege deputati sunt (ut audio) Regentes sub adiectione Cancellariae: quorum munus est nomine magni Cancellarij libellos excutere, priuilegia inspicere, & in memorialibus, ut dicitur decretationes facere: quod est libellos agere,... hi Domini ad latus Regis in Collaterali concilio assumpti assistunt, nec Cancellarij nomine nominatur: sed quia ipsis est imposita cura Cancellariam regendi, Regentes dicuntur ab eo munere: ipsi subscribunt libellos, non magnus Cancellarius. ipsi manus ut ita dicam in priuilegijs apponunt, non magnus Cancellarius. neque etaim scrinea seu regesta penes Cancellarium asseruantur, prout ex norma officij, et iuris regula: sed penes secretarium, qui etiam in concilio pro libellis consistit: fertur hoc ex diuo catholico Rege institutum.' Freccia, *De subfeudis*, fols. 40^v–41.

The imperial chancellery

Ferdinand and his grandson did: namely, the dismantling of those seven great feudal offices of the crown deriving from Norman-Angevin roots and their substitution with Spanish institutions. For in the two decades following El Católico's abrupt appearance in Italy, the new viceregal government spearheaded by the Collateral Council came to intrude upon and assimilate the functions of the traditional offices of Grand Constable, Grand Chancellor, and the other 'grands'–Protonotary, Chamberlain, Justiciar, Admiral and Seneschal. Devoid of content they would nevertheless survive, jealously preserving their external lustre. Thus the office of Grand Chancellor of Naples was already approaching a moribund state when it fell to Gattinara to assume its dwindling responsibilities. There was but one factor, however, that counted in the new Grand Chancellor's favor and would provide him with considerable leverage within the Neapolitan government: his cousin Giovanni Bartolomeo Gattinara was a *reggente*.

According to the privilege issued at Brussels 2 September 1520 Gattinara received the appointment of Grand Chancellor 'del reino de Sicilia citra Faro' (i.e. Naples) at the decease of Ferdinand the Catholic's great secretary, Miguel Pérez de Almazán.[45] In the following year, the Grand Chancellor was to undertake his sweeping investigation into the corruption rampant in Neapolitan offices beginning with the viceroy himself and extending downward in order to explain to his master why he was receiving so little service and equally little revenue from the kingdom of Naples.[46] While still in Flanders Gattinara had pressed for the completion of the new seals for the Neapolitan chancellery but by the time he returned to Spain the grip of the new regime upon this other chancellery still remained insecure. Writing to his cousin Giovanni Bartolomeo from Valladolid on 21 March 1523 Gattinara observes:

Concerning the moneys which your Lordship has derived from the reciprocal seal (*ex sigillo mutuo*) we are both fully agreed that at this time we can expect to receive nothing from your stipends nor from mine nor is there any great hope of this income while these dislocations produced by the wars persist...As for the new seals that must be made I have written now twice before we departed from Flanders and I marvel that the Lord Lieutenant has not received my letters wherein I charged him to have those seals renewed. I thought that he had now accomplished this task. Therefore please take care that they are made according to the form of the existing seals with whatever appropriate changes seem necessary...[47]

[45] *Privilegios*, no. 1075. This work constitutes a most valuable presentation and exposition of the 'Privilegiorum' series of the Archivo de la Corona de Aragón for this period and thus makes available in print an important aspect of Gattinara's chancellery.
[46] This forceful, searching consulta, so indicative of Gattinara's decisive personality, is printed in *Aktenstücke*, I, 401–18 and is analysed at length by Giuseppe Galasso, *Mezzogiorno medievale e moderno* (Turin, 1965), pp. 147–64.
[47] Bornate, 'Doc.', pp. 433–5. The fact that only one financial account exists for the period prior to 1524 suggests the still uncertain grip of the central administration upon the Neapolitan chancellery. See ASV, 8/5, N, Ranzo, 5 June to 10 September 1520.

75

The emperor and his chancellor

Thus, in keeping with the ambulatory government of the Habsburg emperor, there was emerging an arrangement similar to that between the imperial court chancellery and Mainz. The two Gattinara cousins were to have identical copies of a common seal, one to be used essentially within the jurisdiction of the Collateral Council, the other essentially within the context of the Aragonese chancellery.

Barely had the new system been established than Gattinara's mounting debts and unpaid salary compelled him to consider selling the Neapolitan office. On 20 October 1524 Gattinara's appointment to the office was reconfirmed[48] but by 8 November the chancellor was seeking permission to undertake measures for its sale – a request which was most promptly granted on 11 November 1524.[49] By February 1526 the sale of the office had apparently been completed and Gattinara had realized 10,000 ducats once expenses had been paid and monetary exchange incurred. But was it an outright sale? Although the treasury statement signed by Juan de Adurca speaks of sale, on the back of the document Gattinara writes – whether at the time of reception or later is uncertain – 'Compter...en baillant loffice de chanceller de naples', suggesting that he still enjoyed the exercise and prerogatives of the office.[50] In an important statement of personal income and expenses for the period 1524–7 there appears as first item under the former category the following: 'Par la ampliatione del officio de gran Canzeller de Napole per il duca de Martina – 12000 ducatos.[51] *Ampliacion* signifies the right of succession or inheritance to an office at the death of the present incumbent. Gattinara had earlier studied this very practice which had become current in Il Regno during the reign of Ferdinand.[52] Now he seems to have resorted to its application in his own case whereby the inheritance to the office and not the office itself is sold. By a privilege dated 11 May 1526 the presumably delayed permission was granted which gave him the capacity for arranging the inheritance (*dejar en herencia*) of the office of Grand Chancellor of Naples and for conceding to the designee equal emoluments and prerogatives as Gattinara enjoyed while alive.[53] At the end of that summer, culminating in the first weeks of September, Gattinara's financial difficulties became most acute and in a letter stemming from these early days at Granada he presses the emperor now for the *ampliacion* of the seals of Naples apart from that of the office of chancellor

[48] *Privilegios*, no. 1078.
[49] HHSA (Belgien), PA 91/4, fol. 351; *Privilegios*, no. 1079.
[50] Bornate, 'Doc.', pp. 483–4. 'Bailler' here appears to be used in the sense of giving 'bail' or a contract by which the legal possessor of an immoveable cedes the usage or enjoyment of it on certain conditions and for a determined time.
[51] ASV, 8/5, personal income, 1524–7. On Giovanni Batista Caracciolo, Duke of Martina, Count of Nicastro, who is listed among the major titled feudatories of the realm in 1528, see Tommaso Pedio, *Napoli e Spagna nella prima metà del cinquecento* (Bari, 1971).
[52] See Bornate, 'Doc.', pp. 421–2 on *ampliacions par heritiers*.   [53] *Privilegios*, no. 1080.

76

itself and cites the authorization given by Ferdinand to Almazán in a similar instance.[54] The conjunction of the imperial propaganda campaign against the pope with Gattinara's efforts to achieve solvency and even liquidity at the expense of some of his offices contributed to a happy resolution for the ageing statesman. On 21 September, four days after presenting his aggressively Erasmian riposte to Clement VII, Gattinara received two important concessions from the emperor. By the first he obtained the provisional possession of the seals of the Neapolitan chancellery with all the prerogatives appertaining 'because of his great services'.[55] By the second, in accordance with the emerging Spanish royal policy of using crown lands in Il Regno as a vast quarry in which to forage for the rewarding of its servants, Gattinara obtained the barony of Monterone in the province of Otranto in recognition of 'his great diligence, prudence and integrity in treating, directing and ordering day and night the most important affairs and negotiations of our State (*nostri Status*) and in counseling us most prudently and wisely on these matters.[56] Long overdue official praise for decades of dynastic service!

This investigation into Gattinara's office of Grand Chancellor of the kingdom of Naples and his possession of its seals would therefore suggest that the chancellorship and the exercise of the seals, or at least the enjoyment of the emoluments thereto appertaining, were separable and that by the current practice of *ampliacion* he had sold not the office nor its seals but the right to succeed to the same in each instance. In fact a few weeks before his departure for Italy, as if to prepare for any necessary contingencies, he managed to obtain from the crown the power to sell and alienate (*vender y enajenar*) the office of Grand Chancellor as well as his provisional possession (*tenuta*) of the seals and registers of this chancellery.[57] The privilege, dated 1 March 1527, simply confirmed what had been implicit since the beginning of these negotiations.

Turning from the Neapolitan chancellorship to the chancellery itself, one only has to sift through the nineteen *legajos* of the 'Privilegiorum' section for the period 1516–43 to be convinced as to the reality of the effective exercise of the Neapolitan seals during this period within the context of Gattinara's Aragonese imperial chancellery. Grants on the rents to alum production, concessions of rents, assignments from royal customs and taxes, expectatives of naval captaincies in Sicily, given at Barcelona, Worms, Saragossa, Seville, Genoa, Piacenza, Ratisbon or wherever the emperor and

---

[54] AGRB (PEA), 1471 (4), fol. 13. Cf. *ibid.*, fol. 11.
[55] *Privilegios*, no. 1081.
[56] *Ibid.*, no. 1082. On the royal use of Il Regno at this time as a quarry for rewarding government servants and for maintaining the fealty of restless nobles and placeseekers, see *ibid.*, Preface, esp. pp. xii–xix.   [57] *Privilegios*, no. 1083.

The emperor and his chancellor

his government might be, attest to the continuing Aragonese source of Neapolitan government. In each instance the participants in drafting a commission are listed in the upper corners of the document. The principal names of chancellery agents for this Neapolitan business are the two Aragonese Pedro García, a well-established secretary, and Juan Raphael as royal scribe and taxator. Such prominent members of the Aragonese chancellery are expectable but frequently there appears the counter-signature of Lalemand as controller-general for Naples and increasingly after the imperial residence in Seville the counter-signature of Valdés who was to persist in this office up to his death at Ratisbon in 1532.[58]

Of the surviving accounts of receipts from the Neapolitan seals, which are often intermixed with Gattinara's personal accounts, the first stems from mid-1520 but these receipts only become regular later in 1524. Here again Jean de Grey appears as receiver.[59] In a hand recognizable as that of Valdés occurs the following revealing statement six days before the second ordinance for the chancellery in which he would figure so significantly: 'Since 20 August 1524, when the Grand Chancellor gave charge of the chancellery and seals of Naples to Jean de Grey and to me up to the end of the present year, the dues from this seal amounted to 122 ducats *de moneda* worth 106 gold ducats eight reales'.[60] Jean de Grey's departure from the imperial chancellery after 1525 left Valdés in sole command of this function up to his death seven years later. Acting as the Grand Chancellor's executor for the seals of Naples and their emoluments at Ratisbon 8 April 1532, Giovanni Bartolomeo Gattinara would recognize Valdés as imperial secretary and administrator of the Neapolitan chancellery.[61]

Any effort to portray the features of this medieval institution together with its Renaissance aspirations would be incomplete without considering the social and cultural implications of the chancellery. Lacking a firm material base or distinct location, the chancellery followed by necessity the roving habits of the monarch and thereby compelled its staff to an unstable, ambulatory existence. The fact, however, that all documents had to be carried in chests on muleback provided a blessed deterrent to the accumulation of papers. After the establishment of the crown's archives at Simancas in 1543 and the sedentary nature of government in the following reign, the tidal wave of paper and the burgeoning bureaucracy would serve

[58] See ACA (Privilegiorum), 3936–40 *passim*. The pagination in these *legajos* is so badly jumbled that it is meaningless to refer to specific instances. Unfortunately Martínez Ferrando does not provide in his synopses the signatures of the officials expediting the *mercedes*.
[59] ASV, 8/5, N., De Grey, 1525.
[60] *Ibid.*, Valdés, August through December, 1524.
[61] ASV, 8/5, N., Giovanni Bartolomeo Gattinara, 1530 and 1532–3.

78

to announce a new age.[62] Living in an era of administration prior to the realities of Simancas and the Escorial, Gattinara through his ordinances required that the chancellery should be located in a hostel or inn as close as possible to the emperor. Nevertheless we know that its chief could take advantage of the residences of friends or of a rich merchant such as Stefan Centurion at Granada in 1526.[63] At other times, if the structure allowed it, the chancellery might be in a room adjoining the quarters of the emperor or come into being through the simple demarcation afforded by a hung tapestry.[64] Sometimes conditions could be virtually intolerable: a dirt floor, crushing heat, lack of space and physical means, exposure to every form of interruption.[65] Inevitably a certain degree of collegiality developed among the staff. It is probable that most of them ate and slept as well as worked together. The chancellor kept his own table to which members of the staff might be invited.[66]

As a cultural phenomenon the chancellery exercised a special role in the development of the Renaissance. To understand the immediate context or contexts for Gattinara's pursuit of interests that occasionally reflected humanistic influence, it is useful to remember that unlike the scholastic *magistri*, who enjoyed the firm institutional base of the university, our humanists had to create – or locate – their own institutional contexts which were certainly of a more casual, unstable but often more influential nature: the court of the prince, his chancellery, the printing shop, the *sodalitas*, the academy. Of these only two effectively pertain to the present case: the chancellery and the *sodalitas*. The latter particularly cannot be conceived as a discrete institution but as intersecting and overlapping the activity of the chancellery and perhaps being better understood as Gattinara's *familia*, his entourage or household. Like the household of any dynastic servant of the age, Gattinara's had a public character. The best single statement on the existence of such a gathering derives from a letter written by Christopher Scheurl, legal consultant to the government of Nuremberg, who served on the delegation sent to the emperor in 1519. In his fulsome report on the entire government, court and courtiers of Charles he expatiates on 'my Mercurino':

[62] Cf. Fernand Braudel, *La Méditerranée et le monde méditerranéen à lépoque de Phillippe II* (Paris, 1949), pp. 523–5.
[63] See *infra*, Chap. 5, p. 90.
[64] There is no reason to believe that Charles V's chancellery was any more stable than that of Francis I. See Michaud, *Chancellerie*, p. 333, cf. also pp. 287, 290–4.
[65] HHSA (Belgien), PA 91/2, fol. 352ᵛ. It is unclear from the context whether Gattinara here is referring to his household or the chancellery but the two are to a fair extent interwoven.
[66] See the letter of Valdés to John Dantiscus in E. B. Boehmer, 'A. Valdesii Litterae XL', *Homenaje a Menéndez y Pelayo* (Madrid, 1875), I, 398.

The emperor and his chancellor

I say 'mine' for he has quite drawn me into the favorable recognition of the royal council, because as often as he saw a kindred spirit he commanded that person to dine with him, yes he even freely caused the uninvited public official to join daily in his midday meal – this accomplished orator, erudite jurisconsult, faithful counsellor, hard working, articulate, gentle, charming, jovial, kind, well-versed in matters of polite learning (*rerum humanarum*). Never dining alone, he is restored by the company of feasting guests: he makes merry, laughs, converses, mixes jokes with serious matters while eating; moderate, most pleasing in his manner, most accessible, obliging, affable he honors those coming to him and listens indulgently.[67]

Scheurl enjoyed more than sixty days of this treatment. Little wonder that he provides us with one of the most enthusiastically favorable descriptions of Charles' court, and that he paints in such glowing hues the portrait of his host. Little wonder also that the chancellor ran up debts in excess of 34,000 ducats before going back in March 1527 to Italy where he hoped to reorganize his personal finances.[68] Yet according to the scattered statements of other contemporaries there is nothing, despite its exuberance, inaccurate in Scheurl's account of Gattinara's company or his characterization of the man.

Indeed, the chancellor was in the habit of eating only once, recognizing the midday meal and using it as an opportunity to converse with friends and visiting dignitaries. Who attended? Certainly at the time Scheurl wrote, one could find there with some frequency Charles' physician, the Milanese doctor Marliano, Bishop of Tuy, correspondent of Erasmus, described by Peter Martyr as the greatest philosopher of the time and half Gattinara's soul.[69] Then there would have been present members of the chancellery staff:[70] perhaps Maximilianus Transylvanus, who in his *De moluccis insulis* would provide the first account of Magellan's circumnavigation of the

---

[67] Christoph Scheurl, *Briefbuch*, eds. Franz Freiherr von Soden and J. K. T. Knaake (Aalen, 1962), II, 109. Cf. also Scheurl's letter to Giovanni Bartolomeo Gattinara, 7 March 1520, *ibid.*, pp. 99–100. For the diplomatic context and the possible diplomatic intent to Gattinara's dinner gatherings see Johannes Müller, 'Nürnbergs Botschaft nach Spanien zu Kaiser Karl V in Jahre 1519', *Historische Zeitschrift*, *98* (1907), 303–28, esp. 316–20.

[68] Bornate, 'Doc.', pp. 526–7.

[69] Martyr, *Opus*, nos. 696, 723, 724; on their being almost interchangeable in Anghiera's opinion cf. nos. 664, 673 and 704. On Marliano see Earl E. Rosenthal, 'The invention of the columnar device of Emperor Charles V at the Court of Burgundy in Flanders in 1516', *Journal of the Warburg and Courtauld Institutes*, *36* (1973), 198–211.

[70] Unfortunately there is no evidence that the humanistically gifted Gaspar Argillense and Sánchez de Orihuela attended. For these secretaries see Luis Núñez Contreras, *Un registro de cancillería de Carlos V. El MS 917 de la biblioteca nacional de Madrid* (Madrid, 1965), pp. xxvi, xxix. Although the chancellery in question is not specified, it would have been the Aragonese chancellery parts of which had been merged at Brussels in 1516 with a provisional secretariat attendant upon Charles. See Walser, *Zentralbehörden*, pp. 126–9, 224–5.

80

The imperial chancellery

globe;[71] Jean Hannart, *audiencier et premier secrétaire* as well as vice-chancellor, who could have attended until his ill-fated embassy in 1523 to the empire; inevitably the dangerous Jean Lalemand who clandestinely strived to unseat his master and benefactor; later the faithful Alfonso de Valdés, 'more Erasmian than Erasmus', the chancellery's registrar and Latin secretary, brilliantly lettered in the vernacular, and the most strident champion of an imperial messianism; Balthasar Mercklin, Provost of Waldkirch, who by 1524 was unofficially in charge of the German correspondence of the imperial chancellery, and early in 1527 assumed the post of vice-chancellor;[72] and later still Nicholas Perrenot, the elder Granvelle, who would inherit many of Gattinara's responsibilities and a double portion of his spirit.[73]

Beyond the leading personnel of the chancellery there were members of what a later age would call the diplomatic corps. One of Gattinara's closest friends in the last few years of his life was the talented, humanistically gifted vice-chancellor of Denmark, Cornelius de Schepper, or Scepperus,[74] who had been sent by Margaret of Austria to Spain and thereby entered Charles' service and the association with Gattinara at the end of 1524. Distinguished by his prudence and linguistic abilities, he headed an embassy to Poland in 1528 and would later be the imperial ambassador to England in 1545–6. He was among the few who accompanied the chancellor on his hazardous trip to Italy in 1527 and would attend his last moments in the spring of 1530. Perhaps even closer to the affections of the chancellor was the Polish ambassador John Dantiscus later Bishop of Ermland, friend and patron of Copernicus. As leading regular members of Gattinara's innermost circle, Scepperus and Dantiscus referred affectionately to their friend as *senex* and 'our Nestor'.[75] Together with Alfonso de Valdés they stood closest in the affections of the chancellor and served him best in his last months: Valdés as the chief witness to his will, signed at Barcelona 23 July 1529 and executor of his apparent policy of reconcilation with the Protestants at the diet of Augsburg; Scepperus attendant upon Gattinara in his last days and

[71] On Maximilianus Transylvanus see Henry de Vocht, *Literae virorum eruditorum ad Franciscum Craneveldium 1522–1528* (Louvain, 1928), pp. 166–7; also Alphonse Roersch, *L'humanisme belge à lépoque de la Renaissance* (Louvain, 1933), pp. 33–54.
[72] Allen, *Opus*, v, 323; Adolf Hasenclever, 'Balthasar Merklin, Propst von Waltkirch, Reichsvizekanzler unter Kaiser Karl V', *Zeitschrift für die Geschichte des Oberrhins*, *34* (1919), 485–502, *35* (1920), 36–80.
[73] M. Dan Durme, 'À propos du quatrième centenaire de la mort de Nicolas Perrenot de Granvelle', *Bibliothèque d'Humanisme et Renaissance*, *13* (1951), 271–94; and his *El Cardenal Granvela 1517–1586. Imperio y Revolución bajo Carlos V y Félipe II* (Barcelona, 1957), pp. 29, 103–9.
[74] For a sketch of his career see Henry de Vocht, *John Dantiscus and his Netherlandish friends as revealed by their correspondence* (Louvain, 1961), pp. 16–17, 23 *et passim*.
[75] Vocht, *Dantiscus*, pp. 26–30, 172–3, 285–6; Vocht, *Literae*, pp. 639–42.

leading communicant to the larger world of humanism; and Dantiscus who celebrated his late lamented friend in that manner most befitting and distinctive of the humanist world – the publication of a collection of elegies composed by the Netherlandish-Burgundian community of literati honoring the former chancellor.[76]

It would be misleading to compare Gattinara's chancellery as a potential cultural center with the sedentary, well-endowed mid-Quattrocento chancelleries of a Pope Nicholas V or an Alfonso the Magnanimous; the inherently unstable and impecunious nature of Gattinara's secretariat kept it lean under the pressure of political business. Nevertheless, the imperial chancellery was sufficiently important as a political and cultural center to draw the attention of applicants. In April 1524 Archbishop Albrecht had attempted to obtain a position for his client Georg Kurchmuller on the basis of the latter's earlier experience as a secretary of the Emperor Maximilian and because of his mastery of Latin. Nothing materialized.[77] Later, in 1529, Erasmus tried to advance a member of his *familia*, Francis Delfius, but the occasion was inappropriate for the emperor was en route to Italy, and more specifically the finances of Gattinara's household did not permit an additional member to the staff.[78]

In the relationship of the chancellor to the members of his staff one further point needs to be emphasized. Alfonso de Valdés' advancement to the office of registrar and controller-general by August 1524 and the joint appointment with De Grey to the administration of the Neapolitan seals appear surprising in view of the fact that he would not become a permanent secretary until early in 1526, when he succeeded to Nicola's responsibilities. This promotion with new responsibilities would suggest that for the very period which remains undocumented, 1522 to 1524, and thereby lost to view, the young scribe had quickly caught the attention of his chief with whom he would share a common enthusiasm for Erasmus and from whom he would imbibe a marked imperialist outlook. Such a rapid promotion can only be understood as the product of a special affinity between two minds. Ever since their return to Spain in 1522 Valdés and Gattinara had achieved a remarkable working relationship within the chancellery. Indeed as indicated in the Valladolid ordinance Valdés was the chancellor's own (*suum*) secretary.[79] According to the colophon of the propagandistic report that he composed in the spring of 1525 to announce officially the imperial victory at Pavia, Valdés identified himself as the secretary of the Grand

[76] Hilarius Bartel, ed., *Epitaphia epigrammata et elegiae aliquot illustrium virorum in funere Mercurini cardinalis, marchionis Gattinariae, caesaris Caroli Quinti augusti supremi cancellarii* (Antwerp, Joannes Graphaeus, 1531), sigs. [A₂ᵛ]–A₃. I have used the Columbia University copy.
[77] AGS, Estado, 1553, no. 495, fols. 1ᵛ–2.
[78] Allen, *Opus*, VIII, 67–8, cf. VII, 421.
[79] Hasenclever, 'Kanzleiordnung', p. 52.

The imperial chancellery

Chancellor.[80] Admittedly, the whole character and atmosphere of Gatti-nara's chancellery were quite personal, having many of the qualities of a separate barony and merging at times with his household. In a grant of 9 July 1521 Philip Nicola also shares in this personal rather than institutional set of relations, being referred to as 'Secretario del Espectable Mercurino de Gattinara'.[81] Nevertheless, the working habits of the two men as revealed in the fragmentary documentation of the chancellery indicate that Valdés was being entrusted with increasing responsibilities and in one instance dating from late July 1525, when Gattinara's hand tires in drafting a memorandum on Venice's failure to provide financial support for the league that he sought to maintain in Italy, Valdés' hand takes over to complete the document.[82] And yet there exists the threat of Valdés being drawn away, less from ambition than by impending circumstances, out of the context of the chancellery into that of a cameral type of government. As early as March 1526 Gattinara, in writing to the Brussels treasurer Jehan Dadurca, refers to Valdés as *secretaire de l'empereur*.[83] What does the chancellor intend by this title, if anything at all? Does it refer to Valdés' close working relationship to the emperor, which would seem premature as occurring on the eve of the secretary's most intense collaboration within the chancellery and as not being supported by the evidence? Or does the chancellor simply wish to dignify his client and express in the more personal terminology and understanding of the period what a later age would recognize as a secretary of state? Premature or not, the title would stick and its apparently first enunciation here foreshadows the later brilliant relationship of Valdés with the emperor and indicates another striking case of how the ambiguities of secretarial office were resolved to the enhancement of a cameral type of government and to the detriment of the chancellery.

Yet this development lay in the more distant future. For the present Alfonso de Valdés stood on the threshold of his most fateful collaboration with the chancellor. And in the ensuing months the Castilian would be given ever greater responsibilities in trumpeting a Habsburg imperial world-view that surpassed any regional conception of empire.

Although the office of Grand Chancellor hovered upon extinction and would in fact be suppressed at Gattinara's death, the imperial chancellery, if in a somewhat reduced and altered form, would persist. During the succeeding regime of the elder Granvelle it was not to the political interest

[80] 'Los señores del consejo de su magestad: mandaron a mi Alonso de Valdés secretario del illustre señor gran chanciller: que fiziesse imprimir la presente relacion.' Don Fermín Caballero, *Alonso y Juan de Valdés* (Madrid, 1875), IV, 503 – a facsimile reproduction of the original colophon, sig. A^viii.

[81] *Privilegios*, no. 1631.

[82] AGS, Estado, 1454, no. 105.   [83] *Ibid.*, 1553, no. 496.

83

The emperor and his chancellor

of Charles' Keeper of the Seals to promote any further the development of the imperial court chancellery. According to that gifted humanist lawyer and rising statesman Viglius van Zwichem the younger Granvelle, the Bishop of Arras, came to administer for his father the increasingly routine activities of this body. During that charmed moment in the spring of 1550 which saw the gathering of the emperor, his sister and his son at Brussels before the catastrophe of Metz, Viglius drafted an extensive and comprehensive statement on the organization of the imperial chancellery. As chief of the Netherlandish privy council and Council of State and as one who had recently refused the German vice-chancellorship, Viglius wrote with considerable knowledge and authority.[84]

Among the six different earlier ordinances and memoirs which Viglius uses as the historical basis of his memorandum, Gattinara's of 1 January 1522 looms large and is treated with great respect. On the following points he specifically cites and follows Gattinara's first ordinance pertaining to the imperial chancellery: there should be a special registrar to oversee the scribes in the task of registration; such registration should include not only documents with seals appended but also papers with seals impressed, for the latter are often of greater importance; the registration should be based not on the secretarial drafts but upon the completed document which has undergone all corrections and alterations and been subscribed by the vice-chancellor, chancellor or even emperor; summaries, however, may be made of the routine business; a special receiver is to be established to receive the tax, which in some cases is to be waived.[85]

In several instances Viglius' draft illuminates some of the issues presented in Gattinara's ordinances. Concerning the counsellors who move between the privy council and the chancellery receiving and bearing petitions and expediting the processes of the chancellery, Viglius has an extensive section of ten articles entitled *De Consiliariis*. While claiming that ancient chancellery ordinances have said virtually nothing about counsellors, he insists on their present importance for coordinating the activities of council and chancellery. It is thus all the more striking that before coming to the chancellorship Gattinara had sought to integrate these two institutions in Margaret's government and yet when chancellor, he had apparently failed to provide these valuable links.[86] On the question of the precise meaning of *negotia status* Viglius will explicitly declare that *negotia caesarae maiestatis*

---

[84] The document, entitled 'Conceptum ordinationum cancellariae imperialis revisum 9. Aprilis 1550', is published in Walther, 'Kanzleiordnungen', pp. 392–406. For his own analysis of this document cf. *ibid.*, pp. 369–75. On Viglius see Allen, *Opus*, VIII, 56–7.

[85] These points constitute articles 32, 33, 38, 40, 55 and 57 of Viglius' draft.

[86] Gattinara's draft for the reordering of Margaret of Austria's council and chancellery, dated 17 December 1516, is published in Walther, *Zentralbehörden*, pp. 199–203. For an appreciation of its conceptual brilliance see *ibid.*, pp. 102–9, 112–14.

84

The imperial chancellery

pertain to those things which are of greater moment and cannot suffer delay. In contrast to the plurality of counsellors Viglius will treat the office of secretary in the singular as represented by the person of Obernburg, who had earlier served under Gattinara as an aid to Valdés. The secretary will draft documents to be reviewed by the chancellor or vice-chancellor before he distributes them to the scribes for engrossment. Finally, Viglius reasserts the existence of five registers but then adds as a specific correction to Gattinara's ordinance of 1522 that since patrimonial affairs for the Austrian lands are no longer handled in the imperial chancellery, the number of registers is consequently reduced to four. Indeed Gattinara had drawn the same conclusion by August 1524, but the Belgian statesman was manifestly unaware of his great predecessor's later ordinance issued at Valladolid.

Thus, for the retrospective light that it sheds upon Gattinara's chancellery, the continuity and reaffirmation of many of its practices and the condition of the imperial chancellery at mid-century Viglius' draft for the *Ordo consilii* of August 1550 is of capital importance for our study.[87]

[87] Further study of the interlocking Caroline chancelleries and secretariats will benefit from the admirable enterprise of the Constance Project under the direction of Horst Rabe and Heide Stratenwerth with the aid of Peter Marzahl and in collaboration with Christiane Thomas (HHSA). In seeking to inventory the political correspondence of Charles V, based upon the Belgian section of the HHSA, the project is gradually creating a map of unmatched accuracy for this immense archival source and thus a mirror reflecting the exchanges within the Habsburg system. Beginning in 1976, instalments of this research have appeared in the *Mitteilungen des Österreichischen Staatsarchiv*.

5

The imperial propaganda campaign of
1526–1527

Standing at the headwaters of bureaucratic differentiation, the late medieval
chancellery exercised an amalgam of functions – judicial, diplomatic,
administrative – that later ages would gradually sort out into discrete
departments. Certainly by 1500 the properly judicial aspect had been so
clearly distinguished as to be removed from the more secretarial functions
of the chancellery. Within the latter branch the chancellor, as official
spokesman of the ruler, could expect at a moment of crisis or accelerated
diplomatic activity to exercise the functions of a propagandist for his
monarch. Examples of medieval chancellors consciously acting as propa-
gandists, if not many, are still significant: one thinks of the imperial
brilliance of the Hohenstaufen chancellery under Rainald von Dassel and
Piero della Vigna; or more recently the Florentine chancellery under the
direction of Coluccio Salutati whose missives trumpeted the majesty and
virtue of the infant Arno republic from the Baltic to the Bosphorus.[1] In
his exercise of an acknowledged monopoly of official rhetoric the chancellor
sought to promote the prince or polity that he served. It is in this tradition
that we need ultimately to judge the feverish activity of Charles V's Grand
Chancellor within his chancellery during the latter half of 1526. Moreover,
the crisis created in imperial affairs by the League of Cognac had the dual
effect of reconfirming the role and policies of Gattinara and of allowing his
chancellery to operate as a fairly coherent body for what would appear to
be the last time.

    The victory of Pavia in February 1525 had ironically produced a number
of embarrassments for the emperor: the presence of King Francis as a

---

[1] See Ronald G. Witt, *Coluccio Salutati and his public letters* (Geneva, 1976); Nicolai Rubinstein,
'Political rhetoric in the imperial chancery', *Medium Aevum, 14* (1945), 21–43. For some valuable
observations on the nature of early modern European propaganda see Joseph Klaits, *Printed
propaganda under Louis XIV* (Princeton, 1976), pp. 3–12, esp. 10–11, which contrasts the
manipulative character of modern propaganda, based upon psychological assumptions of relativism
and man's irrationality, with the restrained, traditional character of early modern propaganda whose
potential range was greatly confined by notions of human immutability and the unchanging unity
of Truth.

captive in Spain; the fear promoted by the apparent imperial omnipotence in Italy; the heightened expectation of a council. Louise of Savoy, regent of France, and the pope moved toward each other, impressed by their common enemy. The failure of Francis I, once having been liberated, to live up to the obligations of the treaty of Madrid strengthened the reputation of the man who had so bitterly opposed the treaty and was least surprised by the outcome. The discovery and quashing of Morone's plot to unseat the emperor from both Naples and northern Italy had the effect of precipitating the League of Cognac on 22 May 1526 contracted between Clement, Francis, Venice, Florence and Milan. With the army of the League advancing on the imperial position at Milan, Clement VII wrote the first of two fateful briefs to Charles, justifying his resort to arms for the liberty of Italy as well as for the security of his own office and taking the emperor to task for the indignities suffered at the hands of his agents.[2]

During the summer of 1526 Gattinara brooded longer hours than usual over the European situation, and for good reason. The deterioration of the imperial position in Italy, an increasingly hostile pope, the disruptive threat posed by a freed King Francis and the impending danger of a Turkish avalanche upon Hungary began to assume a connectedness in Gattinara's mind. Again Italy seemed the key and the emperor's journey there occupied its usual determinative role in the chancellor's calculations. But the empire itself and German affairs now forced themselves upon his attention in a new way. For if the emperor's brother was to be able to intervene on Charles' behalf in the Italian peninsula, Ferdinand's own position in Germany must be secured. The need to tap central Europe's considerable, if disorganized, resources in order to deploy them both in Italy and against the Turk militated toward a neutralization of the religious unrest that could only be accomplished by a policy of accommodation and moderation. Therefore, Gattinara urged upon the Council of State the publishing of an edict that would cancel the Edict of Worms, and hold out possibilities of amnesty and reconciliation to the Lutherans, who were to be almost flattered by the claim that their sect was essentially based on evangelical doctrine. The proposed edict and its promulgation presents a case of public relations, late medieval style: it was to be posted in all the accustomed places of the cities of the empire, and be directed apparently to Lutheran moderates. Within two months, however, the pressure of events stemming from Italy would serve to transform this effort at public relations, narrowing

[2] For the papal brief of 23 June 1526 and for related documents discussed herein, see the two-fold polemical compilation entitled *Pro divo Carolo eius nominis quinto Romanorum Imperatore Invictissimo, pio, felice, semper Augusto, Patrepatriae, in satisfactionem quidem sine talione eorum quae in illum scripta, ac pleraque etiam in vulgum aedita fuere, Apologetici libri duo nuper ex Hispanis allati cum alijs nonnullis, quorum catalogos ante cuiusque exordium reperies* (Mainz, Joannis Schoeffer, 1527). This is the definitive edition. For the papal brief see sigs. [Bᵛ]–Biiij.

its focus but increasing its intensity through resort to the new technology of the press.[3]

Clement VII's first brief reached Granada where the court was residing; it was formally received and read on 20 August at 9 o'clock in the royal palace.[4] For the past months war tensions had been increasing at court.[5] The unpleasant task of presenting the brief fell to the papal nuncio, that master of tact, Baldassare Castiglione. Indeed all the charm and finesse of *Il Cortegiano*'s author were called upon for the occasion and it is largely from his detailed reports that we are able to understand the genesis of what was to be the centerpiece in the *Pro divo Carlo...Apologetici libri duo*, namely, the imperial response to the first papal brief. Castiglione had asked that he be allowed to present the brief not alone but when other ambassadors were presenting their credentials, a request which appears to have been granted. The emperor's reaction to its presentation was remarkably moderate. While he believed the brief not to have come from a loving father, he was not surprised that the pope had been somewhat outspoken; unwilling to endanger general peace, Charles managed to suppress any suggestion of anger. The papal nuncio tried to sweeten the pill by developing the pope's invitation in the brief that the emperor himself join the league, but Charles declined to join an arrangement which, although proceeding under the guise of the general welfare, he correctly judged to be directed against himself. He did not have time to exchange further subtleties with Castiglione for he was anxious to get off to the hunt in Sante Fé but he promised a formal response soon. One thing, however, was clear to the papal nuncio: His Majesty did not seem to take anger.[6]

Acting in the name of the emperor, Gattinara seized the initiative: he summoned the royal council of Castile to confer on the defense of the emperor's state and dignity. In his *relacion*[7] he set forth the violations by the pope to previous treaties pertaining to the Italian peninsula, his increasing constraints placed upon the emperor's emissaries and his declared animosity to the emperor by all his actions. In its purport and language we have here the genesis of the later notorious imperial response. As a result of Gattinara's vehement appeal to his fellow councillors for their most solemn advice, a document including five recommendations was drawn up to be submitted to the emperor. The councillors first determined that in order to maintain his lands and estates it is just and lawful for the

[3] For Gattinara's discourse of July 1526 on the foreign policy of the emperor see Bornate, 'Doc.', pp. 496–514, esp. 500–3.
[4] *AT*, VIII, 356; *Pro divo Carolo*, sig. M₄.
[5] *AT*, VIII, 356; Serassi, *Lettere di Castiglione*, II, 58, 61.
[6] Serassi, *Lettere de Castiglione*, II, 66–73.
[7] Bornate, 'Doc.', pp. 489–94. Both the *relacion* and the subsequent consulta Bornate has placed in July but the entire context and the material cited in the report argue for a later dating.

emperor to defend himself by taking arms against any attacker, even if he be the pope. Secondly, that in accordance with the customs of the Catholic kings the churches and monasteries are expected to make sacrifices and prayers in keeping with this moment of crisis. Thirdly, in order to give the best appearance before the Apostolic See, all Christendom and to the satisfaction of the kingdoms of Spain, the pope ought to be apprised in the best possible words that can be mustered, while representing the emperor as ready to live and die a faithful son, advocate and protector of the church. Fourthly, the College of Cardinals ought also to be apprised so that it might counsel the pope not to attack the emperor, who is the principal member of the church, but rather to direct the pope against the Turk and Luther. Finally, a full cortes of the realm ought to be summoned to confer on what should be done.[8]

There are times in the life of any regime when it may prove expedient, even necessary, to present itself to the world in a deliberately ambiguous guise: by allowing a responsible agent of the regime to assume a more aggressive posture, the recognized head of state may still hold in reserve a more conciliatory approach and maintain his freedom of action, while confusing his opponents. Such a moment seems to have arrived immediately following the reception of the first papal brief, when Charles' counsellors sought to discover the best posture for his government now to assume toward Rome. Naturally, the recommendations that Gattinara presented to Charles had to give the emperor both freedom of choice and maneuver; he could reject them, modify them, accept and identify himself with them and with the shortly forthcoming response from the chancellery and council. He could also permit the response to run its course and maintain his distance from it, as subsequent events would prove. Charles would use his latitude well.

In the ensuing days the ominous reverberations that came from the Council of State were anything but reassuring to the papal nuncio; they clearly indicated an escalation in the violent tenor of the imperial response. Charles manifested every desire to keep his distance from the course of developments within the council and pressed upon Castiglione written and oral assurances of his benevolent intentions toward the Holy Father. Apparently Charles had returned to the suggestion of entering the league and received the encouragement of his council except for the Grand

---

[8] *Ibid.*, pp. 494–6. Gattinara has endorsed it: 'Consejo real de Castilla.' However, given the fluidity of the councils at this time and the overhaul of the Council of State to make room for more Spanish members, a strict institutional demarcation to each of these councils should not be imposed. On contemporary changes within the Council of State see Walser, *Zentralbehörden*, pp. 235–40; on the preeminently judicial and internal character of the Council of Castile's activities see *ibid.*, pp. 209–12.

Chancellor and the Archbishop of Bari. From the admiring, almost fond statements of the papal nuncio, the emperor seemed to have played his part with the utmost courtliness and circumspection in the eyes of the first gentleman of Europe. In actual fact he was permitting the manufacture of a stout riposte to the pope, while providing shelter for himself from the expectable fallout. In his extended letter of September to the Archbishop of Capua, Castiglione confessed nervousness whenever the emperor mentioned the word 'council'. When pressed by the ambassadors of France and Venice on the matter, Charles sought to exculpate himself from the idea of a general council as something quite alien to his intention and he went on to admit that members of his Council of State were interpreting the papal brief as being harsher than it actually was.[9] Undoubtedly there were periods of violent disagreement and discussion within the council. The English ambassador Edward Lee on 7 September reported the Council of State to be astir over the matter of answering the papal brief; two days later he registered impatience with his observation that 'they show themselves very slow in writing their great book'.[10]

During these early September days the papal nuncio claimed to have identified the best medicine for the first papal brief in the mildness and modernation of the second papal brief, which arrived at court on 7 September;[11] he hastened to press this instrument upon Charles as proof that the first was written in a moment of anger that lasted but a day. Yet some members of the council felt otherwise. With the difference of a day they reasoned, the pope could have overtaken the first messenger had he so wished. It was thus resolved to imitate the papal pattern and reply to each brief successively.[12] By 8 September, nine days before the presentation of the final *riposta*, Castiglione indicated that he had managed to see a draft of the proposed response (*proposta*) which he found full of calumnies and *molto aspro*. Shortly, however, he would deem the final version worse than the draft.[13]

When Gattinara at 9 o'clock on the morning of the seventeenth stood before the assembled members of the Council of State in the house of the Genoese merchant Stephan Centurion, where he and thus the chancellery were residing, and addressed the papal nuncio, he held in his hand a sheaf of twenty-two folios. The chancellor passed the sheaf to the Latin secretary and specialist in the Roman correspondence, Alfonso de Valdés, the presumed author of the response and the one whose name would appear at the end of its several printed editions. What Valdés began to read

[9] Serassi, *Lettere di Castiglione*, II, 75–9.
[10] *Letters and Papers*, 4/2, nos. 2470, 2473.
[11] *Ibid.*, no. 2473.
[12] Fra Paolo Sarpi, *Istoria del concilio Tridentino*, ed. Giovanni Gambarin, 3 vols. (Bari, 1935), I, 62.
[13] Serassi, *Lettere di Castiglione*, II, 80–4, 86–7, 91.

represented the consuming preoccupation of both council and chancellery for the past month.[14] It had shuttled back and forth between the two groups of Habsburg agents, the main features being hammered out in the council, the prose being provided in the chancellery and checked again in council. It had obviously gone through several drafts and had almost weekly been altered in the virulence of its style[15] and the length of its verbiage, swelling at one time apparently to thirty folios before ultimately being pruned to its present sufficiently imposing and thoroughly acerbic twenty-two.[16] Thus to ask who wrote it may seem somewhat beside the point.

The question as to the authorship of Charles' response from Granada, dated 17 September 1526, to the papal brief of 23 June cannot be judged in modern terms as a literary work being the sovereign expression of a single mind and personality; rather, account must be taken of both the institutional context, namely the chancellery and its relation to the Council of State, and the special relationship developing between the Latin secretary, Valdés, and the chancellor himself. From a permanent scribe in January 1522 Alfonso de Valdés had by August 1524 risen within the ranks of the chancellery's officialdom to the post of permanent secretary as well as enjoying the responsible positions of contrarelator and keeper of the four registers. When news arrived in March 1525 concerning the imperial victory at Pavia, it was Valdés who, having ready access to the preceding correspondence and documents in the chancellery, was called upon to compose for the domestic scene the government's official report and response. The subsequent *Relacion de las nuevas de Italia* bore on the title page the explanation 'corregido por el señor gran chanciller y consejo de su majestad' and in the colophon, that the lords of 'His Majesty's council charged Valdés as secretary of the Grand Chancellor to arrange for the printing of this report'.[17] In the case of Charles' reply to Clement eighteen months later we may presume a somewhat similar provenance and operation. Admittedly, Valdés would later claim for himself the authorship of the imperial response to the pope as well as to the King of France.[18] By a royal warrant of 8 February 1526 Valdés had received notice that he was to succeed the ailing Latin secretary Philip Nicola effective from 1 January, and was presently entrusted with the correspondence pertaining principally to Rome and

[14] *Pro divo Carolo*, sigs. L$_{iij}$, [C^v]–C$_{ij}$. In his report of this event to the Serenissima, 20 September 1526, Navagero claims that Lalemand read the riposte of eighteen folios. Bornate, 'Doc.', p. 517. Cf. *ibid.*, p. 524 where again, according to Navagero, Lalemand will read the riposte of 12 February 1527 to the ambassadors assembled in Gattinara's bedroom. I have preferred here the public, official account presented by the chancellery.
[15] Hubert Jedin, *A History of the Council of Trent* (London, 1957), I, 236; cf. Serassi, *Lettere di Castiglione*, II, 91.
[16] *AT*, VIII, 356.
[17] See Caballero, *Valdés*, pp. 489, 503 for a facsimile reproduction of the tract.
[18] *Ibid.*, pp. 324, 335.

Italy.[19] Certainly when the crisis occurred, Valdés was the obvious man to present the imperial response. Furthermore, he enjoyed the confidence of his master, the chancellor, with whom he shared an enthusiasm for the writings of Erasmus and for their promotion in Spain.[20]

On the other hand, there is a ring of authenticity in the Venetian ambassador Navagero's conviction that Gattinara was alone responsible for the harsh reply to the pope. The marginalia in several of the published documents pertaining to the controversy with Francis I appear to have been composed by the chancellor. To Navagero the vehemence and malevolence of these writings could bring only new hatreds rather than peace. And when he expostulated to the emperor that Gattinara made remarks about the church that its worst enemy would never utter, Charles emitted only 'mixed noises'.[21] The papal nuncio Castiglione himself entertained no doubts as to the responsibility for the harshness and calumnies of the reply. He immediately accosted Gattinara as *ministro in questo caso e principale*, rebuking him for his dishonorable action and claiming that his response to the papal brief did not represent the mind of the emperor. After consulting the latter, Castiglione came away with a hand-written voucher from the emperor attesting to Charles' continuing sense of filial obedience to His Holiness which satisfied the nuncio that Charles had been forced unwillingly by his chief counsellors to accept this reply.[22] In short, the chancellor was certainly as much as Valdés the author of the emperor's response to the first papal brief in Book I of *Pro divo Carolo*. While the words of the major replies and the letter to the Sacred College were those of Valdés, their tenor, the subjects treated and main arguments advanced, in fact the formulation of policy, could only have been Gattinara's. To his contemporaries there was no doubt that the amassed materials of the *Pro divo Carolo* were at every point the expression of a single mind, will and policy identifiable with the chancellor. It is inconceivable that it could have been otherwise. While the hand was that of Valdés, the voice was clearly that of his master. Valdés' successful execution of the task bears witness to the conformity of the secretary's mind with that of the chancellor. He would prove in more than one instance more Gattinarian than Gattinara.[23] The same applies to all the other imperialist writings especially that of the refutation to King Francis' *Apology*. While Valdés could be and did claim

[19] *Ibid.*, pp. 319–20; cf. Bataillon, *Érasme*, p. 248, fn. 1.
[20] The classic presentation of this relationship and their Erasmianism is, of course, to be found in Bataillon, *Érasme*, pp. 243–300 *et passim*.
[21] Cicogna, *Inscrizioni*, pp. 193–6, 266.
[22] Serassi, *Lettere di Castiglione*, II, 91, cf. 84.
[23] So much emphasis had been given to the influence of Erasmus upon Valdés that the at least equally great influence of Gattinara has usually been ignored. For a valuable corrective see Sosio Pezzella, 'Alfonso de Valdés e la politica religiosa di Carlo V', *Studi e materiali di storia delle religioni, 36* (1965), 211–68, esp. 265–8.

to be the author, we have express and explicit statements from both Castiglione and the Polish ambassador Dantiscus that Gattinara himself wrote the reply to the French king.[24] As with the earlier report on the battle of Pavia, it is most likely that the chancellor assigned his secretary the task of working up a public statement based upon original letters and documents, but examined, corrected and approved by the chancellor and his fellow councillors. The evidence provided by the surviving manuscripts attests that whatever was not either dictated by the chancellor to his secretary or mutually devised certainly had his assent.[25] Indeed, by its very nature it was bound also to be in part a collective enterprise calling upon not only members of the chancellery and Council of State but also perhaps upon members of Gattinara's own inner circle.[26] Salinas, Ferdinand's ambassador, reported that in the Council of State the proposal for the reply to the papal brief ran to thirty-six sheets.[27] And within the Council of State, Gattinara could expect the support of at least Loaysa, Charles' confessor and president of the council of the Indies, and that the others could be won over by his

---

[24] Serassi, *Lettere di Castiglione*, II, 90; *AT*, VIII, 357.

[25] Of the surviving drafts, probably used as printer's copy, the following are to be found at the Archivo General de Simancas: the imperial response of 18 September to the pope (Estado, 1554, no. 545); the letter of 6 October to the cardinals (Estado, 1554, nos. 546–8); the letter of 29 Nov. to the German princes (Estado, 1554, nos. 549–51); and the preface 'Pio lectori' to the entire volume (Estado, 1554, nos. 575–6). Unfortunately although the Archivo General de Simancas' 'Catalogo XIV', *Estado: Negociación de Roma*, p. 4 refers to the presence of the first imperial *respuesta* of 1526 to the pope, presumably that of the *Pro divo Carolo*, as being present in *legajo* 847, such is emphatically not the case. In fact, Pascual Gayangos, the editor of *Cal. SP Spain*, III/1, 905–22, unaware of the *Pro divo Carolo's* existence and only dimly surmising a possible contemporary printing, used an Italianate seventeenth-century copy of the imperial response in the Biblioteca Nacional de Madrid (Estado 50, f. 44) as the text for his summary translation. Concerning the drafts of those parts of the *Pro divo Carolo* surviving at Simancas, all are in Valdés' hand with relatively unimportant additions and cancellations made throughout by Gattinara. Cf. also Brandi, *Quellen*, pp. 178–9. Later in his autobiography, where he was not averse to depicting himself giant-size, Gattinara claimed his own specific 'instrumentality' for all the compositions of imperial provenance appearing in the Mainz edition, averring that the imperial reply to the pope was 'Mercurini studio', the reply to Francis I was 'ope etiam Mercurini' and the response to the papal French and Venetian ambassadors was produced 'ipsius Mercurini organo'. See Bornate, 'Vita', pp. 332–3, 337.

[26] Cf. Caballero, *Valdés*, pp. 471–4. Culling the correspondence of Gattinara's close friend, the Polish ambassador John Dantiscus, Henry de Vocht, in *Dantiscus*, p. 26, educes evidence that would provide a suggestive variant to what has been presented here: namely, that Valdés received permission from the chancellor at the end of September to introduce some changes in a document *Pro Caesare ad Romanum Pontificem mittend[um]*, and that he sought the advice of Gattinara's two intimates and members of his inner circle Dantiscus and De Schepper, whom he invited to lunch. Apparently, the document in question was a copy of that imperial reply already handed a few days earlier to Castiglione. Have we here a case of further editing by Valdés before the reply went to press? But even more interesting is the recourse to personages outside both the Council of State and the imperial chancellery. For the roles of Valdés, De Schepper and Dantiscus as members of Gattinara's inner circle, see the present author's article cited *infra*, fn. 88.

[27] Rodríguez Villa, 'Cartas de Salinas', *43*, 504.

superior knowledge of Italian affairs. Perhaps Navagero was not short of the truth when he observed immediately after the event that all had been done by Gattinara and Loaysa *consultissimamente*.[28]

The imperial response to the first papal brief represented the opening shot in a propaganda campaign of European scope that would burgeon and develop over the course of the next six months drawing to itself the energies and talents of the chancellery's personnel. For if the *Pro divo Carolo* reflected the mind and policy of a single man, its various parts revealed the efforts of many persons, all associated with the chancellery. Besides Valdés, the composite work bore the signature of Waldkirch, soon to be made vice-chancellor, who would help its promotion in the empire, to which it was chiefly directed. Alexander Schweis, permanent secretary to the chancellery, had the express responsibility of preparing the twenty-two folios of the imperial response for the press.[29] From his background in association with the Archbishop Elector of Trier he also could be expected to promote the expediting of the work in the empire. His counterpart Lalemand had the same responsibility for the public instrument replying to the peace proposals of the League, wherein the reader is told that all these matters were enacted in the hospice of the chancellor.[30] Nevertheless, Valdés, because of his role in the chancellery and because he worked so well with the chancellor, by his multiple contributions, certainly far outweighed all his colleagues in the promotion of the volume.

Even the most superficial consideration of the language, references and sources reveals the collaborative nature of the undertaking and especially the continuous intervention and supervision by Gattinara. The unique marginal note in the imperial response to the first papal brief, correcting the statement in the text that Francis I was 'captured by Lannoy and led away' to 'Not captured by the viceroy but led into Spain' suggests that Gattinara or perhaps a member of the council caught this error after printing had begun.[31] Later the passage that mobilizes a text from the Psalms (84:11) to associate peace and justice and from the *Aeneid* (6:853) to promote clemency is strongly reminiscent of the earlier usage of these passages made by Gattinara, suggesting his direct intervention or Valdés' recourse to materials of the chancellor made available to him.[32] Although

---

[28] Cicogna, *Inscrizioni*, p. 196; cf. Bornate, 'Doc.', p. 517; Vocht, *Dantiscus*, p. 26.
[29] *Pro divo Carolo*, sigs. A₃, [N₄ᵛ]. On Waldkirch see Adolf Hasenclever, 'Balthasar Merklin', *34*, 485–502, *35*, 36–80. On Schweis see Allen, *Opus*, IV, 452.
[30] *Pro divo Carolo*, sig. [d_{vi}ᵛ]; cf. Bornate, 'Doc.', p. 524.
[31] *Pro divo Carolo*, sig. [D_{iij}ᵛ].
[32] *Ibid.*, sig. H_{iij}. In his remonstrance to the Emperor Maximilian of September 1514, entitled 'Remonstrances de Messire Mercurin de Gatinare [sic], President de Bourgongne faictes a Maximilian I Empereur sur les traverses causees a sa personne et au Parlement par le Marschal de Bourgongne' (BMB, Collection Chifflet, CLXXXVII, fols. 116–34), Gattinara exploits these two texts at fols. 120 and 133.

94

no author possesses a monopoly over the use of commonplaces and well-known texts, the use of the Psalms, so strongly evident in Gattinara's other writings, intimates that he had a direct hand at certain points in the composition of the imperial reply. Following Psalm 2 : 1–2 – 'Why have the Gentiles raged and the people devised vain things? The kings of the earth stood up and the princes met together against the Lord and against his Christ'[33] – we read, 'I do not say against the Lord and Christ but against the minister and lamb divinely established by Christ himself from whom all our authority and power depend'. The text's reference, which was ordinarily understood to pertain to David, his kingdom and literally to Christ, is now directed to the emperor as the Lord's anointed. Dante's use of these verses at the end of the first book of *Monarchia* may well have prompted the more explicit application here. The messianic note as it applies to the emperor reverberates in other writings of the chancellor.[34] Its import becomes the more impressive when we realize that the force of the text is directed against that pastor or common father who rather than affirming the established lines of obedience, by his leagues and conspiracies, threatens to violate the imperial state and dignity.[35] The thought as well as the specific Psalm is completed in Gattinara's 'Refutation' of King Francis' 'Apology', a treatise which is far more obviously the direct work of the chancellor himself: to provide an antidote to the corrosive infection of rulers' minds by this Gnatho, the notorious parasite in Terence's *Eunuchus*, in this instance King Francis, the 'Refutation' presents the psalm's injunctions to embrace discipline and good faith, lest they perish from the right way, and urges rulers to exercise their office with honor, conscience and justice that they show themselves inviolate, immaculate of faith and cultivators of religion.[36]

As a means of more readily considering the substance of the *Pro divo Carolo* and its polemical worth, the following table of contents together with the dates of the respective parts can serve as a guide to this composite work.[37]

---

[33] Douay, 1956.

[34] See for example Bornate, 'Vita', pp. 323, 325, 356, 363. On the traditional exegesis of Ps. 2 : 1–2 cf. Nicolaus de Lyra, *Biblia sacra* (Lyons, 1545), III, fol. 88ᵛ. Nevertheless W. O. E. Oesterley, *The Psalms* (London, 1939), I, 122–7 explains that the whole psalm is spoken by the newly enthroned king. The expressions mentioned refer to an earthly king, not to a messianic one. Yet because he is God's anointed, it is understandable that a messianic interpretation should have grown up. On Dante see *Monarchia*, I, 16.

[35] *Pro divo Carolo*, sigs. [K₁ⱼᵛ]; [Lᵛ].   [36] *Ibid.*, sig. Z₁ⱼ.

[37] Because of the difference in wording that sometimes occurs between the title of a section as it appears in the table of contents and at the head of the actual text, I have allowed myself to draw upon both or to prefer one for the sake of the translation. In placing both the pages and the date of composition in brackets, where the latter is not specified in the particular writing itself, I have indicated my source. The *Errata* and two prefaces, items 11 and 13, have been bracketed because they are not included in the Latin tables of contents.

BOOK I

1. The Privilege of the Emperor Charles [Sigs. Aii–Aiii] [2 March 1527]. [Errata] [sig. Aiiiᵛ]
2. Prologue to the devout Reader in which beside other matters Reasons are given for the Pillaging of the Vatican [sigs. Aiiii–Avi] [Mid-February 1527]³⁸
3. The Letter of Clement VII, or as they themselves call it, the Brief in which all the very falsest Accusations that he has been able to compile, he has heaped up against the Emperor Charles [sigs. B–C] [23 June 1526]
4. The Instrument of the Public Response of Emperor Charles to such Accusations with Appeal and Demand for the Summoning of a general Council [sigs. Cᵛ–Liiiiᵛ] [17 September 1526]
5. The Second Letter of the Pontiff sent to his Nuncio, apologising for having falsely accused the Emperor and forbidding the earlier letter from being delivered to the Emperor [sigs. M–Mᵛ] [25 June 1526]
6. The Response of the Emperor Charles to the Second Letter of the Roman Pontiff [sigs. Mᵛ–Miiᵛ] [18 September 1526]
7. The Letter of the Emperor Charles to the Senate or College of Cardinals in which he begs that if the Pope denies or defers the calling of a general Council of Christians, they themselves should summon it [sigs. Miii–Nii] [6 October 1526]
8. The Public Instrument concerning those Matters enacted at Rome when the Letters of the Emperor were presented to the Pontiff and College of Cardinals [sigs. Niiᵛ–Niiiᵛ] [12 December 1526]

BOOK II

9. The Letter of the sacred Emperor Charles to the Most Reverend and Illustrious Prince Electors of the Holy Roman Empire [sigs. O–Oiiiᵛ] [29 November 1526]
10. Apology of the Treaty of Madrid between the Emperor Charles and the French King. Confutation. [sigs. P–Qᵛ] [31 July 1526]³⁹
11. [Greetings to the Reader] [sigs. Qii–Qiiᵛ] [12 October 1526]

³⁸ In his letter of 11 February 1527 the emperor at last responds to the successive communications of Perez: *Cal. SP Spain.* III/2, 61. In its tone the letter's content agrees with that of the justification and hopes expressed in the preface. Further support for the mid-February dating derives from the content of the preface itself, which speaks of a papal bull ostensibly directed against Lannoy, the viceroy of Naples, but actually intended for the emperor. (Cf. *Pro divo Carolo*, sig. [Aᵥᵛ].) By a letter of 16 November 1526 the chief secretary to the Spanish embassy at Rome, Juan Perez, told the emperor of a rumor that the pope had composed a bull depriving Charles of the kingdom of Naples: *Cal. SP Spain*, III/1, 1006. Although the *Magnum bullarium romanum*...contains no such bull, Perez, writing again to the emperor on 10 January 1527, speaks of a monitory delivered by the pope after mass on New Year's day, and directed against Lannoy, that produced consternation within the Spanish community at Rome. *Cal. SP Spain*, III/2, 7–8. Allowing one month for the delivery of this letter, we arrive at a mid-February date. For the draft of this and four subsequent parts to the *Pro divo Carolo* see *supra*, fn. 25.
³⁹ Bornate, 'Doc.', p. 332, fn. 1; *AT*, VIII, 357.

12 Refutation of the Apology of the Treaty of Madrid, namely the Confutation, published for Francis King of the French [sigs. Qiii–Ziiiᵛ] [12 October 1526]⁴⁰

13 [To the devout Reader] [sigs. Ziiii–Ziiiiᵛ] [12 February 1527]⁴¹

14 Chapters of the League, which they call most holy, effected among the Roman Pontiff Clement VII, the French King, the Venetians, Duke Francesco Sforza, and the Florentines against the Emperor. [sigs. a–cᵛ] [12 February 1527]⁴²

15 The Letter of King Francis transmitted to the German Princes [assembled at Speyer] full of obvious Deceits which we have wanted to append here to do justice to the Reader concerning these matters [sigs. cii–ciiii] [6 October 1526]

16 Response for the Most unconquerable Emperor of the Romans, Charles, Fifth of this name, Catholic King of the Spains, to those matters which have been recently proposed by the ambassadors of the Roman Pontiff Clement VII, and of Francis King of the French and of the Venetians for the purpose of achieving a general peace [sigs. d–dᵛ] [12 February 1527]

The division of the material into two books as they appear in the Mainz edition indicates not only that two fairly distinct controversies are at issue – one directed against the pope, the other against the King of France – but that beginning with the Cologne edition there was also the practice of publishing separately the materials involving each controversy. Furthermore, given the habit of publishing in one form or another the work that is to be refuted, the volume was swelled by such opposing materials as Francis I's 'Apology' and his letter to the German estates, not to mention the papal briefs. Thus, any consideration of the emperor's controversy with the pope clearly must focus upon the first reply together with the letter to the cardinals which develops further the conciliar theme; similarly with the second controversy, between Charles V and Francis I over the failure of the latter to fulfill the terms of the treaty of Madrid, Gattinara's refutation of the royal 'Apology' principally demands attention.

Our analysis of the imperial reply cannot concern itself with the specifics of Italian politics present in this letter. Suffice it to observe in passing that Valdés and Gattinara take the opportunity to rehabilitate the reputation of Pescara perhaps as a sort of penance for the chancellor's misjudgment of the marquis' early warnings concerning the conspiracy of Morone – a misjudgment which certainly contributed to the emperor's failure to give his loyal general the support and recognition that he deserved before his untimely death.⁴³ The politics and diplomacy of the Italian peninsula can only be relevant in so far as they bear upon the two principal issues of the

⁴⁰ *Letters and Papers*, 4/2, no. 2532; *AT*, VIII, 364.
⁴¹ Here as with the preceding preface, item 11, the date seems to be fairly clearly dictated respectively by that of the material immediately following.
⁴² Brandi, *Emperor*, p. 251. ⁴³ *Pro divo Carolo*, sigs. Eᵢᵢᵢⱼ–[Eᵢᵢᵢⱼᵛ], Hᵢᵢᵢⱼ.

imperial reply—the pope's violation of the moral and spiritual obligations of his office and the appeal to a council.

In its effort to de-politicize the pope or at least to call him to account before his flock for having entered into armed leagues and become overly involved in the power politics of the moment, the imperial response seems to partake of a widespread notion current among Charles' generals and diplomatic agents in Italy that the political pretensions of the papacy must be annihilated and the pope reduced to his properly pastoral function. Nevertheless, in emphasizing the preeminence of the moral and spiritual role for the pope, the response together with associated materials constituting Book I of a larger polemic reveals itself to be informed by an Erasmian tone that asserts the moral performance and internal disposition of a person conformable to Christ to be the true measure of the Christian. Picking up on Clement's lamentation in the first brief that he does not receive the praise due to a pastor and common father,[44] the imperial chancellery laboriously shapes the claim that the pope has not by his actions lived up to the requirements of a pastor and common father. Beginning cautiously by denying any intention to impugn the office of His Holiness, the case for the emperor against the pope is carefully built up: we have never sought the oppression of Italy nor the diminution of your office; the sword unsheathed by you, Christ commanded to remain sheathed and not even to be used by you against the enemies of the faith; otherwise your actions militate neither to the liberty of Italy nor to peace but to the disturbing of the Christian republic and to the encouragement of heretics and their errors; more specifically you worked to impede our coronation as much as possible and to vitiate the diet of Worms;[45] according to the dispatches of Pescara Your Holiness sought by a single blow to exclude us *ab omni Imperio Italico* so that you might thereby depose us from the entirety of the imperial dignity;[46] Your Holiness may judge whether it is worthy of a pastor to upset the proper order of things, casting tumult and scandal into Christ's Church.[47] The chancellery's use of the text Psalm 2 : 1–2 with its messianic implications has the effect of implicitly identifying the pope as a rebel against the divinely established order. The Letter's tone of reprimand and rebuke culminates in the accusation that in promoting arms under the guise of universal peace the pastor and common father, who should treat all with equal justice, suffers a deformity, for it is a scandal that the Apostolic See must resort to force rather than supporting itself on Christ alone.[48] The letter calls for an end to fear and a restoration of mutual trust leading to mutual disarmament so that the task of correcting the Lutheran heretics and, if possible, leading them back to the fold of the

---

[44] *Ibid.*, sig. [B$_{iiij}$^{v}].

[45] *Ibid.*, sigs. [C$_{iij}$^{v}]–[D^v].

[46] *Ibid.*, sig. [E$_{iiij}$^{v}].

[47] *Ibid.*, sig. F.

[48] *Ibid.*, sigs. K$_{iij}$–[K$_{iij}$^{v}].

Church, may be undertaken. If Clement would assume the office of true pastor and common father, he would find a most obedient emperor ready to expose himself to all dangers in the pope's defense.[49] Otherwise, the pope will appear as a partisan not as a father (*non patris sed partis*), a wolf and not a shepherd (*non pastoris sed invasoris*). Should the transposition to a peaceful Clement not occur, the letter assures him that if something unfortunate (*quicquid sinistri*) happens to the Christian religion, it would not be the emperor's fault.[50]

Beyond the often dreary details of Italian politics, which are not readily susceptible to effective polemical presentation, the reader is continually reminded of the incongruity between a true Vicar of Christ in the full meaning of the title and the present warring, conspiring, even rebellious pope. Such a comparison was common enough at the inception of the Protestant Reformation in the popular woodcuts on Christ and Antichrist. But more immediately there is an undercurrent in the imperial response reminiscent of Beatus Rhenanus' evangelical preface to the recently published *editio princeps* of Marsilius of Padua's *Defensor pacis*.[51] Indeed, there seems to be present a peculiarly spiritual dimension to the chancellery's argument which would suggest that at least some of its members had absorbed the viewpoint of Erasmus or of his school. One cannot read the repeated use of *Vestra Sanctitas*, the proper address to the pope, without sensing a measure of irony. The crying demand to give spiritual reality and effectiveness to those titles and offices becomes quite explicit at one point in the letter where it is stated: 'Indeed our devotion to Your Holiness was deserved so that through such an office holiness itself (*Sanctitas ipsa*) might be performed.'[52] That this thirst for holiness and for a spiritual reawakening within the traditional forms of the old religion is not something occasional or peripheral to the chancellery's criticism of the Clementine Papacy, but the chief polemical weapon in the imperial armory becomes evident when one turns back to Book I's 'Prologue to the devout reader'. In its peroration, the most conspicuous part of the entire volume, designed to impress itself upon every reader stands the following statement:

[49] *Ibid.*, sigs. L–[L^v].
[50] *Ibid.*, sigs. [L^v]–L$_{ij}$.
[51] On intriguing parallels with the Marsilian–evangelical preface see for example: 'Nihil igitur mirum, neque novum, si Evangelicae lucis contemptae poenam merito luimus, si in densissimis humanarum superstitionum tenebris...Quoniam nihil iam corde amplectimur mundum, merito quoque purissimum veritatis radium non assequimur sed mendacio circumventi, penitus a fide & Evangelio excidimus. Quid est enim aliud ab Evangelio excidere, te obtestamur lector Christiane, quam pro Christi lenitate arrogantiam, pietate insolentiam, charitate odium, pace bellum, exinanitione dominationem, & imperium orbus terrarum (ut quotidie fit) usurpare?' Marsilius of Padua, *Opus insigne cui titulum fecit autor defensorem pacis*...(Basel, 1522), sig. Aiij. Cf. also *infra*, fn. 73. On the identification of Beatus Rhenanus as author of the preface see Gregorio Piaia, *Marsilio de Padova nella Riforma e nella Controriforma* (Padua, 1977), pp. 26–67.
[52] *Pro divo Carolo*, sigs. D$_{iiij}$, cf. [C$_{iij}$^{v}].

Wherefore all Christian princes collectively on account of the common glory of Christ and the Christian name about which we so often boast, on account of magnificent titles, if there is true piety, if they are actually to realize their titles, if the *Sanctissimi, Beatissimi, Christianissimi, Catholici*, if the churches, that is the defenders of the entire Christian people, if they want to be truly called protectors of the faith, inasmuch as these belong to the Christian religion and for that purpose the way has been shown by the Emperor, we pray that for those having office or duties they may fulfil them most attentively and by the single consent of the world, all controversies having been set aside, they may prepare for the universal assembly of Christians. It will be accomplished without difficulty, if they will apply Christian attentiveness, if that shall occupy their most earnest breasts. At this assembly Christ Best and Greatest shall preside, the freest opinions are spoken; the judgments of all having been conferred to one evangelical light, it will at last be achieved so that we may discern more conspicuously the matter of Christ which we thus far were so fully overlooking. To none will it be able to appear an injurious assembly at which Christ himself will preside. For on the contrary who may doubt that Christ will be present, if he shall see all to come together there for the supreme improvement of the Christian commonwealth?

The Erasmian resonance even with its appeal to the evangelical light, firmly presented here at the outset, although at the time of composition introduced as an afterthought, is perpetuated in the imperial response itself. On the papal–imperial controversy over Reggio and Rubiera the imperial chancellery seizes the opportunity for registering righteous incredulity that Christ's vicar would ever wish to assume some secular possession at the expense of one drop of human blood, for such an act would seem so alien to evangelical doctrine.[53] In each instance the adjective 'evangelical' suggests a moral content to the gospel, impelling conduct that is conformable to Christ as well as being the ultimate criterion of the Christian religion – thus all the greater scandal in the papal *difformitas*.[54]

Audacious as the imperial response appeared in its reproachfulness and in its lecturing the Vicar of Christ on Christian performance, the real bombshell lay elsewhere. Looking back over the distance of almost a century, Sarpi in his *Istoria del Concilio Tridentino* would observe that the emperor in these letters of Book I had touched upon the two greatest *arcani* of the pope: namely, the appeal to a future council and inviting the cardinals to convoke one should the pope prove too recalcitrant in this respect.[55] In fact it is only at the very end of the first imperial response, as a measure of apparent desperation, that the appeal to a council is made. If the pope chooses to continue to act as a wolf rather than a shepherd, the emperor will carry his case before a general council. But once having enunciated this

[53] *Ibid.*, sigs. [A$_v$^{v}]–[A$_{vi}$], E$_{iij}$^{v}. The later addition in Valdés' hand can be found in AGS, Estado, 1554, no. 576.

[54] *Pro divo Carolo*, cf. sig. K$_{iij}$.   [55] Sarpi, *Istoria*, I, 65.

threat the letter goes on to wrap this intention in appropriate submissiveness and deference to the pope, begging and imploring him to undertake the actual calling of a council.[56] In this regard, therefore, the 'Letter to the Sacred College', completed over two weeks later, is a far more radical document.

Enjoying the brevity and directness of an appeal, the letter to the cardinals bears favorable comparison with its more extensive, labored predecessor. The review of injustices, misunderstandings and complaints in the imperial response had been sustained by the theme of the deformed pastor and common father with its Erasmian reverberations. The later composition can afford to come rapidly to the point. It begins by exculpating the emperor of all malign intentions: he does not seek to extend the limits of empire by the expenditure of Christian blood but simply desires that the imperial dignity, ornamented with authority and power, may be recognized by many and condemned by few that by its benefit peace may be perpetually enjoyed.[57] In the brief justification of imperial actions the letter allowed that at Worms the emperor, against the judgment of some in the Council of State, had turned a deaf ear to the complaints for reform with the result that the Lutheran madness now ran rampant. Furthermore, fearing that the national council to be assembled at Speyer in November 1524 might divert Germany from the Roman obedience, the emperor prohibited its convening, thereby preferring papal interest to German prayers. In fact papal claims have been supported at the expense of alienating some German minds. So much for the crimes and malevolent intentions imputed to the emperor by the pope! But by now all implore a general council which could address the Lutheran impiety and the depredations attributed to the Roman Curia. At this point the emperor calls upon the cardinals to lead the pope away from impious counsel lest all degenerate from our prince Christ. If the pope fails to call a council the cardinals are enjoined and exhorted not to delay in summoning one. And should they refuse –

On account of our duty to God and our imperial dignity by which we perform his free benevolence, with what remedies permissible thereupon we will strive vigorously to provide for these matters so that we may seem in no way to be deficient for the glory of Christ, our justice, or for the peace, tranquility and welfare of the Christian Commonwealth.[58]

Despite the oblique language at the end the reader could be left in little doubt regarding the possibility of the emperor himself taking action. A similarly menacing note had been earlier sounded in the instructions

[56] *Pro divo Carolo*, sigs, L$_{ij}$–L$_{iij}$.   [57] *Ibid.*, sig. M$_{iij}$.
[58] *Ibid.*, sigs. [N^v]–N$_{ij}$.

provided the special envoy Miguel de Herrera.[59] In the present context it appeared more urgent.

While in the midst of launching the chancellery's campaign against the pope, Gattinara had received from the hands of the French ambassador a small volume, being a copy of Francis I's *Apology*, pertaining to the terms of the treaty of Madrid. A brief glance at the work sufficed for him to recognize here an invective against his master as well as a cheap justification for Francis' failure to keep his word and execute the terms of the treaty of Madrid. Incensed by this new challenge, the chancellor threw himself into the task of providing what he considered to be an antidote to the present poison by refuting the claims of the French king.[60] Thus, sometime in early October of 1526 Gattinara entered directly into his own propaganda campaign which now extended itself on a different plain to meet a second most formidable opponent.[61] In responding to the royal *Apology* Gattinara allowed his own work to be shaped in two respects by his opponents: first, as was expectable in such tracts, the author refuted in successive fashion the points raised and challenges presented by the work to be refuted; secondly, because the French *Apology* had tried to make Francis' cause that of all kings and rulers, its refutation was directed specifically to the same audience.[62]

Gattinara addresses a single issue throughout his long and often tangled confutation: the violation of good faith. At the outset he assembles a number of classical references directed against the sycophant and against infidelity on the part of a ruler. Initially he indicates recourse to Plutarch's treatise 'Quo pacto possis adulatorem ab amico dignoscere' which was available to him in numerous editions of Erasmus' translations from the *Moralia* as well as appearing in three editions of the *Institutio principis christiani*. He also presses into service John of Salisbury's *Polycraticus* with its extended treatment of *adulatores* in Book III.[63] He twice cites the historical examples of Regulus in his voluntary return to Carthage, and more recently of King John of France returning to his English imprisonment as outstanding examples of good faith. Yet except for an occasional Terentian sally he will leave his classical authorities behind and, eschewing any obvious humanistic appeal, submerge his argument in feudal history, dynastic politics and the intricacies of the *jus appennagii*.[64] While this line of attack may not be

---

[59] See the present author's 'Ghibellinism', p. 103.   [60] *Pro divo Carolo*, sig. [Q$_{iij}$ᵛ].

[61] *AT*, VIII, 364.

[62] *Pro divo Carolo*, sigs. [Zᵛ]–Z$_{ij}$, cf. P, [Qᵛ].

[63] See A. J. Koster, *Einleitung* to 'Ex Plutarcho versa' in *Opera omnia Desiderii Erasmi* (Amsterdam, Oxford, 1977), IV/2, 106–7. On Plutarch and the reference to the *Polycratus* (*sic*) of John of Salisbury see *Pro divo Carolo* sigs. Q$_{iij}$ and Q$_{iiij}$. For the source of Gattinara's observation: 'tria fecerunt Romanos esse gentium victores, scientia, exercitatio, & fides', see *Policraticus* VI/2 which in turn is based upon Book I, Chap. I of Vegetius' *De re militari libri quatuor*.

[64] *Pro divo Carolo*, sigs. Q$_{iiij}$–Q$_{iiij}$; V$_{iij}$–V$_{iiij}$. For the reference to King John in Gattinara's autobiography see Bornate, 'Vita', p. 327.

The imperial propaganda campaign of 1526–1527

particularly engaging to the ordinary reader, we need to remind ourselves that especially in this work the chancellor understands his audience to be the rulers and potentates of Europe. In attempting to document a long history of bad faith on the part of France's kings, he turns to the treaty of Noyon in 1515 after touching upon the Calais conference of 1521.[65] Péronne and Conflans come up for reconsideration and the seizure of Bourbon's estates is paraded.[66] Delving further into the past he will treat the strife between Angevins and Aragonese and dwell upon an old favorite for one long accustomed to elucidating rights from dynastic politics, namely the marriage of Count Raymond of Barcelona to the only daughter of the Count of Provence, who acquired her inheritance on 1 February 1112. Alas, even Pharamond receives honorable mention.[67] Throughout these dynastic-legal perambulations the intention remains to demonstrate the outrageous violation of the moral law and feudal obligation by the French king.

In order to get around the feudal obligations owed by the Habsburgs for the counties of Flanders and Artois to the kings of France, Gattinara at one point enunciates the most extreme legalistic argument for the exaltation of the imperial authority:

Quite on the contrary, however, when before the time [of rendering homage] occurred, the emperor, as if a new person, was conveyed to the remains (*vestigia*) of Empire and as this very imperial dignity admits no one to be superior in temporal matters, the emperor was not bound, nor by any law whatever would have been able to be distrained so that to the king of the French, especially for those [lands] which [the emperor] previously possessed, he would perform the vow of homage or recognize [the king] as superior. Furthermore all this pretended superiority is considered restrained under the supreme imperial power itself whence it seems earlier to have departed (*digressa*). For from the empire as if from a fountain, as the laws [of Justinian] attest, all jurisdictions come forth and thence they flow and flow back, for certainly anything will return to its original nature. And that indeed so much the more certainly must it be admitted if we should look at ancient records according to which such superiority was in nowise owed to the kingdom of France.[68]

Returning to the fateful language of *Per Venerabilem*, Gattinara claims that when Charles the Bold died in 1476 (*sic*), according to the preamble of the

[65] *Pro divo Carolo*, sigs. R–R_{iij}.
[66] *Ibid.*, sig. [R_{iiij}^v].
[67] *Ibid.*, sigs. [S^v]–[S_{ij}^v], [X_{iij}^v]. Although Gattinara does not provide the date, he could only be referring to the second marriage of Ramon Berenguer III to Dolza, the heiress of Provence, an event which would further involve Aragon and Catalonia in Languedoc and all of southern France. See J. Lee Shneidman, *The rise of the Aragonese-Catalan empire 1200–1350* (New York, 1970), I, 190, II, 294, 296.
[68] *Pro divo Carolo*, sig. R_{iiij}. Gattinara is here following Baldus at 'De allodijs' in the latter's commentary on the *Libri feudorum* (Baldus de Ubaldis, *Opus aureum iuris utriusque luminis domini Baldi de perusio super feudis* ([Lyons, Casper Trechsel], 1545), fol. 72^v): 'Ex premissis ergo apparet iurisdictiones esse apud cesarem tamquam apud fontem a quo fluunt et refluunt sicut flumina ad mare fluunt.'

103

league with Louis XI, he held all his domains including the duchy free and exempt from all superiority of the French realm, *nullum recognoscens superiorem.*[69] Thus while the larger argument remains a moral one, Gattinara's development of legal claims supported by historical precedent seeks to secure the independence of the Burgundian inheritance from the French realm and the ultimate and essentially overriding authority of the imperial dignity. The weakness of his position is evident, however, from his vainly invoking Francis to return to captivity.[70]

In compiling for the press the materials for Book II of the *Pro divo Carolo*, the chancellery could exploit more venturously polemical techniques from which it had been somewhat inhibited in the earlier book by having to contend with the pope, the treacherous shoals of conciliar politics and the danger of alienating Spanish religious sensibilities. With Book II the chancellery's chief concern was to hold the estates of the empire firmly against any French blandishments by showing Francis I to be utterly faithless. Therefore the book begins with Charles' letter to the electors wherein he is represented as ever desirous of peace and the French king ready to spill Christian blood in exploiting the Turkish threat immediately following the Hungarian disaster.[71] Here and throughout the book, with the curious exceptions of the French 'Apologia', marginal glosses are introduced to aid the reader's understanding of the text as well as to maintain his interest by a biting jibe or prompt refutation delivered to the opponent. It uses these marginal glosses to greatest effect in King Francis' 'Letter to the Estates at Speyer' where it successfully neutralizes and refutes the royal argument, while addressing *rex Francisce* with the contemptuous *tu* and *te.*[72] Gattinara must have recognized, if only dimly, the tedious and oppressive character of his 'Refutation' and thus the need to introduce marginal glosses as an apparent effort to distill the argument and aid the reader's understanding. Poorly exploiting any sustained use of classical authors and images, he allows his argument to drag through the underbrush of Burgundian dynastic politics and feudal rights. Two obscure references probably drawn from Servius' commentary on the Aeneid are employed, the first occurring in the emperor's letter to the electors and intending to convey the impression of Francis I as a fetid pestilential pool, the second appearing once in the concluding epigram to the 'Refutation', and again in the marginal gloss to the imperial response to the ambassadors at the very end of the volume. Although the sixteenth-century learned reader knew his Servius a good deal better than the ordinary twentieth-century scholar, one cannot help but question the appropriateness and polemical effectiveness of the two references here. For when Prudencio

[69] *Pro divo Carolo*, sig. [X$_{ij}$^{v}].
[70] *Ibid.*, sigs. Y$_{iiij}$, [Z^v].
[71] *Ibid.*, sigs. [O$_{ij}$^{v}]–O$_{iij}$, O$_{iiij}$.
[72] *Ibid.*, sigs. C$_{ij}$–C$_{iiij}$.

Sandoval came to translate the epigram into Castilian for incorporation into his history, perhaps confused by the classical reference, he or his printers silently dropped the final lines in which one of the two references was embalmed.[73]

In the 'Prologue to the Devout Reader', the penultimate ingredient of this polemical pastiche, the collective authorship of the *Pro divo Carolo* disclaims any pretensions to a Ciceronian style in order to emphasize the naked truth of the arguments that follow. Indeed as is clearly evident in the 'Refutation' an appealing rhetoric often sags under the weight of the legal and political arguments being advanced. Classical influences are not sufficient to inform evenly the style of the several treatises, and thereby strengthen the appeal of the book. There are, nevertheless, moments of stylistic merit, such as at the end of the imperial response to the first papal brief with its contrast between pastor and wolf, father and partisan. An opportunity to derive the maximum effect from word play seems to be missed, however, in the 'Prologue' where after being apprised of Clementine arms, Clementine war and a Clementine league the reader would expect to find, in the depiction of the pope hurling pronouncements against the Colonna allies of the emperor, 'as if to lose by so much Clementine thunder and lightning what clemency alone was able to accomplish'. Unfortunately, however, the printed text reads 'Clementis Papae' and not 'Clementinis'.[74]

Taken together the 'Privilege' and the 'Prologue' of the *Pro divo Carolo* provide some idea as to the nature of the audience for which this collection was intended, as well as the chancellery's own attitude toward the work. The privilege granted to Joannes Schoeffer of Mainz directs the volume to the attention of all, from princes and prelates to subjects and citizens of whatever degree or condition within the empire.[75] This statement applies to both books, although, as is later made evident in the controversy between Charles and Francis, it is the favorable opinion of Europe's rulers that is most immediately sought. It is expected that in the reading of this material one will give vent to expressions of admiration and of indignation, of laughter and of complaint.[76] Unfortunately events would outstrip the

---

[73] *Ibid.*, sigs. O$_{iiij}$, [Z$_{iij}$^{v}], [C$_{iij}$^{v}]. The two Vergilian references are to *camerina* (*Aen* 3; 701) and *Laomedonta* (*Aen*. 2; 241). Cf. *Pub. Vergilii Maronis Opera*, ed. M. Ludovicus Lucus (Basel, Sebastianus Henricpetrus, 1613), pp. 771 and 569; Prudencio Sandoval, *Historia de la vida y hechos del emperador Carlos V* (Barcelona, Sebastián de Cormellas, 1625), I, 685. For the possible intellectual influences upon the composition of the *Pro divo Carolo*, Beatus Rhenanus in his evangelical–Erasmian preface to the *Defensor pacis* also indicates an awareness of the tradition of Vergilian commentary: 'Neque me latet quantam hic Camarinam moveo.' See Marsilius of Padua, *Opus*, sig. [A^v]. However, as both Beatus Rhenanus and Gattinara spell the fetid pond 'Camarinam' rather than 'Camerinam' it is possible that for this reference each is using not Servius but Erasmus' 'Movere Camarinam' (I. LXIIII) which figures in the successive editions of the *Adagiorum Chiliades* beginning in 1500.   [74] *Pro divo Carolo*, sig. [A$_v$^{v}].
[75] *Ibid.*, sig. A$_{ij}$.   [76] *Ibid.*, sig. [A$_{iiij}$^{v}].

best efforts of both the emperor and his chancellery to coordinate the printing of this material at such a great remove from central Castile, thus reducing its pungency and relevance.

The passage from manuscript to print involved the attentions not only of the chancellery but of the emperor and ultimately of his brother Ferdinand. No less than three manuscript copies of the imperial response to the first papal brief, which were prepared for direct communication to concerned parties in Europe, can be identified. The original, forwarded by Castiglione, reached Clement VII well before the formal presentation by the first secretary of the Spanish embassy in Rome, Juan Perez.[77] One copy, much to the distress and over the objections of Castiglione, was sent together with a copy of the papal brief to Uncle Henry in England. The English ambassador consoled the papal nuncio that the likelihood of it being published in England was nil.[78] Another was promised to the Polish ambassador, Dantiscus, to be sent on to the King of Poland.[79] On 4 October Charles writing to his brother included a copy of the papal brief which he described as being 'assez rude et piquant', together with a copy of the chancellery's reply recommending not to publish them because of the mention of a council unless the pope should persevere in his present hostile attitude.[80] As hostilities between the two interested parties did not remit, Ferdinand decided to submit a copy of the first papal brief and its response to the Cologne printer Peter Quentell who brought out his *Epistolae duae altera Clementis VII... altera Karoli* – one a quarto, and another an octavo, whose colophon was dated March 1527. Subsequently, during the same year and certainly by April 1528, Andreas Cratander brought out at Basel an edition of what constituted the later Book I, closely following the Eguía edition.[81]

The Alcalá edition of Miguel Eguía appears to have been published under the direct auspices of Gattinara. From the bill later submitted to Gattinara for its printing, it is clear that publication of the imperial–papal controversy in Spain was expected to be paid for out of the chancellor's own pocket.[82] In his autobiography the chancellor will later mention in passing his deep involvement in the composition of the various replies constituting the *Pro divo Carolo* and his determination to commit them to

[77] *Cal. SP Spain*, III/1, 1046–7.
[78] *Letters and Papers*, 4/2, no. 2531; *AT*, VIII, 356. These copies appear to be distinct from those sent by English intermediaries to Mendoza, the imperial ambassador to England. Cf. *Cal. SP Spain*, III/1, 1039–40.
[79] *AT*, VIII, 357.   [80] Bauer, *Korrespondenz*, I, 477.
[81] Edward Boehmer, *Spanish reformers of two centuries* (Bibliotheca Wiffeniana) [Strassburg, 1874, repr. New York, n.d.] I, 87–8. I have consulted the Marciana's copy of the Cologne octavo edition. The date of 1526, cited in the *British Museum Catalogue of... German Books, 1455–1600* (London, 1962), p. 347 is an impossibility.
[82] Marcel Bataillon, *Erasmo y España* (Buenos Aires, 1966), p. 230, fn. 14.

the press that they might be read indiscriminately, far and wide.[83] Gattinara here evinces an instinctive discernment for the imperial government's exploiting the technique of the printing press. Indeed, the Venetian ambassador Navagero early in 1527 will register alarm at the way Gattinara, in receiving the peace mission of the papal emissary Paolo d'Arezzo, gives to the press all the chapter headings relating to the anti-imperial league so that everyone might know the reasons for the emperor's hostility toward his opponents.[84]

In enlisting the services of Miguel de Eguía of Alcalá, Gattinara chose that printer who since May 1525 had been publishing the fundamental works of Erasmus' piety and paideia, and whose press was becoming a focus for Erasmianism in Spain. Accompanied by orders to set aside all other work in progress, the controversy with Francis I was the first of the polemical materials to be committed to this press. What was later to be designated in the Mainz edition as Book II appeared on 7 January 1527. That the papal–imperial controversy, although the first to be composed, came forth three months later on 10 April raises some questions as to the procedure of its publication. It would seem that some in the Council of State proved hesitant. In reporting to the Serenissima his receipt of a copy of this work exactly a month after its date of imprint, the Venetian ambassador Navagero registered shock on reading it and claimed that Luther himself could not have been expected to be worse. He went on to add that the emperor continued to assure Castiglione, presumably during the printing, that the attack upon the pope was made against his wish and without his consultation. Certainly part of the delay was occasioned by the decision to include in the same volume with the papal–imperial controversy the latest material, namely, the imperial reply of 12 February to the papal, French and Venetian ambassadors. As the latter had protested against some of Gattinara's invectives and vituperation and had actually effected the removal of two of the more offensive paragraphs, Eguía's apparent tardiness becomes more understandable. The small volume emerging from the press of Castile's preeminent printer, which Navagero now sent on to Venice as he had the earlier book, represented the formative version of what was to constitute Book I of Schoeffer's later edition.[85] It would be through a copy of the Eguía edition, conveniently identified as 'excussa Computi per Cancellarium Mercurinum' by Europe's leading humanist, that Erasmus would become familiar with the papal–imperial controversy.[86]

In the subvention of later printings of the two controversies in the

---

[83] Bornate, 'Vita', pp. 332–3.
[84] Cicogna, *Inscrizioni*, p. 194; cf. Bornate, 'Doc.', p. 509.
[85] Bataillon, *Erasmo*, pp. 159–65, 230, fn. 14. Cf. Panzer, *Annales*, IX, 441. For Navagero's letter see Bornate, 'Doc.', pp. 527–8 and *Cal. SP Ven.*, IV, no. 107.   [86] Allen, *Opus*, VII, 146.

empire, the burden may well have fallen on the emperor rather than on his chancellor. According to the date of the privilege awarded Schoeffer at Mainz, 2 March 1527, Charles and his council planned a definitive central European edition of the controversies a month before the Alcalá edition even emerged from the press.[87] For Charles, once having decided to permit the publication at Cologne, entered more positively into the propaganda campaign that he had allowed the chancellery to launch and now engaged the cooperation of his brother Ferdinand. It is interesting to note that differences persist in the viewpoints brought to bear on the same problem by emperor and by chancellor. In telling his brother that he shares Ferdinand's opinion that the edict against the Lutherans must in no way be suspended, Charles reveals a reserve before the policy of accommodation suggested by his minister.[88] With the same letter of 29 November he sent his brother a copy of the King of France's letter to the Estates at Speyer, as well as a copy of the chancellery's refutation and the terms of the treaty of Madrid, with instructions that they be printed together. The emperor asked his brother, if possible, for the original of the king's letter. Three months later Ferdinand's ambassador at the imperial court, Martin de Salinas, explained to his master in greater detail the emperor's intentions regarding publication: Ferdinand should have the diet arrange to get printed in both Latin and German the letter revealing the deceits of the French king and the text of the treaty of Madrid; furthermore, the papal brief and the imperial response should be published and the manuscript originals returned.[89] Not until 14 March did Ferdinand respond to this matter. He regretted that the original of the royal letter was in the hands of the Archbishop of Mainz as chancellor of the empire and would probably not be allowed to leave the empire. Offering to send a copy, Ferdinand went on to state that he had all other materials for the book, which was ready to go to press.[90]

The several editions that came forth from the presses of Antwerp later in 1527 can best be understood as having received some form of financial support from the Habsburg dynasty, although the possibility of a response of the book market to popular demand cannot altogether be discounted. Three complete editions of the two controversies were published, two of them successively and identical by Joannes Graphaeus, the other jointly by Gottfried Dumaeus and Martin de Keyser. Both Michael Hillen and Martin de Keyser each brought out a separate edition of the French

[87] *Pro divo Carolo*, sigs. A$_{ij}$–A$_{iij}$, cf. Boehmer, *Spanish*, I, 84.
[88] On the extent of Gattinara's Erasmianism and conciliarism at this time and its discrepancy with Charles' own views see the present author's, 'Gattinara, Erasmus and the imperial configurations of humanism', *Archiv für Reformationsgeschichte, 71* (1980), 64–98, here recast for this chapter.
[89] Bauer, *Korrespondenz*, I, 497, 499; Rodríguez Villa, 'Cartas de Salinas', *44*, 11–12.
[90] Bauer, *Korrespondenz*, II, 36.

controversy alone and Willem Vorstermann published a French edition of the same controversy. Finally, Graphaeus followed up his first Latin edition of both controversies which appeared on 19 August with a complete low German edition on 12 September.[91] Particularly interesting is the production of these vernacular editions of the polemical confection promoted by the imperial chancellery. On the basis of the limited evidence it is impossible to determine whether the impulse was political, arising from the Habsburg officialdom in a propagandistic effort to reach the lower echelons of society, or commercial, deriving from a shrewd printer's calculations of what the market would bear. The fact, however, that Graphaeus should choose to bring out a second complete Latin edition would suggest that there existed a market and an interested reading public at least in the Burgundian Netherlands. It is thus not surprising that the only suggestion of the polemical work's possible readers derives from this area: both J. L. Vives and Jean de Fevyn, a correspondent of Francis Craneveldt, register appropriate indignation on reading the King of France's *Apology*.[92] Perhaps because it was less dated by events and less vulnerable to ecclesiastical censure, the French controversy proved at the time to be both more politically and commercially viable. Indeed, realignment of emperor with pope culminating in the treaty of Barcelona 29 June 1529 could only make the papal–imperial controversy present in the first book of the *Pro divo Carolo* a source of considerable embarrassment to Charles. Although the terms of the treaty do not specifically refer to the earlier piece of anti-papal propaganda, the spirit of the treaty certainly stood in conflict with any further support of this work's circulation. It appears that efforts were made to withdraw the now offensive work.[93] Nevertheless, a German vernacular edition came out. It is not unreasonable to suppose that an edition of Book I, even in the vernacular, could be employed by a territorial prince to support a middle of the road Erasmian reform program. Such a conjecture would help to explain the German rendering of the emperor's response to the first papal brief which came out in the Dresden of Duke George from the press of Wolfgang Stoeckel in 1529.[94]

---

[91] Wouter Nijhoff and M. E. Kronenberg, *Nederlandsche Bibliographie van 1500 tot 1540* (S-Gravenhage, 1923–), nos. 1263–6, 1269, 3297 and 0721. Regarding Antwerp editions for 1527, Boehmer, *Spanish*, I, 88, cites only one which is attributed to Dumaeus.

[92] Vocht, *Literae*, pp. 533, 549. As both men read the king's *Apology* in the autumn of 1526, they would have had to have used the royal book itself before its later incorporation in any of the editions of the *Pro divo Carolo*.

[93] For the terms of the treaty of Barcelona see Dumont, *Corps*, IV/2, 1–7. On the efforts at suppression see Antonio Palau y Dulcet, *Manual del librero hispanoamericano* (Oxford, Madrid, Barcelona, 1950), no. 44448.

[94] Boehmer, *Spanish*, I, 91–2. According to Georg Muller's biographical sketch in the *Allgemeine Deutsche Biographie*, *36*, 283–4, however, Stoeckel may simply have been an opportunistic printer. After moving to Dresden in 1523, he specialized in publications and ordinances of the ducal government, the works of the Catholic apologists around Duke George, and *Flugschriften*, all with

The definitive and authoritative edition emerged from the press of John Schoeffer of Mainz on 9 September 1527. As privileged printer to the chancellery of the empire located in that city, Schoeffer was the obvious agent for purveying within the Reich the imperial court chancellery's creation.[95] In his printing of the papal controversy Schoeffer followed closely Eguía's splendid earlier edition. The emperor's privilege to Schoeffer claimed validity for a five year period. It indicated that two books each comprising one of the controversies, had already been published in Spain. The privilege also allowed the two polemical books to be printed and circulated in the realms and domains of King Ferdinand.[96] The edition may well represent a collaboration between the two chancelleries as well as between the two Habsburg brothers. Once in circulation the Mainz edition with its imperial privilege had the effect of supplanting the numerous Antwerp editions.

If in print the papal aspect of Gattinara's polemical confection never enjoyed at Antwerp the separate editions of its French counterpart, and seemed to evoke at best only embarrassed silence, in manuscript at Rome during December of 1526 and the first months of the following year it was greeted with consternation by the pope and anxious debate by the cardinals. Acting under instructions from Spain, Perez, who was in charge of the Spanish embassy following the Duke of Sessa's death, provided the utmost legal authentication to his presentation of the imperial response on 12 December in order that it might have the maximum impact. While the imperial reply to the first papal brief was read in consistory on the same day, it was not until the twenty-first that the letter to the cardinals suffered a reluctant reading in consistory. Writing to the emperor on 24 December, Perez, apparently unaware of his government's intentions and even practice concerning the matter, urged that the letter to the cardinals be printed for the people's information.[97] There is no need to rehearse the story of its

an eye to a wide general public. The Dresden edition is especially interesting because Stoeckel has seen fit to spice the chancellery's response by appending two short prophecies. The first one (sigs. Nii^v–Niii) purports to derive from a learned doctor in 1440, although it betrays all the marks of a contemporary re-presentation of the conventional pseudo-Joachimite schema of prophecy. It predicts that Charles, the son of Philip, will be crowned at seventeen and by the twenty-fourth year of his empire he will have extended his power to all peoples from the English and Lombards to the Arabians, Palestinians and Georgians and even across the seas to the heathen, subjecting all to his empire 'und ein gemein Gesetze machen und in aller werlt [sic]/aussruffen lassen'. In the thirty-sixth year of his empire he will come to the holy city of Jerusalem, be anointed and his soul will be assumed into heaven, crowned and hailed by the holy angels 'ein Vater des Vaterlandes' and he will be the next emperor after Frederick III! I am here using the British Library's copy of the *Prognosticon*.

[95] F. W. E. Roth, 'Die Mainzer Buchdruckerfamilie Schoeffer', *Beihefte zum Centralblatt für Bibliothekswesen*, 9 (Leipzig, 1892), 3–11.   [96] Boehmer, *Spanish*, I, 84.

[97] *Cal. SP Spain*, III/I, 1056–7. On the reception of Book I in the Curia see Ludwig von Pastor, *Geschichte der Päpste im Zeitalter der Renaissance und der Glaubenspaltung* (Freiburg, 1956), IV/2, 244–6 who asserts that 'seit den Tagen Kaiser Friedrichs II und Ludwigs des Bayern hatte kein Herrscher Deutschlands mehr eine solche Sprache gegen Rom geführt'.

reception in Rome as well as that of the appeal to the cardinals that with the pope failing, a council be called.[98] With propaganda reverting to diplomacy we are reminded that the polemical efforts of the chancellery had all along been the expression in a different form of a continuing negotiation. The spectre of conciliarism released by Gattinara in Rome at this time might well have convulsed ecclesiastical attentions for several months. But as winter turned to spring the unhappy Medici pope was diverted by the far more tangible spectre of Bourbon's army, as it hurtled apocalyptically southward.

By the time Miguel de Eguía had published his edition of the soon notorious controversy, Gattinara had left court and was on his way to Barcelona and thence to Italy. Among his last acts before departure was the expediting of a brief letter to his friend Erasmus. During these months of intense literary composition, polemical effort and diplomatic maneuver embodied in the twofold propaganda campaign of the *Pro divo Carolo*, Europe's leading humanist had by no means been absent from the mind of Charles' busy chancellor. And it was not accidental that something of his influence is discernible to the careful reader of the anti-Roman polemic.[99] How obvious and natural that Gattinara should now seek the aid of his friend in order to provide the ultimate capping to his propagandistic efforts. Having just delivered to the press the product of the chancellery's preoccupation for the past half year, Gattinara recognized that an author-itative edition of Dante's *Monarchia*, the classic text for imperial claims, critically established and published under the auspices of the greatest humanist of the age, would give the ultimate support to that Ghibellinism which lurked in the manuscript folios of the *Pro divo Carolo*.[100] Based on the evidence available to him, the chancellor's expectation was reasonable enough. Yet it was an expectation doomed to disappointment. For Erasmus could never subscribe to Gattinara's imperial view of Christian polity. Moreover, his request could have only reached Erasmus by the time that the whole European context had been transformed by news of the sack of Rome.[101] Among its many effects *Il Sacco di Roma* cut across the imperial propaganda campaign of 1526–7 muting and disordering some of its more striking conciliar features.

Although the publication of the *Pro divo Carolo*, in whole or in part, was to define a trail that perdured down to the late eighteenth century,[102] the

---

[98] *Cal. SP Spain*, III/1, 1039, 1045–7, 1056–8, III/2, 8–13, 37–43.
[99] See *supra*, fn. 88.
[100] Allen, *Opus*, VI, 470–1.
[101] By 29 May 1527 when he wrote to Warham, Erasmus was aware of Rome's sack. Cf. Allen, *Opus*, VII, 78.
[102] Boehmer, *Spanish*, I, 88–92. If after initial appearances at Alcalá, Cologne and Basel, Book I seemed to be displaced for the moment by the Valois–Habsburg controversy of Book II, in time the greater polemical import of the imperial–papal controversy asserted itself. While the materials of both

The emperor and his chancellor

appropriate conclusion to the present inquiry into its bibliographical history occurs with the Roman editions of 1528. From the press of Nicetes Pistophilus appeared a complete edition of the twofold controversy linked with an additional supporting tract, that was followed by a separate publication of the French *Apology* to which was associated an answer; the answer, however, was not that of Gattinara's 'Refutation' but an entirely new composition whose author remains conjectural. The printer's name, Nicetes Pistophilus, veritably proclaims a pseudonym.[103] Amidst the ruins

controversies can be found distributed through Melchior Goldast's *Collectio constitutionum imperialium* (Frankfurt am Main, 1613) and *Politica imperialia* (Frankfurt am Main, 1614), beginning in 1587 at Antwerp with a partial reprint of the 1527 Dumaeus edition, subsequent publications all pertain to the anti-papal materials: O. Raynaldus, *Annales ecclesiastici* in 1670, 1694, 1755; Edward Brown, *Fasciculus rerum expetendarum & fugiendarum* (London, 1690), in which he condemns Roman errors and abuses and urges reform; in Johannes Christianus Lünig, *Codex Germanicae diplomaticus* (Leipzig, 1732–3); Dumont, *Corps universel* (Amsterdam, 1739); and J. Le Plat, *Monumentorum ad historiam Concilii Tridentini...collectio*, II (Louvain, 1782). It would at first appear odd that the materials of Book I were not pressed into service for probably the most renowned imperial–papal polemical exchange in early modern European history: namely, between Pope Paul IV and the Emperor Ferdinand I which called forth the *editio princeps* of Dante's *Monarchia*. Nevertheless the imperial chancellery's reply to the first papal brief clearly lacks that theoretical definition of universal jurisdictions evident in the *Monarchia* and the similar works of Alciato, Jordanes of Osnabrück, Alexander von Roes and Aeneas Sylvius which accompanied it. On this propaganda campaign see Andreas Burckhardt, *Johannes Basilius Herold: Kaiser und Reich im protestantischen Schrifttum des Basler Buchdrucks um die Mitte des 16. Jahrhunderts* (Basel, Stuttgart, 1967), pp. 194–212. For the same reason the absence of any reference to the 1526 materials in Simon Schard's compilation, *De iurisdictione, autoritate, et praeeminentia imperiali ac potestate ecclesiastica* (Basel, Oporinus, 1566) is quite understandable. For the impact of Book I upon the collective sensibility of Italian reformers see Delio Cantimori's suggestive article 'L'influence du manifeste de Charles-Quint contre Clement VII (1526) et de quelques documents similaires de la littérature philoprotestante et anticuriale d'Italie', *Charles-Quint et son temps* (Paris, 1959), pp. 133–41. Apparently assuming that his audience is thoroughly conversant with the imperial 'rescript' – the first reply to Clement – and the appeal to the cardinals for a council, Cantimori, working from the later reprints in Goldast and attributing the two relevant documents to Valdés, perceives in much of the later imperial universalist aspirations of Italian reformers 'toujours les idées de 1526'.

103 Boehmer, *Spanish*, I, 88. I have used the Marciana's copy of the *Apologia Altera Refutatoria Illius Quae est pacti Madriciae conventionis dissuasoria* [Rome, 1528]. The author was perhaps Nicholas Perrenot (Granvelle) or more probably Gattinara's cousin Bartolomeo, a highly placed Neapolitan councillor who had attended the chancellor at Granada in the presentation of the imperial reply and who would shortly provide a justification and description, *Il sacco di Roma nel 1527*, eds. G.-B.-G. Galiffe and Odoardo Fick (Geneva, 1866). The tract's concentration upon the impending loss of ducal Burgundy to France and the proto-national reverberations recommend it for more careful attention than is possible here. Henri Hauser, *Le traité de Madrid et la cession de la Bourgogne à Charles-Quint: Étude sur le sentiment national bourgignon en 1525–1526* (Dijon, Paris, 1912), p. 92 does not mention it. On the tract's printer, the sole publication appearing under this apparent pseudonym in Fernanda Ascarelli, *Le cinquecentine Romane. 'Censimento delle edizione romane del XVI secolo possedute dalle biblioteche di Roma'* (Milan, 1972), p. 9 is the following entry: 'Apologia altera refutatoria illius quae est pacti Madriciae conventionis dissuasoria et quasi totius rei et pace, et bello gestae inter Caesatem [sic] et Francum succinta narratio...Romae, Nicetum Pistophi, [sic] 1528, 4°, p. 22'; cf. Boehmer, *Spanish*, I, 88, item 9. Despite the claim of the Roman edition to be 'iam primum in lucem aedita', the reference in the colophon to Emmeus – 'Excudebat Emmeus' – a Basel printer, would suggest that the Roman edition based itself on an earlier Basel edition cited in *British Museum. Catalogue of...German Books 1455–1600*, p. 346. On the sometime

The imperial propaganda campaign of 1526–1527

and desolation of the shattered city well might our unknown printer feel
somewhat embarrassed about bearing the imperial chancellery's propaganda
campaign into what remained of *caput mundi*, the common mother of all
peoples.[104]

Basel printer John Faber Emmeus see C. W. Heckethorn, *The Printers of Basle in the XV and XVI Centuries* (London, 1897), p. 162.

[104] Allen, *Opus*, VII, 510, II, 34–8. (Erasmus to Sadoleto, 1 October 1528).

6

The last years of the chancellorship

During the final five years of the chancellorship in the Habsburg *monarchia* personal elements assume greater prominence. Gattinara's correspondence with the emperor, at least until the autumn of 1527, abounds with appeals for money to meet his debts and his obligations as lord of a household and family. These letters tell us little about the chancellorship except in so far as Gattinara's debts had created so much anxiety, according to his own opinion, as to impair his service to the emperor,[1] and that the apparent failure of repeated appeals revealed the corrosion of their relationship. In considering this period, which saw Gattinara's removal to Italy, the fall of Lalemand and the ultimate triumph of the chancellor's Italian policy, we must attend to biographical and personal elements only to the extent that they help to explain the demise of the chancellorship.

The emperor's most loyal servant might have departed Spain in the summer of 1526 had it not been for the League of Cognac and the emerging crisis over Italy. None in the imperial service had as comprehensive a grasp of Italian and European politics as he. The acceleration in the tempo of diplomatic affairs kept him apparently at the center of governmental action. Or so it seemed to Castiglione who exaggerates the paramount role played by the chancellor in the period after Pavia.[2] Certainly from the perspective of diplomacy, Gattinara stood forth as preeminent in the dispatching of the new imperial peace mission to the pope, the reception of the papal emissary Paolo d'Arezzo, the review and rejection of the powers committed to the special envoys of the pope, Venice and France in their credentials and the overseeing of the publication of the *Pro divo Carolo*.[3]

An unnecessary cloud of uncertainty has been allowed to settle on Gattinara's self-exile from the management of imperial affairs and his temporary removal to Italy.[4] In the light of his repeated requests to be allowed to visit his estates in Italy in order to organize his affairs, there

[1] AGRB (PEA), 1471 (4), fol. 11ᵛ (Gattinara to the emperor, 7 September 1526).
[2] Serassi, *Lettere di Castiglione*, II, 100.
[3] *Ibid.*, II, 127–35, 144.   [4] Cf. Brandi, *Emperor*, p. 254.

can be little reason for surprise unless it be that of the Venetian ambassador
Navagero who was astounded that a leading minister of the emperor should
choose to remove himself from the center of affairs, particularly at a time
when he appeared to be all-powerful.[5] On the contrary, everything in the
last four years of Gattinara's service to the emperor, and most particularly
his debts, now amounting to 34,000 ducats, conduced to make him seek
his Italian homeland. His predilection for astrology, his possible identification of himself with the predictions of a court astrologer who believed
that a man of jovial temperament would conclude peace in Italy, may have
hastened his departure at this particular time but the astrological motif is
hardly necessary for understanding the chancellor's leaving the imperial
court for Italy in March, 1527.[6] The emperor granted him permission to
depart on 18 March but not before first having him assemble and address
the estates of Castile at Valladolid. By the end of the month he was on his
way first to Montserrat to accomplish a novena, and then on to Barcelona.[7]
Although the imperial license was for three months, Navagero reported the
uncertainty as to whether he would return or be recalled by the emperor,
or if recalled, whether he would comply. In his own opinion the Venetian
ambassador confided that he would not be recalled, for it was the emperor's
nature not to convey the sense of anybody being indispensable to him. While
Salinas, intent upon netting Milan for his master, implied that the court
and government would be better off without the chancellor, Navagero,
despite his harsh criticism of Gattinara, grudgingly admitted that they
would be the poorer by his absence.[8]

As Gattinara turned his face to Italy, the lengthening lines of the post
which moved between him and the court indicated that despite Charles'
apparent indifference the business of imperial government still adhered to
the person if not the office of the present chancellor.[9] The aged statesman
left behind him two secretaries to whom he entrusted his interests – Jean
Lalemand and now Alfonso de Valdés, who had enjoyed a considerable rise
within the chancellery and in the affection of his master during the past
year. Not simply the different personalities of these two men, but their
different relations to the emperor, the chancellery and to the chancellor
himself provided the ominous setting for future strife and a fateful rupture.
From the abbey of Montserrat on the evening of Easter, 21 April 1527,
Gattinara wrote to Lalemand addressing him in the most affectionate terms.

[5] Bornate, 'Doc.', p. 528; cf. Cicogna, *Inscrizioni*, pp. 196, 267.
[6] Bornate, 'Doc.', p. 525; cf. Serassi, *Lettere di Castiglione*, II, 141.
[7] AGRB (PEA), 1471 (4), fol. 11 (7 September 1526); Bornate, 'Doc.', pp. 525–7 (8 March and 2 April 1527).
[8] Bornate, 'Doc.', pp. 526–7; Rodríguez Villa, 'Cartas de Salinas', *44*, 19, 27, cf. *43*, 495. On Gattinara's plans to return after three months see AGRB (PEA), 1471 (4), fol. 8.
[9] Bornate, 'Doc.', p. 527.

Incapable of turning his back upon politics, or of desisting from rendering counsel to the emperor, even if unsolicited and undesired, the chancellor sought to establish his line of communication to his master, apparently first by way of Valdés and then Lalemand. Although claiming to write more fully to Valdés, he made Lalemand his principal representative. At midnight on the same evening Gattinara, writing to Charles, affirmed that he would communicate at greater length to Valdés regarding his counsel and the contents of some letters sent from the Archduchess Margaret.[10] Having arrived at Barcelona and remained fifteen days awaiting a favorable wind, Gattinara, amidst a few parting volleys of counsel to Charles, resolved on 12 May to leave for Palamos the following day. From Palamos, while suffering further delays, he instructed the emperor to hear the letter he had written Valdés, wherein he gave the time that he thought he would return.[11] Then in his final letter to Charles, again on the same day as he set sail, 28 May, Gattinara, while imparting his characteristic sense of profound loyalty to the emperor's service, raised for the first time the spectre that someone close to Charles might be working to undermine him:

Sire, I have heard by letters from some of my friends that those who do not seek your service nor my good, believing unworthily to move Your Majesty against me in order to alienate me ever more from your grace, have bruited it about that I have left Your Majesty to his sorrow, showing myself ill-content and that I had said I would not return to your service unless Your Majesty wrote me and commanded it expressly and that even in commanding me I would not return unless Your Majesty gave me for my maintenance ten or twelve thousand ducates of income. Sire, these are indeed false rumors and lies invented to induce Your Majesty to do something to my prejudice and against my honor in order to alienate me entirely from your service and good grace and to cut the path for being able to return there. I do not consider this to be your intention and I am sure that by your prudence you will consider the intention of each one and will not trust such sinister inventions, even knowing what has passed between you and me [and] of the causes which constrain me to go to order my small affairs... in order to be able afterwards to serve you better and more freely without importuning or annoying you. And Your Majesty knows well that in asking leave of him to this effect and in promising him not to remain more than three months to dispose of my affairs, that at the latest I would return in the month of September. And that if before my embarkation there should supervene certain news of the pope's coming to Barcelona, I would detain myself there in order not to fail the service of Your Majesty... And Your Majesty should not believe that I am waiting to be recalled, not expect Your Majesty to write me about this, for I am far from·these pretensions and ambitions and there is no particular interest that would deflect me from your service... But if it pleases God to give us peace and put an end to these tribulations, I hope to recompense myself for past harm and to be able to serve you without

[10] HHSA (Belgien), PA 94, fols. 438, 442.   [11] *Ibid.*, fols. 444, 445.

necessity. Or if misfortune continues as a means of penance for my sins, my heirs may be able some day to have the enjoyment of my labors and pains. And I beg you, sire, always to hold me for your good and loyal servant, as I have been and desire to be as long as I live. And if anyone would want to charge me with the contrary saying that I had said or done something opposed to your service or that truly ought to displease you, I would come from wherever I might be, even from the end of the earth, in order to reply to him and to maintain the contrary up to death.[12]

The emperor could have been left in no doubt that his chancellor intended exactly what he said. The letter evoked from Charles a most uncharacteristically appreciative and reassuring response in which the emperor mformed his *tres chier et féal chancellier* that there was no effort or movement afoot to subvert him and went on not only to wish a safe voyage out also a safe return, when he could be certain of being most welcome to his very good master.[13] The absence of the chancellor may have been felt by Charles in the daily workings of the imperial government even before his most loyal, if trying, servant had departed Spain.

During the abortive trip of Gattinara to his Italian estates, Charles' government managed to creak along. The Chancellor's withdrawal from court allowed Lalemand to take the final step in securing the preeminence

[12] *Ibid.*, fol. 446. 'Sire, jay entendu par lectres daulcungs mes amys que ceulx qui ne desirent votre service ny mon bien cuydans indigne et inanimer votre maieste contre moy: pour me aliener de plus en plus de votre grace: ont estore ung bruyt par dela que je me suis party de votredite maieste a son regret me monstrant mal content: et que je deusse avoir dict que ne retourneroye a votredicte service: si votre maieste ne le mescripvoit: et le me mandast expressement: et que encoures en le me mandast ne revendroye: si votredite maieste ne me donroit pour mon entretenment dix ou xij mil ducas de rentes. Que certes sire sont choses faulcement controuvees: et menteryes inventees por [*sic*] induisre votre maieste a innover quelque chose en mon preiudice et contre mon honneur: pour me aliener du tout de votre service: et de votre bonne grace et pour me couper le chemin dy pouvoir retourner: que ne pense estre de votre intencion: et suys sehur qui par votre prudence considererez la intencion de ung chascun et ne donrez foy a telles sinistres invencions mesmes sachant: ce quest passe entre vous et moy: des causes que constraindoient a aller donner ordre a mes petitz afferes...a fin de vous pouvoir apres mieulx et plus librement servir: sans vous importuner ny ennuyer: Et scet bien votre maieste que en luy demandant congie a cet effect: et en luy promectant de non demeurer plus de troys moys a disposer mesdites afferes: et que au plus tard seroye de retour au moys de septembre: Et que si avant mon embarquement survenoit nouvelle certaine de la venue du pape en barcelone je me detiendroye illeques pour non faillir au service de votre maieste en telle coniuncture...Et ne croye votre maieste que en ce jaye de actendre: que je soye appelle ny que votre maieste sur ce mescripve: car je suys bien loing de ces ceremonies et ambicions: Et ny ha nul interes particulier que me sceust destourner de votre service:...Mais sil plet a dieu de nous donner paix et de mectre fin a ces tribulacions: jespere de me recompenser du mal passe: et vous pouvoir servir sans necessite. ou si le malheur dure en moyen pour penitence de mes pechez: pourront mes heretiers quelque jour avoir joyssance de mes labeurs et peines. Et vous supplie sire me vouloir tousiours tenir pour votre bon et loyal serviteur comme lay este et desire estre tant que je vive: Et si quelcung me vouldroit charger du contraire disant que jeusse dict ou faict chose contre votre service ou que meritement vous deust desplaire: je viendray de quelque part que je soye quant ce seroit du bout du monde pour en respondre et maintenir le contraire jusques a la mort.'

[13] Quoted in Brandi, *Quellen*, p. 183.

of his own position and influence. Lalemand together with Loaysa took
charge, introducing themselves into all affairs and doing the greater part
of the business of state. Salinas describes Lalemand as the key in the
Council of State and 'el fiel del juego'.[14] Navagero represents Lalemand
as carrying on protracted secret negotiations at night with the French and
English ambassadors at the house of the latter.[15] Although Salinas
understands Lalemand as having the greatest credit among those around
Charles and as being occupied in all that Gattinara undertook, it is
questionable just how much attention the secretary gave to the chancellery.[16]
For by Salinas' own admission Waldkirch, who had replaced Jean Hannart
as vice-chancellor early in 1527, delayed his mission to Germany in order
to attend to the chancellery during the first weeks of Gattinara's absence.
Furthermore, it appears that Juan Manuel assumed the temporary superintendence of the imperial secretariat and was aided by the young gifted
Latinist Diego Gracián de Alderete, formerly an assistant of Valdés and
earlier of Maximilian Transylvanus. Gracián complains of being weighed
down by the burden of correspondence.[17]

The chancellery now seemed to suffer a further step toward its
impending demise. Gattinara's good friend, the Polish ambassador John
Dantiscus, complained loudly that the business of the chancellery dragged,
confusion prevailed, affairs were conducted by two or three nobodies and
one trudged profitlessly from office to office. Navagero would have us
believe that with Gattinara's absence, writing in Latin stopped and the
alternate use of French and German had caused some confusion.[18] To
accept this observation as a general truth would be to overlook the activities
of the imperial chancellery's Latin secretary, Valdés, who, as with Lalemand,
saw his position enhanced by the temporary withdrawal of his master from
affairs. For to Valdés fell the responsibility, following the sack of Rome,
of acting upon the advice, or at least part of the advice, proferred by
Gattinara to Charles from Monaco: namely, that the emperor should purge
himself before all Christian princes by getting Valdés to write good Latin
letters. The further suggestion that these letters to Europe's rulers should
press for the convocation of a council to heal divisions and extirpate
heresies, Charles saw fit not to follow for the present.[19] The letters duly
appeared.

Meanwhile, Gattinara's efforts to penetrate to his Piedmontese estates
proved in vain: French galleys, French troops and that perennial and most

[14] Rodríguez Villa, 'Cartas de Salinas', *44*, 16, 23; Cicogna, *Inscrizioni*, p. 197.
[15] Cicogna, *Inscrizioni*, p. 198; cf. Rodríguez Villa, 'Cartas de Salinas', *44*, 143–4.
[16] Rodríguez Villa, 'Cartas de Salinas', *44*, 144.
[17] *Ibid.*, p. 13. On Alderete see Bataillon, *Érasme*, pp. 286–7; and Allen, *Opus*, VII, 265.
[18] *AT*, IX, 135, 148; Cicogna, *Inscrizioni*, p. 199.
[19] For the Latin version of Valdés' letter see Manuel Fernández Alvarez, *La España del Emperador*

The last years of the chancellorship

intimate opponent, the gout, forbade it. Pursued by enemy warships and besieged in Genoa, the chancellor barely managed to flee that city before its fall and return by way of Corsica to Barcelona. By 1 September his presence in Spain was known at court, for Salinas wrote confidently to his master that he would not be received there, that he would not return to what he had before and that he had so little credit that he would be ignored.[20] As if to heighten expectancy and increase speculation Gattinara, after a second novena at Montserrat lingered in Catalonia, choosing his time to reappear at court. He caught up with the court on 4 October shortly before it removed from Palencia and to the surprise of many, as well as the disgust of his enemies, he was welcomed by the emperor, who seemed genuinely pleased to have his old chancellor back; according to Navagero he was restored to all his previous authority *e forse maggiore*.[21]

The subsequent thirty-odd months remaining to Gattinara challenge satisfactory analysis on account of the paucity of reliable sources. It is very probable that at least formally Charles restored his chancellor to more than his former authority, but by this time the channels of power hacked out by Lalemand and his fellow secretaries during the course of the decade were not to be rerouted and the obviously declining health of the chancellor did not allow him to capitalize upon new powers or political opportunities. Against a tense diplomatic background, the final period of Gattinara's chancellorship comprised two salient events: the fall of Lalemand and convincing the emperor that he must go to Italy. The impending issues of Henry VIII's divorce and a religious settlement in Germany were barely grasped during the final months and had to be left to his successor Nicolas Perrenot, Lord of Granvelle. Despite the unavoidable friction between the rigid, demanding personality of the aged minister and the still youthful, searching temper of his master, Charles needed and thus could tolerate the great dynastic servant during the time remaining. According to Dantiscus, the emperor came to recognize the singular faith, integrity and prudence of his chancellor in the forthcoming negotiations with France and after heading off a plot on the part of his enemies to give Gattinara an Italian assignment away from court, Charles began to confide in him more confidently than ever before and consult with him in private. Furthermore,

Carlos V, historia de España, XVIII, ed. Ramón Menéndez Pidal (Madrid, 1966), pp. 332–4 (to Henry VIII), or *AT*, IX, 240–1 (to the King of Poland); for the Spanish version see Valdés, *Diálogo*, pp. 78–81. For Gattinara's letter from Monaco see HHSA (Belgien), PA 94, fol. 451. According to Dantiscus, his friend Valdés urged the Polish ambassador to move his king to promote a council; *AT*, IX, 257.
[20] Rodríguez Villa, 'Cartas de Salinas', *44*, 147–8.
[21] Bornate, 'Vita', p. 354; Cicogna, *Inscrizioni*, p. 200; Dantiscus gives 5 October and claims that Gattinara was recalled by the emperor. *AT*, IX, 332–3, cf. 259, 260. For cases expressing individual pleasure and welcome at Gattinara's return see the letters in Caballero, *Valdés*, pp. 343–4, 349–50, 367, 410–11; *Cal. SP Spain*, III/2, 772; and *AT*, X, 46.

if we are to believe Gattinara's autobiography, the business of the chancellery had been impaired by his absence and thus he was not allowed to go far away from the emperor who kept him close at hand.[22] And with the chancellor's passing the emperor could act upon his earlier menacing promise to suppress the office. In the context of Gattinara's declining health and the imminence of a resolution in Italy a *modus vivendi* was reached during these last months in the relation between the emperor and his chancellor.

Gattinara returned to a government dominated by his former creature Jean Lalemand. Indeed the first secretary attained the peak of his power in the twelve months following the chancellor's return. His influence and activities are discernible not simply from accounts of contemporaries but also from the trail of signatures to important documents, some of which conspicuously lack that of Gattinara whether from illness, aloofness or disfavor. To Lalemand fell the brunt of the fruitless negotiations with Henry VIII and Francis I which culminated first in the delivery of the defiance to Charles 2–27 January 1528 and later during the cortes of the Crown of Aragon held at Monzón early in the subsequent summer. At the vortex of affairs, Lalemand, as if to secure the inside track for himself, graciously put the French herald up at his own lodgings in Monzón where he could more easily rummage through the herald's papers.[23] When at an earlier stage of the interchange the French herald conveyed a disparaging remark from his king about the Grand Chancellor, Charles, in the reply drawn up and signed by Lalemand, rebuked Francis for his abusive reference to a servant simply because he had served his master well; would that Francis might have such a servant who could hold him to his word. In concluding his own account of the proceedings Lalemand listed those present but failed to include the chancellor who did in fact participate.[24] Moreover, although the instructions to Miguel Mai, as the imperial agent seeking to effect an understanding between pope and emperor, were drafted by Gattinara's hand, 10 July 1528, two months later he was conspicuously absent at the gathering in the royal palace at Madrid where Lalemand, Castiglione, Perrenot and others signed a preliminary agreement between Charles and Clement.[25] Similarly in the final negotiations and signing of the all important agreement with the Dorias and Genoa on 10 August, Gattinara, who had prepared the ground for such a vital alliance as early

---

[22] Bornate, 'Vita', pp. 357–8.
[23] Charles Weiss, ed., *Papiers d'État du Cardinal de Granvelle* (Paris, 1841), I, 361; Rodríguez Villa, 'Cartas de Salinas', *44*, 175; Santa Cruz, *Crónica*, II, 428–9; cf. *Letters and Papers*, 4/2, no. 3826.
[24] Weiss, *Granvelle*, I, 369–70, cf. 366. For the negotiations of Charles with Henry and Francis over the defiance see *ibid.*, pp. 314–427.
[25] HHSA (Belgien), PA 95, fols. 112–13ᵛ, 118.

as September 1523, was conspicuously absent and Lalemand appears as chief negotiator.[26] Nevertheless, despite the considerable activity of Lalemand and his seeming ability to capture the limelight, it was the hard line of Gattinara that prevailed in the negotiations. And when it came to attempting to moderate the harsh words of the chancellor in the imperial response of 21 January 1528, Charles prevented Lalemand from making the change. Perhaps the English ambassadors were not far from the mark when they judged the relationship between the chancellor and the secretary as that of rivals during these months.[27] Looking back at the moment of Lalemand's imprisonment 17 December 1528, the same two ambassadors Ghinucci and Lee would observe to Wolsey that the secretary and the chancellor had 'for some time' not agreed.[28] The two statements bracket the year 1528 as the period in which their relationship soured. What had happened?

In his autobiography Gattinara never mentions Lalemand in 1528, nor indeed at any other time. It would seem that he had never existed, or that by silence the chancellor sought to obliterate from the eyes of posterity this man, around whom the politics of the Habsburgs and of Europe had moved for almost a decade. Likewise, his correspondence with the meagre exception of a single letter does not in any way relieve the darkness that has settled over the fall of one of the earliest state secretaries in European history. To Lalemand himself and to Salinas, anything but impartial, it was simply a case of Gattinara, acting out of jealousy and fear, having deliberately connived to bring down his rival.[29] But the chancellor's motives were complex. Reading among the fragments of evidence, one gains the impression that he acted less in anger than sadness and that a profound disillusionment and embarrassment urged him to get the whole affair behind him and bury it in silence. Here the critical document written by Lalemand's chief accuser six months after Gattinara's death is the memoir of Antoine Perrenin, for six years in charge of enciphering and deciphering, and chief clerk to the accused. Those few scholars who have concerned themselves with the memoir have had their credence weakened by the violence of the characterization of Lalemand and the effort to portray him as a second Judas.[30] But the weight of evidence drawn from others and Lalemand's own wretched efforts to frame the very man who had been his

---

[26] *Ibid.*, fols. 173–5; *Cal. SP Spain*, III/2, 756–7; *Cal. SP Ven.*, III, no. 746. Cf. *Cal. SP Spain*, IV/1, 117 for Gattinara's absence in the signing of the marriage treaty between Alessandro de'Medici and Charles' natural daughter Margaret, 8 July 1529, Barcelona.
[27] *Letters and Papers*, 4/2, no. 3826.
[28] *Letters and Papers*, 4/2, no. 5039.
[29] Rodríguez Villa, 'Cartas de Salinas', *44*, 209–10; HHSA (Belgien), PA 21 (alt 24)/4, fol. 27.
[30] *Ibid.*, fol. 44ᵛ. The Perrenin memoir constitutes folios 35–49.

benefactor and friend lead one to suspect that the substance of Perrenin's depiction is not too far from the mark.[31] At least at the very beginning of the memoir, when describing the triangular relationship between Charles, Gattinara and Lalemand, there is a ring of authenticity, most alarming in its import. For Perrenin affirms that Lalemand owed everything to Gattinara and that he repaid his master with something worse than ingratitude by conspiring to sow dissension between him and the emperor. According to Perrinin, Lalemand communicated alternately to the chancellor and then to the emperor in order to incite the former to make several remonstrances and complaints concerning his treatment and the preeminence of his authority. And on the other hand he shamelessly told Charles that his chancellor was too difficult to please and even went so far as to say to the emperor that he need not have any chancellor and that the present one was too old and enfeebled and only useful for making announcements to the ambassadors. When the chancellor departed for Italy to set his household in order, the secretary accelerated his campaign of subversion by interpolating the correspondence between emperor and chancellor to promote mutual mistrust.[32]

Although Perrenin was hardly impartial in the whole affair of Lalemand's fall and apparently hoped to succeed the first secretary, there is too much evidence from other sources to allow us to ignore some of the clues suggested by his accusations. On the other hand, to assert the essential veracity of Perrenin's accusations in this particular regard is not to argue that Lalemand in any way caused the dissension between the emperor and his chancellor. The basic institutional and personal elements quite apart from Lalemand himself worked to create the strained relationship between the two which we have attempted to reveal here. Lalemand, opportunist that he was, simply served as a catalyst, adroitly seeking his own advantage in promoting the decomposition of that relationship. When in October 1527 Gattinara returned to Spain, his creature was moving rapidly toward the attainment of an ascendancy in the government which the chancellor was either unwilling or slow to recognize and which Charles, desirous of maintaining a precarious balance, would ultimately not have countenanced.

It is probable that the affair involving Alfonso de Valdés and his dialogue on the sack of Rome had the effect of forcing Gattinara to recognize the arrogance and pretensions of Lalemand and of shaking his former confidence in the man. In the conflict between the two secretaries Gattinara revealed how far he had removed himself during the course of 1527 from any dependence upon Lalemand and in turn had vested an ever increasing trust

---

[31] See Lalemand's letter to the emperor *ibid.*, fols. 26–8, and especially fol. 27, for his resurrection of the false charge, first concocted by Marshal de Vergy, 1513–15, against Gattinara.
[32] *Ibid.*, fols. 35ᵛ–36.

and reliance in Valdés. The Latin secretary's account of his imbroglio with Lalemand helps to provide the chronology and context for the mounting accusations against the first secretary which paralleled this literary scuffle. In explaining to Erasmus the origin of his *Lactancio* dialogue, Valdés represented himself as being cajoled by the urging of friends, gathered at his house for dinner, to write something on the sack of Rome shortly after the news had 'been received. The notorious dialogue, which, in affirming the sack to have been an act of divine providence, became the semi-official defence of the emperor's position, saw the light of day amidst the enthusiastic acclaim of Valdés' Erasmian friends – Coronel and Virues; even Sanctio Carranza pressed for its publication. Valdés hung back. With manuscript copies already leaking into circulation, the secretary wisely consulted the government.[33] He first turned to no other than Lalemand, then to Juan Manuel and the chancellor all of whom made emendations. As the work began to receive increasing acclaim, Lalemand for reasons unknown shifted his ground. He began by resorting to the emperor to alert him to this dialogue that he claimed to be rife with heresies and ripe for the flames. Charles demurred, incredulous that his secretary should be considered so impious. He referred Lalemand to the Council of State where the first secretary to the consternation of Valdés denounced his former friend and called for the burning of his heretical work. Valdés' chief supporters Juan Manuel and Gattinara were absent at the time, but since the emperor's confidence in him never at any time faltered, he was in no great danger despite the storm that swirled around him. The matter was referred to two most influential imperial councillors, Louis de Praet and Nicholas Perrenot (Granville). When their examination only served to vindicate Valdés, Lalemand, now having aroused the papal nuncio Castiglione and in conjunction with him, made the ecclesiastical rounds, first appealing to the Archbishop of Seville, who as an Erasmian should hardly have been expected to share Lalemand's alarm, and subsequently to the

---

[33] Caballero, *Valdés*, p. 476, also found in Allen, *Opus*, VIII, 168–74; and Valdés' letter of early autumn 1528 to Castiglione: Serassi, *Lettere de Castiglione*, II, 173. John E. Longhurst, *Alfonso de Valdés and the Sack of Rome: Dialogue of Lactancio and an Archdeacon* (Albuquerque, N.M., 1952) has here in his translation of the letter incorrectly interpellated, instead of Gattinara, Lerma, the chancellor of the university of Alcalá, although earlier in his narrative he correctly included Gattinara (cf. pp. 100 and 12). It should also be noted that Longhurst (p. 116) has dropped three lines of Castiglione's letter which are valuable for understanding the papal nuncio's view of the chancellor: 'Perchè notissimo è che sempre il Sig. Cancelliero ha persuaso all'Imperatore quello, che S. Maestà ha posto in opera: il medesimo ha fatto il Sig. D. Gio Emanuel, e l'uno, e l'altro' (Serassi, *Lettere di Castiglione*, II, 199–200). The passage should therefore read: 'Nor will you really persuade me of that which was stated in your letter: namely that the Grand Chancellor, Don Juan Manuel and so many theologians have seen and approved your book. For it is most obvious that the Chancellor has always persuaded the Emperor of whatever His Majesty has put into operation and Don Juan Manuel has done the same and both alike have always grieved over the ruin of Rome as a misfortune for all of Italy.'

Archbishop of Santiago. Disappointed, the first secretary now found his position far more directly threatened. For concomitant with these exchanges that consumed the late autumn of 1528 a government inquiry into Lalemand's conduct had been proceeding and had by December reached a decisive stage. At the moment that Gattinara became convinced of his guilt and moved with full force against him (*graviter in se concitatum*), the secretary broke down and threw himself on the mercy of his former victim, Valdés, begging for his support.[34]

At what stage and how did the chancellor become convinced as to the culpability of his former aide and confidant? Although Valdés' account derived from two letters dated 22 April and 15 May 1529 to Maximilian Transylvanus and Erasmus respectively, by a letter, since lost, of 16 January to the Polish ambassador Johannes Dantiscus, Valdés had reported the whole proceedings of Lalemand's fall from favor and removal from court.[35] The English ambassadors Ghinucci and Lee reported to Wolsey on 17 December 1528 that they had just learned of Lalemand being sent to prison for ostensibly providing the French king with information regarding the emperor. They went on to volunteer the opinion that the chancellor would not be sorry, for the two had not been in agreement 'for some time'.[36] This intriguing scrap, which would suggest that Gattinara had been working over an extended period, perhaps ever since his return to court, in order to rid himself of a dangerous rival, would seem to be corroborated by Salinas. Ferdinand's ambassador, it should be noted, relied heavily upon Lalemand for the attainment of his goals and had the most to lose by his fall. Writing home in mid-March of 1529 at a time when Lalemand's detention had been considerably relaxed and he was merely required to remain two leagues away from court and from Toledo, while the emperor undertook a more extensive investigation into the case, Ferdinand's ambassador lamented to his master that malevolent passions were driving a good servant from his brother's service. For both Gattinara and his friend, the Grand Master, Gorrevod, were motivated by passion and their own interests; the chancellor particularly believed that his abilities were not given due recognition and to remove the source of his embarrassment, he spread suspicion with little to support it.[37] Here Salinas provides the ambassadors' view of the imbroglio as seen from the outside.

From within the government and the chancellery the picture is somewhat

---

[34] Caballero, *Valdés*, pp. 432–4 (Valdés to Maximilian Transylvanus, 22 April 1529), pp. 476–7 (Valdés to Erasmus, 15 May 1529). In a letter of 1 February 1529 to Valdés, Dantiscus indicates the mutual pleasure he experiences in amusing his friends with pasquinades on Lalemand, *ibid.*, pp. 408–9. An example of these can be found in HHSA (Belgien), PA 21 (alt 24)/4, fols. 24–24ᵛ: 'Ad Lalemantum'.
[35] Cf. Caballero, *Valdés*, p. 408; Vocht, *Dantiscus*, p. 42.
[36] *Letters and Papers*, 4/1, no. 5039.   [37] Rodríguez Villa, 'Cartas de Salinas', *44*, 209–10.

different and to be preferred. If Perrenin was responsible for instigating by his accusations the investigation into the conduct of Lalemand, it can be safely presumed that he emerged in August. For after 10 September there is ample evidence that the government was undertaking an extensive and thorough investigation into the first secretary.[38] The arrival of the important memorial of articles composed by Guillaume Des Barres, Margaret's principal secretary, helped to precipitate the imprisonment of the accused. The value of the Des Barres articles as documentary evidence rests not so much on their continuous denuciation of Lalemand based upon reports and hearsay from secretaries in the Netherlands, Naples and Spain, who had been exposed to the movement of documents and chancellery affairs during the past decade, but rather in the marginal comments of Gattinara as he sifted through this sort of evidence. The chancellor's reactions were of three kinds to these charges involving pensions and the taking of money particularly in Flanders and Naples: Lalemand confesses it and 'ce nest cas de crisme'; more formal evidence speaks to the contrary; His Majesty will look into it and justice will be done.[39] Gattinara here appears cautious, sceptical of some of the charges, scrupulous and conscientious in the pursuit of justice. It is probable that it was not this type of evidence that sent Lalemand to prison but the reports that he had imparted documents and information to the emperor's enemies – particularly Francis I. By 13 October Lalemand was quite convinced in his letter to the emperor that Gattinara must be his chief accuser. But a bad conscience could have driven him to this conclusion.[40]

It is most probable that Guillaume de Montfort, the emperor's ambassador, returning from his mission to Ferdinand and the Archduchess Margaret, brought the Des Barres report and other incriminating documents that now raised the case against Lalemand to a new level of intensity. He arrived at court sometime during the first week of October.[41] The emperor's chamberlain Jean de Vandenesse speaks of Montfort bringing several types of evidence that placed Lalemand in greater danger.[42] The ambassador reported that Des Barres, who also came from Burgundy, had

---

[38] HHSA (Belgien), PA 21 (alt 24)/4, fols. 53–57ᵛ, cf. fols. 23, 66ʳ–66ᵛ.
[39] *Ibid.*, fols. 7–20 (the Des Barres memoir with Gattinara's marginal comments), cf. fols. 82–3 (Lalemand to Hannart, 16 February 1529, on his participation in this memoir).
[40] *Ibid.*, fols. 26–8.
[41] The date of Montfort's arrival from Flanders and France is uncertain. Vandenesse says that he reached Charles at Toledo which according to his chronology could be any time between 31 October 1528 and March 1529. But according to Gachard Charles left Madrid and reached Toledo by 8 October. (Cf. Vandenesse, *Journal*, pp. 44, 81.) Furthermore, Granvelle began drafting Montfort's new instructions at Madrid on the same day, to be completed at Toledo on 10 November. (Bauer, *Korrespondenz*, II, 295–308, esp. 296 and 304). It would appear, therefore, that unless Granvelle's action is to be understood as being anticipatory to Montfort's imminent arrival, Vandenesse has telescoped dates and places, and Montfort first caught up with the court and chancellery at Madrid sometime during the first week of October.   [42] Vandenesse, *Journal*, p. 81.

said that Lalemand was a native Burgundian but secretly French. In
Burgundy the belief was current that Lalemand was *bon francois*. And when
Montfort in his passage through France stopped off to speak to the king
about Lalemand, Francis intimated that he had given him 30,000 livres.[43]
Lalemand therefore had good reason to write the emperor on 13 October
and protest his loyalty.[44] Although continuing to press a wider inquiry into
the matter, Charles, if we are to credit the present chronology, delayed his
decision more than a month. The last document that Lalemand countersigned was the final version of Montfort's new instructions on 28 November.
Two days later a note was introduced into the chancellery register that Jean
Lalemand had formerly handled all this business.[45] Charles, still reluctant
to cashier his useful secretary, probably suspended him in some of his
functions but did not yet throw him into prison.

Sometime between 28 November and 13 December, when Montfort
departed for Flanders and the empire,[46] Gattinara moved against Lalemand.
Sometime in this same period of two weeks the secretary took fright at the
chancellor being *in se concitatum* and threw himself on the mercy of Valdés.
What motivated Gattinara's decision to declare against the secretary arose
from the arrival of some revealing letters from the collegiate church of the
Magdalene in Besançon whose members had been known to be in a state
of rebellion. The case involved the apparent forgery of documents that had
led to the violation of the rights of a powerful ecclesiastical corporation
which had resulted in much unrest. On 30 September from Madrid Charles
had had Lalemand compose and countersign a letter to Margaret inquiring
what had transpired with the Chapter of the Magdalene in Besançon
concerning the *primarias preces* assigned to Anatole Bourgeois and the
subsequent disobedience and rebellion of that chapter, the most powerful
in the diocese. Identical enquiries were sent to the Archbishop of Besançon,
the magistrates of the city and the Dean of Poligny.[47] Gattinara had drawn
his own conclusions as to what had happened on the basis of newly arrived
explanatory letters from the collegiate church of the Magdalene: Lalemand
had concocted a false instrument, whereby one of his relations would be
received to the parochial cure of the Magdalene even though this same
person had accepted another benefice in virtue of the *primarias preces*.
Failing this, Lalemand had resorted to an act that would have confiscated
the collegiate church to the emperor and the Archduchess Margaret.
According to this information, Gattinara accused Lalemand of having
procured the emperor's signature to letters virtually confiscating the
temporal revenues of the church in an action which he considered to be

[43] HHSA (Belgien), PA 21 (alt 24)/4, fols. 89ᵛ–90. [44] *Ibid.*, fols. 26–8.
[45] Bauer, *Korrespondenz*, II, 345. [46] Cf. *ibid.*, II, 308.
[47] HHSA (Belgien), PA 21 (alt 24)/4, fols. 59–60, cf. 61, 62, 63.

a brutal forgery and a perversion of justice. In closing he added: 'Moreover, Sire, if your Majesty may wish to communicate anything concerning your affairs I beg Your Majesty most humbly that it be through one from your Council of State, either De Praet or M. de Granvelle or another but not by the asaid Lalemand in whom I am not able to find truth'.[48] Thus very simply but most effectively did Gattinara snap the link in an association of work, collaboration and trust that had lasted a decade. Since the chancellor's statement implies that Lalemand was still not only at court but either in the Council of State or capable of communicating between council and chancellery, it appears probable that Valdés' report refers to this decision which directly preceded and significantly contributed to Lalemand's arrest.

The emperor received his chancellor's recommendation as the final influence impelling him to arrest Lalemand. It must have been plain to him by now that whatever the result of the public investigation, the *primero secretario* was only an embarrassment to the regime and could not be allowed to continue in any capacity. He was seized on 14 or 15 December[49] and placed under the guard of the Seigneur de Sylly, marshal of the household, who took him first to a place a short distance from Toledo for a week, then on to Monzón where he remained in prison until the emperor left Toledo for Barcelona on 9 March 1529.[50] Subsequently, he was brought back under house arrest to a place two leagues from Toledo where

---

[48] *Ibid.*, fol. 64: 'Sire. Jay entendu que M. Jehan Lalemand a fect signe a votre maieste des lettres adressans a madame votre tante/aussy a Larchevesque de Besancon et a ceulx dela cite de besancon pour de plain fault mectre subz votre main et de madite dame le temporel et revenu de ceulx de leglise collegiale de la Magdaleine dudit besancon/a Loccasion quilz nayent voulsu recevoir ung sien parent a la cure parochiale de ladite eglise/en vertu des primarias preces de votredite maieste/Jacoit ce que commil scet que lesdits de La magdaleine ayent de pieca envoye Leurs excuses qui sont en mes mains par les quelles entre aultres choses ilz dient que ledit parent se fonde en ung instrument faulx/et que desja il a accepter ung aultre benefice en vertu desdites primarias preces/et encoires quil nest Lectre ne souffisant a ladite cure quest la primiera [*sic*] de tout Le diocese/et peult sembler soubz le bon plaisir de votredite maieste que lesdites lettres sont violentes/et que Ladite mainmise seroit scandaleuse et pervertisant Justice actendu les Susdites excuses que ne sont contre auctorite de votredite maieste a La quelle commilz dient/ilz sont tousjeurs [*sic*] est obeissans/et mesmes en ceste partie dont ilz alleguent a tesmoing monseigneur Le grand maistre que aussy Le tesmoingne par ses lettres quil a escript a votredite maieste/Et pour ce sire que comme je entends ledit Lalemand a envoye lesdites lettres par monfort/il me semble soubz votre bon plaisir que votre maieste doit depescher audit monfort luy commandant quil envoye en voz mains le pacquet dudit Lalemand dresse au doyen de poligny et votre maieste verra cela/et aultres belles matieres comme je croys./ Au surplus sire: Sy votre maieste vouldra communiquer aulcunne chose de voz afferes/je supplie tres humblement a votre maieste que ce soye par quelun de votre conseil destat soit monseigneur de Prat au monseigneur de grandevelle ou aultre et non par ledit Lalemand au quel je ne puys trouver verite.'

[49] Cf. Bauer, *Korrespondenz*, II, 308, 358; *Cal. SP Spain*, III/2, 864–5.

[50] *Cal. SP Spain*, III/2, 903. Writing on 16 February 1529 Charles was either not aware or more likely was interpreting imprisonment broadly, for Lalemand's confinement had just been relaxed and he was on his way back to Toledo. See *infra*, fn. 51. *Cal. SP Spain*, III/2, 908–9 is misdated and can only refer to February 1528, not 1529.

his detention was relaxed and he was allowed to associate with the court of the empress at Toledo.[51]

Certainly by the beginning of the new year the evidence sought as far afield as Flanders, Franche-Comté and Naples presented a picture of one who, if he had not betrayed state secrets to the French, was culpable of other misdemeanors: falsifying documents, garnishing, general misuse of his official position.[52] In the course of the next six months Lalemand was to make repeated appeals to the emperor, alternating doses of flattery and of humility, pleading his good faith and the baseless suspicions of his enemies, professing his exemplary loyalty and at one point, quoting scripture, he depicted himself as a sort of Christ figure surrounded by accusers.[53]

The wheels of Habsburg justice ground slowly but with considerably more clemency than their Tudor counterpart. From the court of Malines Wolsey's representative wrote back on 25 January 1529 communicating his fears that Lalemand had by now probably suffered the death penalty.[54] Indeed, an agent of Henry VIII's would have had his head cropped for a good deal less than the charges facing the former *primero secretario*. Even if there were no substantive basis to Gorrevod's charge that Francis I had boasted of Lalemand being in his employ and serving as an invaluable promoter of French interests,[55] his excessive improprieties had damaged the effective functioning of the imperial chancellery as well as the emerging secretaryship. At the trial his judges seem to have been readily willing to dismiss the charges of treason against him and to emphasize his taking of gifts, which was such a common practice that the accused could here claim all courtiers as his associates and defiantly require a yardstick. Yet his meddling with dispatches to his own advantage posed a very real occupational hazard to the operation of the chancellery.

Among the charges levelled by Perrenin was one which for its enormity exceeded the accusation that Lalemand had deliberately sought to foment misunderstanding between the emperor and his chancellor. Perrenin claimed that Lalemand in 1524 had sought to displace the first secretary

[51] I am relying here principally upon Vandenesse, *Journal*, p. 81 as controlled by the fragments of Lalemand's correspondence in HHSA and the correspondence in Bauer. Both Keniston, *Cobos*, p. 112 and Salinas' letter of 12 March 1529 (Rodríguez Villa, 'Cartas de Salinas', *44*, 209–10) fail to indicate Lalemand's removal to Monzón. However, beginning with the letter of 22 December 1528 to the emperor, HHSA (Belgien), PA 21 (alt 24)/4, fol. 86, followed by another 26 December (fol. 87), and one to Granvelle 14 February 1529 (fols. 98–98ᵛ) all dated from Monzón (Mocejon) attest to the veracity of Vandenesse's account concerning Lalemand's removal to Monzón. On the other hand, Vandenesse is incorrect in claiming that he was later brought back to Madrid: on 16 February Lalemand writes to Jean Hannart from Burgos, (fols. 82–3); and on 20 March to Granvelle from Toledo (fol. 125).
[52] Walser, *Zentralbehörden*, pp. 258–9.
[53] HHSA (Belgien), PA 21 (alt 24)/4, fols. 86, 120–22ᵛ, 126, cf. fols. 129, 130–30ᵛ, 132–3.
[54] *Letters and Papers*, 4/1, no. 5208.   [55] Keniston, *Cobos*, p. 113.

and *audiencier* Jean Hannart by promoting friction between him and the chancellor and misunderstanding between the emperor and his brother. To effect this end he had introduced a number of deliberately misleading directions into Hannart's instructions as the emperor's special ambassador to the Reichstag of Nuremberg and to his brother in the spring of 1524.[56] Whether true or not the fact remains that the conduct of this experienced and trusted dynastic servant in the empire helped to alienate the imperial estates from Habsburg policy, threatened the relationship between the Habsburg brothers and convulsed Charles' government to a degree not surpassed by the Lalemand affair itself. From the subsequent investigation, which dragged on from September 1524 to September 1526, no satisfactory explanation emerged and Gattinara himself remained puzzled. As chancellor he was of course ultimately responsible for the drafting and expediting of ambassadorial instructions, a task which he performed with the utmost scrupulousness. But whether from overwork, illness or delegation to another whom he trusted, faulty instructions may have been issued. The imperial government intended that Hannart was only to attend the diet at the pleasure of Ferdinand and that at all times he was to act in accordance with Ferdinand's will. Instead, in his appearance before the imperial estates he behaved with an arrogance and independence that irritated the assembly and enraged Ferdinand. Some concluded that his instructions were self-devised and the chancellor had not seen them. The investigation produced nothing conclusive but tended to shift much of the blame to Ferdinand's greedy all-powerful minister, Salamanca, who was rapidly becoming accustomed to the abuse from his contemporaries, deserved as well as undeserved. As for Hannart, his promising career was shattered; he was sent home to assume a lesser charge and perhaps with greater justification than he was aware, felt aggrieved in having his office of first secretary reassigned to Lalemand.[57]

The fall of Lalemand signified a turning point in Charles' government and the decay of the imperial court chancellery. Although the case would drag on until late January 1531 and Lalemand, while cleared of the charge of treason, would be banished from the court and suffer a fine of one quarter of his estate, the government was well rid of him.[58] It was the only instance in a forty-year rule when Charles showed express disfavor to a high ranking

[56] HHSA (Belgien), PA 21 (alt 24)/4, fols. 36–36ᵛ.
[57] On Hannart at Nürnberg and in the empire see *Deutsche Reichstagsakten*, IV, *passim*, esp. pp. 292, 676, 783–5; on Habsburg reactions see Bauer, *Korrespondenz*, I, 182–4, 204, 224 (Gattinara), 246; and on the progress of the investigation see Rodríguez Villa, 'Cartas de Salinas', *43*, 156, 182–4, 186, 193, 202–11, 217–19, 431, 468, 473, 489–90, 504.
[58] For a review of and determination on the charges against Lalemand see Escudero, *Secretarios*, III, Doc. 84, 787–91. For a highly illuminating treatment of the pretensions of Lalemand and his successors to the ranks of the old feudal nobility see Jules Gauthier, 'Du degré de confiance que méritent les généalogies historiques', *Société d'Émulation de Doubs, 7* (1902), 186–201.

official so as to drop him. The case bears favorable comparison with that of Antonio Pérez during the reign of Charles' son, Philip. The accomplishment of Lalemand's removal from the government has been judged as an indication of Gattinara's personal influence with the emperor.[59]

In the period following the chancellor's return from Italy his influence with the emperor and the development of the chancellery seemed to move in inverse ratio to each other. While Lalemand remained in the Council of State, he could expect competition for control. Salinas would have us believe that during these months of early 1528 Charles was aching to get rid of him, and yet the emperor's refusal to send Gattinara on that special mission to Italy which he craved, seems to support the counter-argument that the emperor wanted his chancellor henceforth in close attendance.[60] Certainly after December 1528 Gattinara, while he did not enjoy anything like an ascendancy over Charles, still exercised more influence than anyone else. It was he who along with Loaysa held Charles during these years to the policy of continuing the war until France was driven out of Italy – a policy that was unpopular both at court and throughout Spain in general, but one that would ultimately be vindicated.[61] Moreover, the apparent easing of Gattinara's most pressing financial difficulties would suggest a material improvement in the relationship between emperor and chancellor. For the pleas of monetary distress of the former period are now absent and Gattinara's will, dated 23 July 1529, before his elevation to the cardinalate with its perquisites, indicates one who was not faced by intense financial problems. Nevertheless, his circumstances were far from unconstrained. When in the winter of 1528/9 Francis Dilft, a *famulus* of Erasmus sent by the prince of humanists to seek employment in the imperial chancellery, arrived at Gattinara's door, Valdés had to explain that expenses simply did not permit any further additions to the staff and that in fact the emperor had repeatedly cautioned his chancellor to hold down his expenditures.[62]

[59] Walser, *Zentralbehörden*, p. 260.
[60] Rodríguez Villa, 'Cartas de Salinas', *44*, 159–60; cf. Bornate, 'Vita', pp. 357–8.
[61] Walser, *Zentralbehörden*, pp. 256–7.
[62] Gattinara's testament was edited by Vincenzo Promis and first appeared as a separate publication *Testamento del Cardinale Mercurino* (Turin, 1825), and published later in *Miscellanea di Storia Italiana, 18* (Turin, 1879), 61–147. I wish to take this opportunity to express my gratitude to the late Marchese Mercurino Francesco Arborio di Gattinara who sent me a copy of the first edition. Cf. Baumgarten, *Geschichte*, II, 634. On 20 April 1528 Gattinara had received 'el Sello de las Indias' for the *audiencias* of Hispaniola and of New Spain and was recognized as 'chanciller de las dichas audiencias'. Although the office did not long survive his death, in 1623 Philip IV resurrected it in order further to reward and remunerate his *privado* Olivares. See Ernesto Schäfer, *El Consejo real y supremo de las Indias* (Seville, 1935), I, 48, 220–5, 353. Although from my own survey of the family archive I have not encountered any record of the emoluments received by Gattinara from the American *audiencias*, they appear from the grant to have been respectable. For the definitive treatment of this office in its American colonial context during Gattinara's incumbency see Luigi Avonto, *Mercurino Arborio di Gattinara e l'America*, Biblioteca della Società Storica Vercellese (Vercelli, 1981). The date for Gattinara's investiture can be established by the document

The last years of the chancellorship

Nonetheless, by seeking to draw to the imperial court and chancellery in 1529 such an exotic personality as the recently widowed Cornelius Agrippa of Nettesheim, Gattinara allowed his natural expansiveness to spill out, if in vain, in another direction.[63]

In these final eighteen months of his chancellorship the greatest single achievement of Gattinara as well as the most convincing testimony to his influence with the emperor reveals itself in Charles' decision to go to Italy. Ever since that day at Molins de Rey when the chancellor had accepted the imperial dignity for his master, he had pressed Charles to come to Italy and be crowned. At Worms and again in Spain over the subsequent years he had dinned into his ears this imperative which could only set Gattinara apart from the emperor's Spanish counsellors.[64] For seven years his efforts bore no fruit in the alien environment of Spain and only served to increase the distance between him and the emperor. But in the course of 1528 Charles himself came to recognize the need to leave Spain for Italy and the empire. Beyond obtaining the imperial crown and thereby allowing his brother Ferdinand to become King of the Romans, Charles had by the autumn of 1528 three reasons for going to Italy: to achieve through the pope a calling of a council that would root out heresy and reform the church, to pacify Italy and to become acquainted with the kingdoms, states and vassals in the peninsula.[65] Before the Council of State, meeting at the Alcazar of Madrid on 16 September, Charles announced his determination. The almost miraculous collapse of French strength in Italy, the twin threats of the Turk and the heretic in the empire, and the necessity of reaching an understanding with the pope now coalesced, impelling Charles to commit himself to an expedition that his chancellor had long advocated. As if to mark this moment as the attainment of political maturity, he deliberately sought from his councillors not their opinions but their understanding. The formulation and language of the long justificatory statement that Charles delivered to the council may have been Gattinara's, but the decision was very much his own.[66]

Before posterity Gattinara would shortly seek to claim a greater role than he actually performed in moving Charles to this decision. The chancellor's autobiography is a disappointing document, too lacking in personal detail and self-revelation, too burdened with the *res gestae* of others. But there

of institution in BRT (Misc.), fol. 460ᵛ, which reads Madrid, 22 April 1529, but since Charles was here in 1528 and outside of Saragossa on this day in 1529, the commission must have been given in 1528. See Avonto, *Mercurino Arborio di Gattinara*, pp. 105–7. Cf. Vandenesse, *Journal*, pp. 79, 82. On Dilft's appearance see Allen, *Opus*, VIII, 67.

[63] Agrippa of Nettesheim, *Opera* (Lyons, n.d.), II, Bk. V, Letter 48, p. 934, Bk. VII, letter 21, p. 1022.

[64] Cf. *Letters and Papers*, 3/1, nos. 1098, 1155.

[65] Peter Rassow, *Die Kaiser-Idee Karls V dargestellt an der Politik der Jahre 1528–1540* (Berlin, 1932), pp. 17–20.

[66] Santa Cruz, *Crónica*, II, 454; cf. Brandi, *Emperor*, pp. 272–3.

is one shining exception, a brilliant depiction of emperor and chancellor confronting each other in a discussion that turns upon the emperor's decision to go to Italy. Gattinara prepares his reader for this decisive encounter by emphasizing how, despite his bed-ridden condition, his own will to promote once more the Italian venture revived at the news received in Madrid during July and August: the French threat to Naples and indeed to all of southern and central Italy had collapsed. His enthusiasm is infectious and the emperor begins to make the necessary preparations for the expedition to Italy. But these preparations are committed to the hands of those who oppose the venture with the result that they languish in their initial stage. Sick at heart as well as physically ailing, the bed-ridden chancellor is visited in his quarters at Toledo by the emperor. The latter imparts his hope that the fleet might leave in January. Smiling wryly, the chancellor retorts that he did not believe it. Then seizing the opportunity before the emperor can recover from his confusion, he pressed his own disbelief in the whole venture by reviewing the lack of preparation, the years of lost opportunities, the wasted advantages, the present dangers and weaknesses. No, there would be no fleet until the spring, if then. Thus by playing devil's advocate, the chancellor swept the ground from beneath his opponents and firing the will of the emperor, purged him at least for the moment of all doubts and hesitations. The chancellor would have us believe, and Brandi implicitly follows him, that it is this encounter which steeled the emperor and precipitated the fateful decision announced, according to Santa Cruz, at Madrid on 16 September. But this is impossible, for according to his own statement preparations for the expedition had already begun, if only in a dilatory fashion before the encounter occurred. Furthermore, Charles did not reach Toledo, the locus of the encounter, until 15 October – one month after the announcement in council – there to remain until 8 March 1529.[67] Sometime in early November would be a more likely date for the event. Consequently the Toledo encounter did not inspire the imperial decision to cross to Italy. On the other hand, perhaps more significantly, it stimulated, redirected and galvanized the emperor to act upon his own decision.[68] And repeated stimuli seemed to be in order during the winter and spring months. The English ambassadors reporting to Wolsey on 17 December observed that preparation for the Italian journey had begun to slacken and the emperor had been colder in his purpose since the tenth, though men were still being levied. As reason for this relaxation of effort Ghinucci and Lee opined that the chancellor had left court to go on a pilgrimage and without him nothing

---

[67] Vandenesse, *Journal*, pp. 44–5.
[68] On the encounter between Charles and Gattinara see Bornate, 'Vita', pp. 362–7; cf. Brandi, *Emperor*, p. 273.

The last years of the chancellorship

was done.[69] Later we learn that Charles left Toledo, 8 March, more resolute to go to Italy. By the time he reached Barcelona in mid-May Charles had shed all his former irresolution.[70] Despite his rapidly failing health, the old chancellor in his zeal seemed to sweep during these winter and spring months of 1528/9 a dilatory emperor, his obstructive counsellors and a protesting Spain toward Italy.

Since Gattinara's return to Spain, his relationship to the emperor reflected an apparent change. Never close, affectionate or warm, always respectful, that relationship had come to mellow and attain a certain tense stability in the course of the subsequent months. When in the opinion of the Polish ambassador, Dantiscus, Gattinara appeared to be appreciably growing in the affections and attentions of Charles, who seemed increasingly to confer with him, the chancellor corrected his close friend with a more detached view: that the emperor visited him on several occasions and consulted with him on many matters, he admitted, but on the other hand his favor was essentially superficial and that he, Gattinara, inwardly sensed no real improvement and at such a point in his own affairs he was unable to have a resolution.[71] Although he spoke while Lalemand was still in full career, one may wonder whether his relation to the emperor ever progressed beyond this point of what must be deemed a modest improvement.

In the period from Gattinara's first departure for Italy in March 1527 and the final departure of July 1529, the imperial chancellery as the centralizing and directing institution of the Habsburg *monarchia* virtually disappears from sight. Only in the months immediately preceding the emperor's passage to Italy is there evidence for brief flurries of activity that can be associated with the chancellery. Following upon the assent of the cortes at Monzón to have Valencia provide 100,000 pounds (*libras*) as its quota, Charles dispatched no less than thirty letters through the Aragonese chancellery, dated 7 April 1529, to recalcitrant, reluctant or delinquent groups and persons asking each to hasten his contribution. These were particularly directed to the Valencian military estate from which he expected 50,000 of the 100,000 pounds.[72] Among the final acts before taking leave of Spain the emperor on 12 July 1529 issued a mandate directed to those imperial estates protesting the recent Speyer recess with its nullification of the 1526 recess which had in effect permitted religious innovations to occur. The emperor called upon this now declared Protestant faction to adhere to the will of the majority in its decision to abrogate the Speyer recess of 1526. The application of the new technology of printing to the business

[69] *Letters and Papers*, 4/2, no. 5039.
[70] *Cal. SP Spain*, IV/1, 33–6; Rodríguez Villa, 'Cortas de Salinas', *44*, 216.
[71] 'Caesar eum aliquoties visitaverit et cum eo de multis rebus consultaverit; sed tamen gratia haec esset extrinseca et quod nihilominus intus nullum sentiret profectum et quod hucusque in rebus suis non posset finem.' *AT*, x, 397–8, cf. 46.   [72] ACA (Secretorum), 3950, fols. vi–xxii.

of the chancellery is especially noteworthy in this instance: 3000 copies of the Barcelona mandate were printed and signed by the emperor.[73] And for parting from his Spanish peoples, Charles, as with the earlier occasion in the spring of 1520, had recourse again to both chancellery and press to bid his subjects farewell. The address which was published in both Latin and German imparts a strong sense of imperial *providentia*: would that he might remain with his people without ignominy, but necessity calls and by his labors and vigils he will provide for their peace as well as for the welfare of the Christian commonwealth. He asserts three reasons – somewhat different from those of the previous year – which compel his trip to Italy: zeal for attending to the needs of religion; the conservation of his honor; the effecting of peace among Christian princes. The widespread devastation demands remedial action. Here it would seem that it is an Italian presence who is responsible for dwelling upon the destruction of Italy: her towns, cities and countryside must be restored and Rome which has been ravaged by his soldiers, although he absent and ignorant, must be succoured. Charles ends by exhorting his Spaniards neither to fear nor grieve, for he will most diligently provide and care that they may be able to remain in perpetual peace and their empire may be extended far and wide.[74]

Nevertheless, the continuing activity of Francisco de los Cobos in the emerging Castilian secretariat, the whole impact of Lalemand's tenure of office and the secretary's fall, and the six months' absence of the chancellor himself could only accelerate those forces eroding this medieval institution in its present expanded state. For the dismantlement of the imperial chancellery as the potential bureaucratic center of the Habsburg monarchy did not wait upon Gattinara's death. Rather, during the last years of his life it completed a transformation that led to the clear emergence of two secretariats: one of Castile and the Mediterranean lands under Cobos; the other constituting the Franco-Burgundian lands guided by the rising star of Granvelle. As he had increasingly leaned on the state secretary, Lalemand, so now he turned to his successor Nicholas Perrenot, Lord of Granvelle. Perrenot had been trained by Gattinara since his beginnings at Dole in Franche-Comté.[75] Most recently he had acquitted himself well as the imperial envoy to Francis I. Like Lalemand and several other Habsburg servants who derived from or had association with the free county of

---

[73] *Deutsche Reichstagsakten*, VIII, 136, 694–6.

[74] Münchner Universitätsbibliothek, Hist. 591/74, [no.] 17, for the German version see [no.] 5. Palau y Dulcet (in *Manual*) indicates no publication in Spanish.

[75] Fritz Walser, 'Die Überlieferung der Akten der kastilish-spanischen Zentralbehörden unter Karl V: Geschichte und allgemeine Grundzüge', *Berichte und Studien zur Geschichte Karls V*, VIII, *Nachrichten von der Gesellschaft der Wissenschaften zu Göttingen*, Philologisch-Historische Klasse (1933), pp. 94–102, 107–110. For the relations and parallels between the elder Granvelle and Gattinara see M. Van Durme, *El Cardinal Granvela 1517–1586. Imperio y revolución bajo Carlos V y Felipe II* (Barcelona, 1957), pp. 19, 29, 36, 101–3, 109.

The last years of the chancellorship

Burgundy, he was not bound by any proto-national or territorial links and in his unique devotion to the emperor was capable of a policy European in scope. The burden of government began to devolve increasingly upon Perrenot, who had imbibed some of the perspectives of Gattinara – and upon Cobos. By being able to promote Lalemand's successor, Gattinara gave a decisive impulse to the formation of the state secretariat and the development of the cabinet regime. For although the former *primero secretario* had no direct successor, Perrenin assuming the actual chancellery functions of drafting and expediting documents, Perrenot assimilated Lalemand's other roles, particularly that of sitting in the Council of State; by June of 1529 he was firmly established. Lacking a knowledge of Spanish and of Spanish matters, Granvelle could all the more easily dismiss to the purview of Cobos what it had been impossible for the Grand Chancellor to forsake. Indeed, formalization of this split, which had been maturing during the entire chancellorship of Gattinara, became evident with the naming of Cobos on 24 October 1529 as secretary of state. The few remaining months left to Gattinara merely disguised a reorganization already achieved that became apparent only after his death.[76]

The last year of his life witnessed a close collaboration between Gattinara and Granvelle. Since the fall of Lalemand and the reduction of the French hold upon Italy, Gattinara, assured of the emperor's support, was able to gather in the fruits of his policy. The treaties of Barcelona with the pope, Bologna with Milan, Venice and Ferrara, and the renewal of the Italian league were his work, but only with the masterful aid of Perrenot.[77] Again it was the dying chancellor who introduced the young aspiring secretary to negotiating the perilous shoals of English and German affairs. In April 1529 the opening moves of Henry VIII's divorce had suddenly come to focus upon the validity of the papal brief of Julius II that had served as the dispensation for the fateful marriage with Catherine of Aragon. In the chancellor's absence Granvelle presided over the act of the exhibition of the dispensation brief on 3 April.[78] On the thirteenth of that month Granvelle met with the English ambassadors Ghinucci and Lee and their notaries in the apartments of the chancellor to let them examine and copy the crucial document. Although by the end of the month Gattinara was being represented back in England as responsible for stiffening Charles' attitude toward the divorce, there would be little reason to rejoice soon after at the news of his death, for Granvelle had the continuing interests of the emperor well in hand.[79]

[76] Rodríguez Villa, 'Cartas de Salinas', *44*, 222; Walser, *Zentralbehörden*, pp. 260–1.
[77] Walser, *Zentralbehörden*, p. 263.
[78] *Cal. SP Spain*, iii/2, 967, cf. 805–7.
[79] *Letters and Papers*, 4/3, nos. 5423, 5471, 5487, 5489, 6158, 6355, 6496.

The emperor and his chancellor

Likewise, Granvelle attended Gattinara in the first encounter of the imperial court with the Protestants.[80] Given Gattinara's conciliatory attitude and his developing policy of accommodation with the Protestants, his succumbing to illness and the shifting of responsibility for the negotiations to Granvelle probably had an adverse effect upon the outcome, thus helping to prejudice future negotiations with the Protestants. From the first moments of the encounter on 9 September 1529 at Piacenza matters went awry, suspicion developed and the Protestant embassy was placed under temporary house arrest. The difficulty was two-fold: first, in the course of the negotiations the chancellery secretary Alexander Schweis, upon whom fell increasing responsibility as the court approached Germany, misconstrued one of the two major documents of the embassy, namely the 'Appeal' for a free Christian council, as intending an appeal beyond the express imperial mandate of 12 July; secondly, the Landgrave of Hesse had indiscreetly sent to the emperor a book by Francis Lambert, which appeared subversive to episcopal authority and was the reason for some caustic remarks directed by Nassau and Schweis against the landgrave as well as for the protracted house arrest of the Nürnberg delegate. The mishandling of the negotiations with the Protestants augured ill for later relations of the emperor with the Reich.[81]

Once in Italy, Charles allowed his actions to be dictated by a most scrupulous adherence to the terms of the treaty of Barcelona with the pope. He sought thereby to reassure Clement as well as the princes and powers of the peninsula in order to achieve the pacification of Italy. Consequently, the imperialists were consciously on their best behaviour and from the Prince of Orange besieging Florence down to the least Spaniard in Rome Charles made huge efforts to prevent any bad incidents that might shatter the pacification which he saw within his grasp.[82] At the very time when his chancellor was slipping from this world, Charles looked to him as the most authoritative mind at court on Italian affairs and leaned heavily upon him for a myriad of problems that ran from the tricky negotiations with

[80] For the best modern account of the Protestant embassy to Piacenza see Wolfgang Steglich, 'Die Stellung der evangelischen Reichsstände und Reichsstädte zu Karl V. zwischen Protestation und Konfession 1529/30', *Archiv für Reformationsgeschichte*, 62 (1971), 161–92, esp. pp. 161–76. It should be noted that Steglich is not concerned with the general supervision afforded by Granvelle and Nassau but focusses upon the immediate agency of Alexander Schweis. For a convenient assemblage of the relevant documents see J. G. Walch, ed., *Dr Martin Luthers Sämmtliche Schriften* (St Louis, Mo., 1881–1910), XVI, 452–518.

[81] *Deutsche Reichstagsakten*, VIII/1, 141–5, 163–77 on the negotiations and their breakdown, 336–48 on the arrest of the embassy, 253, 275, 325 *et passim* on reactions throughout the Reich. Cf. also Joannes Sleidanus, *De statu religionis et republicae Carolo Quinto Caesare commentarii* (Kaufburen, 1785), pp. 384–90.

[82] Cf. *Cal. SP Spain*, IV/1, 484–5, 568–9, 585.

The last years of the chancellorship

Milan to apparently minor legal technicalities. On 5 September 1529 Charles, pressed by the pope and the College of Cardinals to take an oath concerning the cities of Parma and Piacenza, sought to discover from his chancellor whether such an act might prejudice the rights of the Holy Empire. When repeated couriers were unable to reach Gattinara, the emperor delegated the matter to Granvelle to resolve in consultation with the legates.[83] Indeed Charles was now working closely with Granvelle, checking occasionally with the chancellor to keep him informed.[84] By this time, 9 September, Gattinara was again ill. But whatever energies he could muster, as they ebbed away in these last months, the seriously ailing statesman directed towards the advancement of the house of Habsburg. In early October he was seeking to resolve difficulties with the estates of Flanders so that money might be obtained to prosecute war against the Turk.[85] At Cremona on 25 October accompanied by the faithful Valdés Gattinara was well received by Duke Francesco Sforza and shortly after urged the emperor to drop all charges against him.[86] And as the coronation loomed more urgently, a host of new problems presented themselves: moneys obtained from Naples should first be directed to the forthcoming election of Charles' brother Ferdinand as King of the Romans and only thereafter to the 'Hungarian war';[87] no, the decree of imperial election is not among the papers of the chancellery, for it was exhibited at Aachen and does not need to be exhibited now; no, there is no need to take the crown of Lombardy, for it is royal not imperial, the ceremonial expressly says that it is not necessary, and Frederick Barbarossa never took it. Having arrived at Bologna 30 October he has an audience with the pope, who affably offers him apartments near to his own in the palace, but Gattinara, recently elevated to the cardinalate, declines to accept without permission from the emperor; with the Turks in retreat and Germany no longer in danger, he now recommends that the coronation occur at Rome where it could be performed with greater solemnity and in keeping with the glory and

[83] *Cal. SP Spain*, IV/1, 197–8.
[84] Cf. *ibid.*, 188 on the Florentine embassy at Savona. In his 'Vita Andreae Doriae', *Opera Omnia* (Milan, 1733), III, 1116–1272, Carolus Sigonius includes valuable documents on the negotiations between Charles and Genoa in which it appears that Gattinara was not only absent from the Barcelona agreement of 10–11 August 1528, but also from the pact of 10 March 1530, cf. pp. 1238–45.
[85] *Cal. SP Spain*, IV/1, 265–6.
[86] *Ibid.*, 309.
[87] *Ibid.*, 187. This brief consulta has the style and authoritative ring of the chancellor, but Pascual de Gayangos is wrong in claiming that it is written by the hand of 'Gattinara'. Nor does it appear to derive from that of his cousin, Juan Bartolomé Gattinara. The chancellor may well have dictated it, as his left arm at this time was painfully affected by the gout. (Felix Contelorius, *Pars altera elenchi S.R.E. cardinalium ab anno 1430 ad annum 1549*...(Rome, 1659), p. 145.) The consulta is included here to suggest the range of problems preoccupying the counsels of the emperor and his chancellor.

137

reputation of the emperor who might afterwards visit his kingdom of Naples; more time would thus be granted to prepare the attack on the Turk.[88]

But the coronation took place at Bologna, Charles having determined that the problems of Germany must take precedence over those of Naples. As at Aachen a decade before, illness prevented from attending that man who had contributed more than any other to the realization of this proud moment. As the court made its way northward towards a rendezvous with King Ferdinand at Innsbrück, Gattinara became dangerously ill in early April at Mantua and was not expected to live.[89] Over the course of the past year repeated illness had compelled his gradual removal from affairs. Although to the end he never relaxed his sense of service to the emperor and the dynasty, his work was done: the emperor had been crowned, Italy pacified, a favorable peace with France achieved. More important still the chancellor's reluctant pupil had attained to his true political maturity as the Emperor Charles V. None can read that long dispatch to his brother Ferdinand, written out in his own hand from Bologna, 11 January 1530, and sent with the utmost secrecy, without being impressed by the maturity of the writer and how despite himself he had absorbed much of the comprehensive view, the careful weighing of alternatives, the sense of multiple obligations, the devotion to duty that had been so much a part of Gattinara's educative role as chief counsellor.[90] Ultimately the consultas had been read; ultimately the constant attendance of the passionately devoted Habsburg servant had not been entirely in vain.

Death came to the chancellor at Innsbrück during the rendezvous of the Habsburg brothers. So gradual and smooth had been the transition of effective power from Gattinara to Granvelle and the longer, more deep-seated process of dismantling the chancellery for the aggrandizement of the two secretariats, that except for the Protestants, who believed to see in Gattinara a moderate, even receptive mind, his death barely produced a ripple in the onrushing political world.[91] Toward the end of his career and

[88] *Cal. SP Spain*, IV/1, 319–21. On the uncertainty that prevailed as late as 31 Dec. 1529 concerning Bologna or Rome as the site for the coronation, see Dantiscus to the King of Poland and to his vice-chancellor Petrus Tomicki, *AT*, XI, 332, 330.
[89] *Cal. SP Spain*, IV/1, 494–5.
[90] *Ibid.*, 396–409; cf. Brandi, *Emperor*, 283–6. On the posthumous evidence for Gattinara's general influence upon the political thinking of Charles see also the interesting observations of Karl Brandi, 'Die politische Korrespondenz Karls V. Alte und neue Editionspläne. Die politische Testamente Karls V', Berichte und Studien zur Geschichte Karls V, *Nachrichten von der Gesellschaft der Wissenschaften zu Göttingen*, Philosophisch-Historische Klasse (Berlin, 1930), pp. 270–9. Brandi also notes in his 'Eigenhändige Aufzeichnungen', pp. 247–8, that Charles, in writing to his brother on 27 July 1526, simply copied into his letter that section of Gattinara's great memorandum of the previous week wherein he presents reasons for the emperor's going to Italy.
[91] Cf. Baumgarten, *Geschichte*, III, 40. On Luther's reaction to Gattinara's imminent death see *D. Martin Luthers Briefwechsel* (Weimar, 1934) V, 339; on his friend Justus Jonas see Gustav

The last years of the chancellorship

certainly after the trip to Italy in 1527 the chancellor's emotional and intellectual life had come to focus on Erasmus and the Erasmian and it was among the humanistically inclined kindred spirits of the chancellery – Valdés, Maximilian Transylvanus, Waldkirch and diplomatic associates such as Dantiscus and Cornelius de Schepper – that he would be profoundly mourned and memorialized.[92] As for the emperor's reaction there is only silence. In a self-pitying, bitter letter to Dantiscus ten years later, De Schepper, bemoaning the times, would recall Gattinara's services and his fate. He concludes that they are horses, esteemed while young and strong but to be dumped aside when weak and old.[93] The Habsburgs tended to be hard on their servants and neglectful of rewarding their services. Gattinara had once warned Lalemand of the dangers incurred by such a practice.[94] Yet it is possible that Charles delayed his departure from Innsbrück for Augsburg until his chancellor had died. For weeks anxiously awaited at the diet, the Habsburg brothers seemed to confer endlessly. Was it then only coincidence that Gattinara, after a protracted, final illness, should expire on 5 June and the emperor set forth to the Augsburg diet on the following day?[95]

Kawerau, ed., *Der Briefwechsel des Justus Jonas* (Halle, 1884), I, 151, 157, 159, 161; on Melanchthon's elaborate response and interesting distortion see Adolf Hasenclever, 'Kritische Bemerkungen zu Melanchthons "Oratio de congressu Bononiensi..."', *Zeitschrift für Kirchengeschichte, 29* (1908), 154–73. The persistence of Gattinara's image in Protestant historiography and the Melanchthonian tradition, as conciliatory toward Wittenberg, and defiant toward Clement VII at Bologna, would require a separate study leading through Chrytaeus and Coelestinus to Goldast and Lünig, culminating in Hane's 'Memoria'.

[92] See the collection of humanist epitaphs to Gattinara in Hilarius Bartel, ed., *Epitaphia; epigrammata et elegiae aliquot illustrium virorum in funere Mercurini cardinalis, marchionis Gattinariae, caesaris Caroli Quinti augusti supremi cancellarii* (Antwerp, Joannes Grapheus, 1531); cf. Vocht, *Dantiscus*, pp. 15–17.

[93] Vocht, *Dantiscus*, p. 329.

[94] HHSA (Belgien), PA 18 (alt 21)/2, fol. 257 published by Vander Linden, 'Articles', pp. 277–9. Cf. also Augustin Redondo, *Antonio de Guevara (1480?–1545) et l'Espagne de son temps* (Geneva, 1976), p. 601, fn. 113.

[95] On the time of Gattinara's death and Charles' departure see Alphonsus Ciaconius, *Vitae et res gestae pontificum Romanorum et S.R.E. cardinalium ab initio nascentis Ecclesiae usque ad Clementem IX. P.O.M.* (Rome, 1677), III, 505, who gives 5 June as it appears on the chancellor's tombstone; cf. Vandenesse, *Journal*, p. 47; on the anxious waiting for the emperor's arrival at Augsburg see *D. Martin Luthers Briefwechsel*, v, 289–95 and esp. 346, 351.

Epilogue

As Grand Chancellor for all the lands of the emperor Gattinara had sought
to create an imperial regime of supra-national character and dimensions for
the total empire of Charles. The conception was monarchical in the sense
of universal and not locally Castilian. Yet effective political power resided
for Charles in Castile and even during the twelve years' chancellorship,
Castile came to localize Gattinara's universal conception while absorbing
something of his imperial vision. Narrowly conceived and from a purely
administrative point of view this territorializing, if not nationalizing, of an
imperial-universal conception can be measured in terms of two institutions –
the imperial court chancellery and the Council of State. Their institutional
authority for the whole Habsburg world empire remained unattained at
Gattinara's death, and it has been said with justification that both the
chancellery and the Council of State became stuck each in its beginnings,
manifesting at best a political rather than a legal and institutional
character.[1] Yet judged more narrowly from the perspective of administrative
minutiae Gattinara's chancellorship was more the end of a long medieval
development than an abortive beginning. In contradistinction to the French
chancellorship which early emerged and persisted as a preeminently judicial
office, its Burgundian counterpart developed political as well as political–
administrative characteristics which were pushed beyond the limits of the
chancellery to the breaking point during the period of Gattinara.[2] Moreover,
the effort to impose the local institution of the Burgundian chancellery and
chancellorship upon a medley of lands in varying stages of administrative
development had the effect of accelerating centrifugal forces within the
chancellery and of hastening its own demise. In the Iberian peninsula that
venerable institution encountered the recent growth of state secretaries
which was a development common to all European governments and

[1] Walser, *Zentralbehörden*, pp. 270–1.
[2] On the preeminently judicial character of the French chancellery see *Encyclopédie Méthodique*,
Jurisprudence (Paris, Liége, 1783), II, 469–70 and François Duchesne, *Histoire des chanceliers et
gardes des sceaux de France* (Paris, 1680), 'Discours'. Of course it would be foolhardy to press
anything like clear distinctions between the political and the judicial and between the judicial and
the administrative in a pre-Montesquieu age.

Epilogue

perhaps best evinced in the papal chancellery itself.[3] Here the rapid increase in the volume of political correspondence that greeted the beginning of the sixteenth century promoted the need for greater differentiation and specialization. Indeed Gattinara, responding creatively to this pressure, aided and abetted this development by his overhaul of the Spanish central administration in the period 1522–6 proliferating functional as well as territorial councils with their accompanying secretaries. He thus unwittingly affirmed that already strong tradition of Castilian-Aragonese secretaries which challenged the continuity of the medieval chancellery as the bureaucratic center of government. In principle, his reform revealed the modern idea of ministries in rational separation and the grouping of individual administrative areas.[4] Gattinara emerges at once as the last medieval chancellor and the first modern bureaucrat. Judged by any standard, he was an administrative genius of the first order.

The personal element also served to accelerate the deterioration of the chancellery during the twenties. Gattinara's severe, exacting character which placed heavy demands upon equals, inferiors and above all himself extended also to the emperor who from the beginning reacted ambivalently to this continuous pressure.[5] On the one hand he sought to distance himself as much as possible from its source; on the other he happened in the process of struggling to attain his own freedom of mind and action to have absorbed inadvertently a fair amount of its content. Gattinara's trip to Italy probably had the desired effect of making the emperor realize how much he needed his chancellor.[6] Only in the final eighteen months, however, did chancellor and emperor reach a more agreeable relationship promoted by the needs of the Italian expedition and the apparent imminence of Gattinara's end.

Gattinara's relative success in monopolizing the business of Habsburg government was less institutional than personal. All contemporaries who met him attested to his monstrous productivity.[7] Yet, as we have attempted to show, his monopoly was more apparent than real. In the first place Cobos, by building up the Castilian secretariat, sheared off a large amount of the paper work. Secondly, in the area of foreign affairs Charles himself took an active hand in Netherlandish matters, while Lalemand directly managed the correspondence with England as well as the Netherlands. In the end, however, Gattinara's expertise in Italian affairs would prove crucial.

---

[3] On the emergence of the state secretariat from papal chancellery and camera in response to the need for expediting political briefs and on the very personal and private relationship between the pope and his *secretarii domestici* see Andreas Kraus, 'Die Sekretäre Pius' II ', *Römische Quartalschrift*, *53* (1958), 25–80; *idem*, 'Secretarius und Sekretariat', *Römische Quartalschrift*, *55* (1960), 43–84.
[4] On this particular point see Walser, *Zentralbehörden*, p. 271.
[5] On Gattinara's demanding nature see Valdés remarks in Vocht, *Dantiscus*, p. 38.
[6] Cf. M. Van Durme, 'À propos du quatrième centenaire de la mort de Nicolas Perrenot de Granvelle', *Bibliothèque d'Humanisme et Renaissance*, *13* (1951), 275.
[7] Baumgarten, *Geschichte*, III, 38–9.

The emperor and his chancellor

While introducing the qualities of a much needed professionalism amidst the club of Habsburg chevaliers, Gattinara virtually alone of Charles' servants combined workman-like habits with a disciplined, far-ranging mind that responded warmly to the contemporary learning and was fired by an imperial vision. By combining a humanistic sensitivity with the professionalism of a lawyer, Granvelle proved in this respect to be a most worthy successor. For their parts, Cobos and Lalemand were mere clerks, incapable of any intellectual pretensions and distinguished only by their knowledge of the ramifying complexity of bureaucratic procedure. They and their ilk recommended themselves as obviously safer persons and the future would certainly justify their good sense. For the administrators, not the meek, would inherit the earth.

After 1530 there would exist independently beside one another a Spanish state secretariat, which links itself to the tradition of the Catholic kings, and a French cabinet secretariat, deriving from the Burgundian *Audience*, and having its links with the subordinate German imperial chancellery. Charles V did not need another Grand Chancellor; he had Granvelle and Cobos. After the didacticism and importunateness of his zealous chancellor, made all the more irksome by Gattinara usually being correct, Charles must have felt more at ease in association with these two secretaries of state so similar in their subtle, genial natures.[8] And yet the suppression of the grand chancellorship was more an expression of political judgment and practical administrative convenience than an act of personal distaste on Charles' part. The emperor's own style of rule by means of a 'cameral regime' and the insuperable problems of attempting to deal with his diverse lands through a single secretariat both argued for a division of labor. Furthermore, good medieval precedents, as evidenced by extended vacancies in the office of the chancellor during and after the reign of Philip Augustus, testify to the occasional need of a prince to remove that imposing official who exercised

---

[8] See *supra*, Chap. 6, fn. 75. On the office of state secretary in name and in fact see Walther, *Zentralbehörden*, pp. 163–5, who does not find the actual term used until 1531; and Walser, *Zentralbehörden*, pp. 244–6 *et passim*, who uses the term freely with reference to Lalemand's office after 1524. Although Walser justifiably attributes the institution of the state secretaryship to the memorandum of late 1523/early 1524, the term itself does not appear in the text. Cf. Brandi, 'Kabinettsakten', pp. 197–8. Lalemand seems not to have had a direct follower. Antoine Perrenin assumed the actual chancellery functions; he was to be called *premier secrétaire d'État*. Granvelle assumed the authority of that office. Cf. Walser, *Zentralbehörden*, p. 261. According to Van Durme, *Granvela*, p. 29, Granvelle was sometimes referred to simply as 'canciller'. Nevertheless the title and office of Grand Chancellor had been abolished. In vain did the Archbishop of Toledo, taking the occasion of Gattinara's death, apply to the emperor for the office of *chanciller mayor* which he claimed the Catholic kings had always had pertain to the primatial dignity. (RAH, Salazar (G), 23, fols. 196–196ᵛ). Escudero, *Secretarios*, I, 99 believes that the collaboration of Cobos and Granvelle poorly concealed a disequilibrium – Cobos being a Secretary of State, while Granvelle was more properly keeper of the seals.

Epilogue

such an accumulation of functions so close to the royal person.[9] Indeed, for the Papacy itself Boniface VIII had removed this constant threat by assimilating the chancellorship into the papal office and relegating its secretarial functions to a vice-chancellor who would later become the papal secretary of state.[10] Having attained political maturity by 1530 and the development of his own political style within a cameral regime, Charles, relying now upon his two secretaries, could politically as well as personally derive satisfaction from the extinction of that potentially dangerous office.

Illustrative of the triumph of the secretaries in 1530 was an event that occurred barely two weeks after the Grand Chancellor's death. The imperial ambassador at Rome complained to Charles, now at Augsburg, that they were lacking many of the necessary legal documents for their negotiations. At this point Cobos scrawled in the margin that he had among the papers of the chancellery the original of the papal brief so greatly desired by Henry VIII.[11] Thus had the secretary *par excellence* come to invade and occupy the domain of his great rival.

It was only just that the last word should come from Alfonso de Valdés, who, as if to vindicate his master, denounced for all time in a composite figure of Lalemand and Cobos the predatory, arrogant, avaricious secretary of the new age.[12]

---

[9] On this last point see Tout, *Administrative History*, I, 15, 285–6.
[10] Pietro Giannone, *Istoria civile del regno di Napoli*, ed. Antonio Marongiu (Milan, 1970), III, pp. 75–6.
[11] *Cal. SP Spain*, IV/1, 587–8.
[12] Valdés, *Diálogo*, pp. 104–9; cf. Keniston, *Cobos*, pp. 113–14.

Appendix I

The Summary by Philippe Hanneton, *audiencier* of the Burgundian chancellery, regarding the office of the Grand Chancellor (BRT (Misc.), fols. 683–86ᵛ)

(The following documents (Apps. I–IV) have been most conservatively transcribed with every effort to preserve the original spelling, punctuation and format. Only in one respect has there been editorial intrusion: for the sake of intelligibility all contractions and abbreviations, often numerous and sometimes obscure, have been silently expanded.)

Ung chancelier de bourgoingne a tousiours este fort exstime et auctorise | tellement quil a este tenu pour la seconde personne de la maison

Et comme tel a tenu et garde les seaulx du prince desquelz il a use a la despeshe et sigillature des lettres qui ont este ordonnees et commandees tant pour les affaires du prince et de ses pays | comme des parties qui en ont eu a besoigne

Ledit chancelier a este | et est chief de la justice | preside en tous consaulx tant secretz et privez que aultres | et en iceulx propose et mis en deliberacion toutes matieres qui ont este tractees es lesdits consaulx tant en la presence du prince comme en son absance | demande et recully les oppinions des assistens tant de courte que de longue robe | et icelles oyes et resumes a dit la sienne au prince quant il a este presente pour y conclure | et en son absance luy mesmes a fait et pronunce les conclusions | ordonne et commande aux secretaires les expedicions et despesches tant de lettres closes et patentes memoires instrucions que aultres provisions selon lesdites conclusions |

Le chancelier | a tousiours acoustume de faire assembler [683ᵛ] les conseaulx devers le prince et aillieurs mis en termes les matieres qui se devoient traicter | et se a en la congnoissance de tous affaires tant de justice comme de guerre et de finance et mesmement decelles dimportance tellement que riens ne sest acousteume de traicter et despescher son sceu |

Quant le chancelier se trouve a malines | le secl du grand conseil ordonne pour le fait de la justice audit lieu doit cesser et sont tenuz les conselliers dudit grand conseil aller a la maison ou au logiz du chancelier pour y besoingner a la despeche des affaires qui leur surviennent et se tractent devers eulx en la presence dicelluy chancelier ou en son absance ou il les peut faire demourer au palays comme pour y besoingner comme dessus si bon luy sambler.

Philippe Hanneton's Summary

Le chancelier peut faire appeller et assembler les maistres des requestes et aultres devers luy a son logis ou ayllieurs toutes et quantesfoiz quil luy plaist | leur communiquer les matieres qui surviennent despecher les requestes Et affaires des parties et aultres ordonner et commander lespedicion des lettres et provisions qui se concluent comme si elles se concluoient devers le prince.

Le chancelier par ladvis du conseil peult faire toutes [684] manieres de constitucions statuz ordonnances restrincions, reformacions et moderacions quil treuve servir au bien du prince utilete et commodite de la chose publicque toutes et quantesfoiz que bon luy semble et que le cas le requiert

Le chancelier est acoustume de secller ordinairement deux foiz la sepmaine | Assavoir le mecredi et le samedi avant le disner et est tenu laudiancier luy faire porter et presenter toutes les lettres et mandemens qui se doivent secller et apres quelles sont seclles et que le secl est recloz les raporter a son logiz pour avec le contreroluer tauxer et arbitrer le droit et emolumens des seaulx des lettres qui se secllent et se aulcunes lettres se secllent hors desdits jours ordinaires ledit chancelier les doit envoyr audit audiancier ou a son commis pour y garder le droit du roy sans les delivrer aux parties ne aultres que audit audiancier ou sondit commis

Quant le chancelier est assiz pour visiter les lettres qui se doivent secller et que le secl est ouvert nul ne peut parler a luy sil ne lappelle a payne de payer lipocras et est tenu laudiancier ou son commis ou le chaufecire faire la chalange recouverer ledit ipocras Et en respondre au chancellier

[684ᵛ] Si les secretaires ou leurs clercs faillent au tiltre ou en la date des lettres quilz despechent Ilz les doivent amender dune couple de chapons a chascune foiz qui la faulte se trouve et est tenu ledit audiancier et son commis ou le chaufecire les recroiuier et delivrer comme dessus

Les secretaires sont tenuz de faire les despesches des lettres et provisions qui leur sont commandees selon que par ledit chancelier leur est ordonne et commande et non aultrement

Et fault noter que toutes chartres de previleges et confirmacions diceulx remissions a volicions de cas capitaulx admortissemens anoblissemens errectionmens de baronnies contez principaultez legittimacions octroys de marchiez et franches foires rappeaulx de ban de cincquante ans et au dessus se doivent secller en laz de soye et cire verd

Item les octroz pour vendre rentes faire imposicions dassiz et maltotes et aultres concessions sembles pardons de cas criminelz qui ne sont capitaulx rappeaulx de ban de dix ans et au dessus jusques a cincquante exclusement saulvegardes pour eglises et aultres samples se seclent en double queue

Lettres de requeste maintenues complaintes en cas de nouvellete debitis relievemens recisions requestes [685] sim[p]les graces a plaidoyer par procuracion et toutes aultres provissions de justice et rappeaulx de ban au dessoubz de dix ans se secllent en simple queue

145

Appendix I

Fait encores a noter que les lettres de remission de cas criminelz et capitaulx et les rappeaulx de ban de cincquante ans et au dessus | ou il y a partie interessee et non satisfaicte doivent estre chargees damende civile et interviennent larbitraige du juge ordinaire du pays ou province ou quel le cas a este commis et le ban prononce et les lettres dadmortissemens a noblissemens et ligittimacions doivent estre charges de finance a la tauxacion et arbitraige des gens de comptes du province ou limpetrant desdites lettres est residant et demourant

Quant les secretaires despechent aucuns mandemens dimportance commandez par le prince ou par le chancelier en son conseil prive ilz doivent mectre et nominer en la signature les principaulx personnaiges dudit conseil qui ont este presents a ladite despesche et pour le chancelier doivent mectre | vous | sans aultrement le nominer et le coucher en son lieu qui est incontinent apres les cardinaulx grans prelatz et princes du sang saulcuns en y a [685ᵛ] Et doit ledit chancelier preceder tous les chivaliers de lordre et tous aultres et pour exemple en doit user en la maniere qui sensuyt Par le roy le cardinal de tortose les marquis de Brandeburg et darshot | vous | larchivesque de palermo les evesques de corduba et de Badajoz le gouverneur de Bresse les signeurs de saniscelles et de la chaulx et aultres [—]*

Quant lon apporte au chancelier aulcuns mandemens dimportance commandez par le prince en son absence pour secller et il trouve aucuns difficultz notables il les doit reverter sans les secler jusques a ce quil a adverti le prince des difficultz et luy remonstrer lincivilite ou incompatibilite desdits mandemens et si apres les remonstrances faictes le prince de sa puissance absolue ordonne lesdits mandemens estre seclles il le peut en faisant mectre pour la despeche par ung secretaire a la partie dextre de la queue diceulx mandemens sur le ply les motz <u>sigillata de expresso mandato regis</u> | avec signe dudit secretaire pour approbacion dicelle clause

[686] Le chancelier doit entretenir tous les officiers et serviteurs de la maison et aultres chascun en son droit auctorite preminence sans les laisser fouler et doit aussy faire observer et entretenir estroictement les ordonnances et restrinctions qui se sont tant sur lestat de hostel comme des finances et des monnaies et aultres et faire corriger et pugnir les transgresseurs dicelles sans port faveur et disimulacion a exemple de tous

Le chancelier | le premier chambellain | et le grand maistre dostel doivent faire leur serement es mains du prince les aultres chambellains sommeliers de corps escuiers et varletz de chambre forrires et aultres officiers servans en la chambre es mains dudit premier chambellain les conseilliers maistres des requestes secretaires huissiers et aultres supposiz du conseil es mains dudit chancelier les gentilz hommes de quatre estaz et officiers de la pantterie eschancconerie fruyterie sausserie es mains des maistres dostel et ceulx de lescuerie es mains du grand escuier les officiers de justice et de recepte doivent faire leur serement et bailler caucion es mains des gens des comptes devant les quelz ilz sont tenuz de compter de leurs exploix et intermises Assavoir ceulx de flandres artoiz haynnau namur lille

* MS. illegible.

146

douay orchiers et malines [686ᵛ] En la chambre des comptes a lille et ceulx de brabant luxembourg et oultremeuse en la chambre des comptes a bruxelles et ceulx de hollande zellande frise voirne brielle et pute en la chambre des comptes a la haye et doivent les retenues et comissions desdits officiers estre charges dudit serement et ladresser comme dessus

Appendix II

'The Doubts of [Alonso de] Soria', lieutenant protonotary, concerning Gattinara's proposals for reforming the Aragonese chancellery (extract from BRT (Misc.), fols. 385–87ᵛ)

[385] Enel articulo que habla delos secretarios ha de advertir v.s. que la negociacion de gracia tiene mas necessidad de ser libre que otra ninguna porque la de justicia provesse se por todo el consejo de manera que puede hazer poco bien nj mal el secretario alas partes enella | lo que enla negociacion de gracia es porel contrario que muchas vezes siendo el secretario señor dela negociacion sin que otro secretario nj scrivano demandamiento pueda poner la mano enella estara en su mano hazer perder a uno un officio o una merced y hazer lo ganar a otro segun la buena o mala voluntad que tuviere y poresta via haura forma de tener tirannizada la negociacion y sojuzgar se los secretarios los officiales y otras personas delos Reynos tratando bien y mal aquien les pareciere que no estara en mano de nadie remediarlo | porque quien recibiere un agravio | o maltratamiento en una cosa de servicio sabiendo que para qualquier otra cosa que se le offrezca ha devenir de necessidad a sus manos no solamente no osora quexarse mas antes procurara de le granjear para le tener propicio en otra cosa | y assi convendria y muy mucho al servicio de su majestad y al beneficio publico de sus Reynos que la negociacion de gracia fuesse libre y se pudiesse despachar por qualquier secretario o scrivano de mandamiento conforme a las ordinaciones y pragmaticas de la Casa y cancelleria como se hazia en todo lo passado y finalmente en tiempo del Rey catholico | y no hazer a un secretario absoluto señor de una negociacion | . Que poner adelante que despachando se por muchas manos hay confusion en los negocios y que podria haver bariedad y contradiction de provisiones no puede militar esto | porque [385ᵛ] toda la negociacion viene a un registro y a un sello y esta a cargo delque tiene la administracion dellos de no despachar una cosa contra otra ahunque venga a su poder sino si se ha despachado una y viene otra contraria detenerla y consultar la | y specialmente enla Cancelleria de aragon el prothonotario y su lugarteniente tienen pena por ordinacion si despachan enel sello carta contra carta | y eneste articulo me parece señor que justamente puede dar se me credito y no pensar que me mueve passion por dos respectos | el uno porque v.s. sabe quan cudicioso voy tras negocios particulares | y el otro porque provihendo se lo que v.s. ordena por la pragmatica me viene tanbien mi parte dela ganancia que mas provecho me cabra enlos negocios de gracia demallorquas y cathaluña siendo solo que no acompañado | y quedo muy satisfecho de haver dicho lo que a loauco enello v.s. haga lo que fuere servido | pero quiero le dezir una cosa que demas del dano publico | con esta

ordinacion se echar a perder veynte dos officiales escrivanos demandamiento que hay muchos dellos muy hombres de bien habiles y que han muy bien servido.

Quanto a lo delos Registros y sellos hablare como parte para que v.s. se informe de quien fuere servido y como cabeca de justicia y naturalmente bueno y zelador del servicio de su majestad despues de bien informado proveha la cosa sin agravio ni injuria de tercero comolo accostumbra | Que ya sabe que como tal la repellio enla entradad de su officio en Caragoca con mucha gloria suya y vilipendio de los que havian feho (*sic*) el contrario | Para lo qual ha de saber v.s. que el officio de prothonotario fue instituhido por el rey don pedro desde el principio que se [386] instit ordeno la casa y cancelleria de aragon y se ha conservado enel mesmo exercicio que se le dio estonces fasta la felice succession de su majestad | que el Canciller sauvage como cudicioso lo altero como v.s. sabe | y estuvo alterado hasta que por v.s. fue restituydo que fue el primero acto que hizistes enlo de la Corona de aragon despues que jurastes por Canciller. Y su exercicio principal entre otras cosas | o de su lugarteniente que es officio creado antiguamente y que provehe su majestad y no el prothonotario es de tener en su poder y administrar los registros y sellos de la Cancelleria de aragon desta manera que haze registrar en los dichos Registros por los scrivanos de registro que le son enesto subordinados todos los despachos que vienen assi de justicia como de gracia | y despues de registrados el dicho prothonotario o su lugarteniente ha de comprobar los despachos originales conel Registro de palabra a palabra para dos effectos | el uno para ver si los despachos vienen bien y congruamente ordinados y scritos | y si trahen las clausulas ordinarias de stillo de Cancelleria | o otras exhorbitantes | y corregir y reformar los conforme al stillo no tocando enla sentencia | y dexar de despachar los que truxeren clausulas insolitas fasta consultarlo | y el otro para que enel registro queden registrados correctamente | y despues desto ha de tassar y recibir el drecho del sello dellos conforme a la tassa que esta ordenada | del qual drecho ha de pagar y paga las quitaciones ordinarias que estan assentadas sobre el | y assi da Cuenta dello enel officio de mastre rational | el qual | orden se ha guardado y guarda continuamente sin dexar lo un solo punto | con mucho concierto | Lo que no se haze en ninguna de las otras Cancellerias | y deponerse por execucion lo que se contiene enla pragmatica se siguirian dos cosas | la una alterar y supprimir officios tan antiguos y tan ordenados y tan necessarios com estos en mucho prejuhizio y agravjo del prothonotario [386ᵛ] y mio que tenemos los officios de su majesdad para durantes nuestras vidas concedidos | que los tengamos en la mesma manera y conel mesmo exercicio y preeminencias que ellos se ordenaron y como los havemos tenido en la passado | y no sin harta nota de nuestras honras las quales esperamos y havemos siempre sperado de v.s. que ha de ayudar y acrecentar pues no havemos deservido sino servido | en quanto havemos podido y podemos a su majestad y enla particularidad de v.s. no le somos desservidores | que bien sabe que no tenemos aca otro señor | y la otra que seria preterir y anihilar todo el orden dela dicha Cancelleria porque v.s. puede ver que teniendo fuera de donde posamos el exercicio della no podriamos el uno ni el otro vacar el tiempo que fuesse necessario para administrar nuestro officio y assistir al despacho de la negociacion conel orden y concierto que se deve y lo hazemos en nuestra Casa y assi la cancelleria de aragon que esta bien ordenada y contodo concierto se reduziria a todo desorden y desconcierto como no dexan de estar lo las otras y pensando v.s. poner orden en todo seria desordenar lo todo que si enlos scrivanos de registro hay desordenes enlo delas cancillerias de napoles y sicilia como creo que lo hay | no merecemos el prothonotario nj yo el castigo delas culpas dellos nj para ordenar los seria justo nj servicio de su majestad desordenar y anihilar nuestros ófficios | yo los he señor muchas vezes reprehendido de no servir bien specialmente a la Cancelleria de napoles y escusan se que no es suya la culpa porque dizen que quando van una vez no hallan aquien tiene cargo delos Registros y otra vez no registran y que quando los hallan no tienen donde screvir y que de aqui se sigue el desorden de no yr ordenadamente a registrar sus horas como lo hazen a lo de aragon y de sacar fuera los registros algunas vezes para registrar | y puesto junctamente conesto lo de aragon [387] pareceme que se reduziria la cosa aque donde hay desorden en parte lo hoviesse en todo | que especialmente entiendo entre otras cosas que se despachen y sellan | algunas provisiones privilegios y otros despachos sin registrar con minutas que despues se pierden | y no se hallan registrados | lo que no se haria sino se pusiesse el sello fasta que fuesse probada la original conel registro | como se haze enlo de aragon | Suplico v.s. que le plega informarse de la qualidad e importancia del officio de prothonotario y si por ventura se mueve por alguna sinistra informacion que tenga de su persona | o dela mia en la administracion de nuestros officios | proveha que estemos al abla | y informe se delos del consejo y delos demas que fuere servido | si delo que tenemos a cargo hay algunas quexas de malos officiales | y si tales nos halla que nos castigue que es muy justo | que muy poca pena seria la del anichilar nos los officios y quitar nos la poca auctoridad que con ellos tenemos | pero si halla que los hazemos bien | y que en lo de nuestro cargo no hay desorden antes orden | haga v.s. su natural officio que es no abaxar sino honrrar y acrecentar a los que bien sirven | y quanto al desorden delos scrivanos bien lo puede v.s. mandar proveher como conviene | que ordenando alque tiene los registros de napoles que assista enel officio las horas para ello ordenadas de manyana y detarde puede apenar a los scrivanos que assistan las dichas haras los que fueren menester dellos | repartiendo se entre todas las Cancellerias so pena de perder el emolumento que ya ellos tienen sus ordinaciones como han de hazer por scrivanos y como lo hazen en lo de aragon que yo le prometo que haziendo se esto no falten | y si por ventura v.s. ha acordado de dar este orden por remediar algun otro desorden que haya en alguna otra Cancelleria que no sea [387ᵛ] la de aragon la qual seria la de sicilia | muy differente | señor desto otro | porque aquel exercicio no le haze cuyo e officio y puede su majestad mandar al que tiene el officio que veng[a] a servirle y sino lo hiziere como no lo hara | eneste caso pued[e] su majestad encomendar le aquien fuere servido | A v.s. suplico quanto puedo | que porquien es le plega jnformado de todo est[o] attender ano hazer agravio aquien no le merece | y me haga merced de me perdonar por lo que enesto jnsistiere | que ahunque demj mesma honra y officio quisiesse acontentarme | no lo podria hazer | por lo del prothonotario sin que me fuesse muy mal contado | alqual y aun soy cierto que v.s. no negara justicia y razon eneste caso | pues con nadie ha fecho jamas nj haze otra cosa | que es la principal cosa que illustra y da gloria a la persona de v.s.

Appendix III

Gattinara's 'Brussels Remonstrance' (extract from AGRB (PEA), 1471 (4), fols. 14^r–24^v)

[14] Sire. Combien que desia par fois reiterees. Jaye donne particulier advis a votre maieste | comme a mon souverain seigneur et maistre. des justes causes | qui me semble que jay de me douloir | concernantes autant et plus votre service | que mon honneur | sur lesquelles eusse bien desire | le remede | et que les choses eussent peu demeurer secretes | sans venir a notice | dautres que de votre maieste | . Neantmoins veant la dilacion | et faulte du remede | et que les causes du mal croissent tousiours | dont votre maieste nen est de riens mieulx servie | ains en vaillent pis voz affaires | comme vous declaireray cy apres dont sen pourroient ensuyr inconveniens irreparables | les quelx ceulx qui nentendent les causes | et ne scavent la racine dautre mal procede | les pourroient attribuer | a ma culpe | a cause de loffice que jay | pensans que ja ne me fusse acquicte a mon devoir | a vous en faire les remonstrances necessaires. Pour ces causes et a fin que lon ne men puist cy apres charger vous ay supplie davoir ceste audience | en presence de messieurs yci assemblez | pour estre leurs personnes telles que ayment votre bien et honneur et de voz bon serviteurs | desquelx votre maieste meritoirement se doit confier plus que de nulz autres | Comme ceulx avec lesquelx avez eu plus de familiarite | dez de votre tendre eaige jusques a present | Et ausquelx sont ordinairement communiquez tous les gros affaires de votre estat me semblant convenable que eulx mesmes entendent en votre presence les raisons de mes doleances Et les devoirs esquelx je me suis mis pour votre service | Et pour evicter culpe | de sorte que les choses bien entendues ung chascun puist congoistre ma descharge et me tenir et reputer pour tel et si entre serviteur | comme je lay tousiours este | et pense estre non deviant de droit chemin de loyaulte | et integrite | . Et pource Sire que comme savez je suis assez mal arengueur | desirant estre mieulx entendu | et qui conste cy apres dece que diray. sans que lon puist alterer ou mal interpreter mes parolles | jay bien voulu mectre le tout par escript | Et feray premiers aucunes premisses que ne seront dehors de propos. Et vous pourront servir cy apres | en les bien conseilerant | .

Sire les grans roys et princes comme vous estes | pource quelque se peuvent trouver presents a toutes les choses qui se font en leurs royaulmes et seigneuries ny veoir et congoistre tous les services que lon leur fait ont neccessairement de pourveoir aux affaires [14^v] et disposer les graces et mercedes selon les relations que leur font ceulx qui sont ordonnez a cest effect | Et pource que telles provisions de grace

151

| et mercede | se doivent faire conforme a la justice distributive | quest donner a ung chascun selon ses merites seroit mestier que avant que pourveoir ny dispenser les graces ilz fussent bien advertez et informez a la verite de trois choses | La premiere de ce quilz donnent. La second des personnes ausquelx lon donne. La tierce des causes pour lesquelles se donne | Et a faire ceste relacion et informacion ne se doyvent a pluesier personnes apassionnees ny partiales | qui pour leurs interestz veullent preferer leurs parens et amys | ou ceulx dont ilz pensent avoir prouffit | ou dont ilz pensent avoir faveur ayde et assistence | a soubstenir leurs passions | mais se doivent a ce choisir | et deputer personnes indifferentes | et alienees de toute partialite | qui se puissent informer tant de lune parcialite que de lautre | des merites dung chascun | et de la valeur et qualite de ce que sera a donner | de sorte que les relations puissent estre veritables et que les roys et princes puissent clerement savoir ce que lon donne | a cuy se donne et pourquelle cause | Et ce pour non offender ladite justice distributive donnant a ung plus quil na merite et servy. Et laissant de donner a autre qui aura bien merite et servy | ou baillant a ung seul | ce que pourroit satisfer a plusieurs qui eussent bien servy. ou faisant la merite a personne | que non seullement nauroit servy | mais auroit desservy | laissant sans provision cellui qui tousiours auroit este bon serviteur | Car en tous ces cas se offend ladite justice distributive | . Et si en la provision des offices et benefices que jusques icy a este faute par votre maieste | se a tenu le poix et mesure que ladite justice distributive requiert | Et si aucuns ont este pourveuz que votre maieste ne les congnoisset ny james vous avoient servy. laissant sans provision aucuns que vous estoient assez congneuz et vous avoient bien servy. Je la laisse penser a votre maieste qui le scet mieulx que nul autre | Et pource que des provisions que se font | sans garder les qualitez de ladite justice distributive sen ensuit que les roys et princes nen sont si aimez de leurs subiectz | et les bons serviteurs tumbent en desespoir. veant que a ceulx sont preferez ceulx qui ne sont congneuz | ny ont servy Pour ces causes sire ce minent au service de votre maieste que ayez [20] personnes comme dit est indifferentes | et non partiales ny interessees | pour se informer a la verite de ce que dist. Et vous en bailler linformacion clere | de sorte que puissez ensuyr ladite justice distributive | Et que voz subiectz et serviteurs puissent congnoistre | que par vraye informacion et pour leurs merites | ilz recoivent de votre main | et non par requeste ou persuasion dautruy. Les graces et mercedes que leur faictes | quest la chose plus propre pour evicter les inconveniens avantdits. Et vous faire aimes generalement de voz subiectz. Et puis sire que dieu vous a fait le plus grant prince du monde | et vous a donne tant de royaulmes et pays | et sera pour vous en donner encoires plus En consernant voz bons subiectz et serviteurs | Est raison que usez envers eulx de ladite justice distributive | Par laquelle pourrez attraire | et inciter plusieurs autres a vous bien et lealment servy. Et si en bien usant dicelle | et cognoissant la grace que dieu vous a donne | vous sauriez ayder a bien choisir les personnes qualiffiees comme dessus pour vous bien conseiller sans passion ou partialite | Et sans avoir respect a leurs interesez particuliers pourez bien dresser | et encheminer les grans affaires a present avez parles mains | et evicter les malices de aucuns | qui soubz espece de charite et monstrans estre fort affectez a votre service traverssent et divertissent les affaires sans que vous le sentez. Et si vous tenez les yeulx ouvers lesprit esveille | vous

cognoisiez que james naurez temps ny disposicion plus propre pour mectre paix
en toute la chretiente | et pour subiuguer les infideles Et extirper la secte de luther
| aller prendre voz coronnes | que lavez a present. Ayant le roy de france votre
prisonnier et loportunite pour passer en ytalie sans nul danger | pourveu que ce
soit tost | et que natendez les inconveniens qui de la dilacion pourroient soldre
mesmes pour les abbus que voz gens de guerre font | lesquelx certes sont
abhominables telz que turcz et infideles ne les feroient | et au lieu de vous nommer
Liberateur dytalie | ilz pourront dire estre entrez en la plus grande et excessive
tyrannie | qui onques fut | car ny les gottes ny les lombardes ny attyla lequel fut
nomme flagellum dei qui par long temps tyrannisarait Lytalie | james ne firent telles
cruaultez Et si bien tost ny remediez sen pourroit ensuyr tel desroy que vous
trouvieriez sans exercite | et sans riens tenir en ytalie | que ne seroit pour culpe
des ytaliens mais pour le mauvais ordre | et pour [15ᵛ] [20ᵛ] faulte de voz ministres
Parquoy est plus que necessaire le souldain remede de votre allee | sans lequel tout
se perdra | Mais sire je me doubte fort | que ce remede | ne vous soit indirectement
empesche Et le dangier est que pour non avoir les personnes de la qualite que jay
dit | Et pour non bien congnoistre le cueur dung chascun pourra estre que aucuns
de ceulx ausquelx plus vous fiez faisant semblant de desirer conseiller | et solliciter
votredite allee en ytalie | et se monstrant chauld de bien dresser le gouvernement
de voz royaulmes | pour iceulx bien regir durant votre absence | seront eulx mesmes
qui par indirect | et sans que vous en puissez appercevoir trouveront les
empeschemens | pour faire que soyez constrainct | de dylayer votredite allee pour
cest annee | et soubz umbre de paix. vous fourrer | envie plus grande guerre en
ytalie et vous faire hazarder la reste | de sorte | que ny contre infideles ny contre
luthere | ne pourriez faire chose bonne | ains vous trouverez en plus grosse
neccessite | vous faisant perdre le fruict de si glorieuse victoire | Et vous yci attachez
pour leurs particuliers prouffitz. Et en cas quilz ne puissent ainsi destourber
votredite allee | tacheront par indirect de vous faire choisir les personnes que soyent
a leurs propoz | tant pour entendre aux affaires du gouvernement du royaulme |
que pour lestat et offices de la maison de limperatrice | et reyne votre compagne
| a fin que riens ne se puist faire | que ne se passe par leurs mains ou de ceulx
qui deppendent deulx Et vous ay bien sire voulu faire ces premisses a fin que myeulx
puissez entendre ce que diray cy apres de mes doleances et que sachez que ceste
est lune des choses qui me touche austant au cueur que nulle autre. voyant voz
affaires en tel hazard et me trouvant si reboute | et quil me semble alyene de votre
grace | que ne treuve lieu | et opportunite pour vous dire et declairer pluseurs choses
que jentends journellement par lesquelles seriez plus saige en voz affaires et en
pourriez mieulx preveoir | et remedier les icoveniens Et ainsi me vous puis faire
le service que je desireroye | et que la qualite de mon office requierroit parquoy
nest de merveilles si vous estes bien souvent deceu | et trompe | en lexercice de
ce que concluez [16/21] ou pensez faire. Et pource sire en ce que a present labourez
sur les advis de ce que auriez affaire | pour votre allee | et pour laisser bon regime
| et gouvernement en ce royaulme | et choisir les personnes qui demeuront auprez
ladite imperatrice | vous y fauldroit proceder si saigement | que pour evicter les
passions et partialitez | ne communiquez les advis de lung a lautre | ains les tenez
secretz. Et quant auriez tous les advis que desirez que sans intervencion de nul

espagnol faictes veoir enquoy ilz saccoutdent | ou discourtent | Et avec personnes indifferentes | et non parciales | choisir la meilleur | et prendre sur ce votre resolucion. | Et apres en plain conseil | declairer ce que entendez estre fait et le publier | ayant esgard aux personnes que choisirez quilz ne soient tous dune partialite | mais quil y en ait de cheus pour faire le contrefoix | de lun a lautre | Et ainsi ne pourrez estre deceu ny trompe | .

Sire il vous pourra sembler | que ce que jay ainsi prevus soit dehors du propoz pour cequel vous avoye demand ceste audience | mais quant auriez bien entendu le surplus cognoistrez | que ce sert aux doleances que diray cy apres. Et pour vous tourner a la memoire les choses passes | et les causes de me douloir | bien savez sire que au temps que je pensoye me retirer de tout devoir et aller reposer en ma maison | il vous pleut de votre benigne grace | et sans nulz mes merites me appeller en cest office | quest en soy le plus grant estat | et le plus honnorable | que nul homme de ma qualite pourroit avoir. Et combien quil ait son contrepoix de grant travail quest neccessaire a suppourter pour y bien rendre son devoir a cause des grans royaulmes et pays qui sont submis a votre obeissance | et que bien pouroye preveoir que ce me seroit labeur sans cesse traveil sans repoz. et charge quasi insupourtable | . Neantmoins [16ᵛ/21ᵛ] trois choses le me firent accepter. desir dhonneur | Espoir de remuneracion | Et intencion de service a dieu | .

Sire | quant au premier poinct de lhonneur encoires qui semble que la dignite de loffice de soy mesmes le me viulle | . neantmoins me levant | et quictant lauctorite et preheminence dudite office et preferant en icelle | personnes inferieures qui devront estre subordonnees audite office | tant par loix et ordinnances que par coustume | Et faisant que ceulx ausquelx ce devroye mander et ordonner | ce quilz ont a faire | viennent eulx mesmes a me bailler ordre | de ce que se doit despecher. Et que eulx consultent | ce que je devroye consulter | et facent les repors | et proposicions de affaires que je devroye faire |. En retournant ce dessoubz dessus | et faisant les varletz maistres | Et ne me laissant user dudit office ainsi que tous autres chancelliers mes predecesseurs ont accoustume den user | cest me priver dhonneur | et me faire grande honte | Et donner a cognoistre a ung quelquun quil y ait cause en moy pour laquelle ne me reputez digne | de user de telle auctorite et preheminence | Laquelle se ainsi estoit | ne se devroit seullement me estre levee lauctorite de loffice | mains jen devroye este depourte du tout combien que je ne pense que mon service vous ait estre infructueulx | ny que en icelle lon ait trouve faulte reprehensible | car ores | que eussiez peu trouver personnes plus apparantes et myeulx parlantes |. et alaventure plus saiges pour vous servir audit estat Neantmoings suis certain | quil ny a homme en la monde qui vous eust servy plus loyalment et nellement sans corruption illicite ne avec plus grand amour affection et integrite que jay fait | et men remectz aux oeuvres que sont assez congnues et notoires non seullement a voz subiectz mais a voz ennemis Et encoires que le bon succez de vosdits affaires se doit [17/22] principalement attribuer a dieu | et non aux hommes neantmoings quant dieu choisit les ministres et instrumens pour exploicter ses oeuvres ne se peut nyer que lesdits ministres ne doignent estre participans de ladite grace que dieu fait Et pource meritoirement en devroye avoir ma part ayant este lung des principaulx ministres qui lont ayde dresser encheminer

Gattinara's 'Brussels Remonstrance'

| et construer | le plus souvent tous loppinion des autres lesquelx par ce me tenoient oppiniatre si se la succez en eust a rebours la culpe | et peyne tumboit principalement sur moy parquoy seroit aussi raison que je me excluz dicelle portion de lhonneur et merite quest deu au ministre dont dieu a voulu user en cestuy affaire par ma main | mais il est assez apparant que en diminuant lauctorite de mon office | et me quictant la faculte de pouvoir servir selon que le devoir de mon estat le requiert | non seullement seray foule cloz de lhonneur et merite des biens fuis passez. mais pourroye encherir au premier dangier de me vouloir charger de culpe et peyne | des autres maux que sans nulle faulte myenne pourroient succeder ce que vouldroye yolunties evicter Et non demeurer ainsi suspens que soubz couleur de loffice | je fusse charge sans cause | et deusse pointer la peyne des pechez dautruy. Et certes sire | si je congnoisseye que pour me desauctorizer et abaisser les preheminences de mon office | voz affaires sen puissont mieulx pourter | et que parce fussiez mieulx servy. non seullement me tiendroye pour bien content deu | mais que je me ostissiez le demeurant de tous les biens que jay en ce monde car en ce cas ce me seroit honneur | et non honte | et les pourroye tenir pour bien employez si je les perdoye pour votre service |. Mais sire considerant que jaie desauctorisacion | et pour me faire honte |. et pour monstrer que ayez suspicion et diffidence de moy | ce nest votre service | et ne peut proffiter a la bonne adresse de voz affaires | ains en vaillant beaucop [17ᵛ/22ᵛ] pis comme pourrez particularement estre informe | quant vous plaira | dy entendre | et en faire diligente inquisition Je ne men puis bien contenter |. car en travaillant jour et nuyt pour voz affaires | et ayant pour tel travail gaigner la goutte | qui macompagnera jusques a la mort nay merit davoir tel guerdon que lon me quicte lauctorite de mon office sans juste cause | Et certes ce mest chose fort dure | et ce mest ung morceaul que je ne puis bien anuller Et mesmes | que pour non avoir la personne auctorisee a laquelle lon ayt respect | et a laquelle lon puist revertir quant les ministres inferieurs font quelque extorcion | ou exaction illicite | ou commectent autre faulte reprehensible de ce sensuit que aucuns prendent hardiesse de despecher les choses a sa volunte | et sans consulte |. et sans signature myenne | En mesprisant | et contempnant lauctorite de loffice | de ce lon se usurpe lauctorite de donner | et prendre de voz biens largement | Et semble que ung chascun fait du maistre |. Lon fait prendre et processer les innocens donnant a entendre que ce sont griefz cas | que apres se tournent en fumee. | En suppourtant les coulpables | desquelx lon pourroit grandement proffiter | de ce viennent les corruptions concussions | et internes exactions de ce se font riches non seullement les secretaires mais leurs clercs | qui bien savent pourchasser les expedients sans que votre maieste le sache |. de ce se descouvirent les secretz au tres grant preiudice de voz affaires comme bien pourrez le tout savoir si vous plet |. Pour ces causes sire ne me puis bien contente | ny satisfaict a votre service ny a mon devoir dexercer ledit estat | ainsi desauctorize | puis que avec lauctorite deue | se pourroient remedier les abbus |. et auroient a cuy recourir | et declairer leurs plaintes pour vous en informer a la verite | et ne se vendroient les despeches [18/23] des saulfconduictz legittimacions pardons et autres choses de grace qui se font sans consulte | ny se donneroient presans pour les autres mercedes que votre maieste fait | pensans que ceulx qui les despechent soient ceulx qui les donnent cesseroient les corruptions que les loix

155

prohibent Et se remedieroit le discord et differend quest entre ceulx du conseil de la chambre | A cause duquel le secretaire sen fait absolut seigneur | a voz depens | et quant les deux sont discords | et que lung ne veult consentir au despeche ainsi quil vouldroit | Il despeche avec le seul signe de lautorite que satisfait a son desir | Et quant mon auctorite seroit garde | et que je y deusse mectre la main comme je faisoye paravant je ne souffriroye riens despecher par ung signe seul. sans savoir la raison de lautorite que nauroit voulu signer | et si la raison estoit juste rebouteroye le despeche | et sil nauroit raison juste de la resfuser | le constraindroye a signer | et ainsi la chose yroit seure | et craindroit lon plus de faillir | Et non ayant lauctorite dy pourveoir | lardiesse de mal faire croistra tousiours | et pourvoit lon cuyder que ne fust pour ma negligence | et men bailler la culpe | laquelle desire evicter de mon pouvoir | Et pource faire sire ayant entendu | que ceulx qui ne veullent avoir supperieur qui puist entendre congnoistre et reprendre leurs faultes desirans empescher que les choses ne soient reduictes a la raison | vous pourront alleguer en contredisant trois choses |. La premiere que les roy et reyne catholiques neurent jamais chancellier en espagne | Ains despechoient le tout par leurs secretaires | et que ainsi cest office ne soit neccessaire | La seconde que si votre maieste me bailloit auctorite telle que mon office le requiert que lon pourroit dire que je vous veulx gouverner que seroit mal prins en espagne et aileurs | La tierce [18^v/23^v] que non ayant des preheminences de mondit office aux affaires despagne |. et estant votre allee dytalie si prouchainne | que je devroye avoir patience comme je lay du passe |. mesmes estant assez charge daffaires destat que jay par les mains | sans me occuper en autres Il ne semble sire convenable que je responde a ces trois obiections pour remonstrer quelles sont impertinents | et fondes en malice pour pouvoir perseverer en leurs abbus. | A la premiere sire je confesse | que lesdits roy et reyne catholiques en usurent ainsi | Combien que soubz autre tiltre | eussent tousiours une personne auctorizee | que faisoit | tout ce que ung chancellier eust deu faire | auquel tous recouroient | et le craindoient et extimoient |. Et quant votre maieste | en eust voulsu ainsi user | Et que eussiez trouve estre pour le mieulx de voz affaires de non avoir nul chancellier et supprimer le nom de cest office | je neusse cause de me plaindre |. Mais sire de mavoir baille le tiltre de grant chancellier de tous voz royaumes | et pays |. sans me bailler lauctorite deue | ny me laisser user desdites preheminences de loffice Cela ne fut jaimes veu | en royaulme du monde. Et les loix despaigne en disposent le contraire selon lesquelles mon predecesseur en a use et moy aussi devant le partement de ce royalume | et apres le retour jusques au temps de ma maladie | de palence | et de valladolid Et daustant plus en pourroye user maintenant puis que par les courtes generales suis habilite a tous offices | et dignitez comme naturel du royaulme sans lavoir demande quest assez signe que je leur suis aggreable | en cest office | et ne suis mal extime ny hay | parquoy ny auroit contradiction de user de mon office selon leurs loix. | Et la seconde | [19/24] obiection | Je dis que votre maieste scet le contraire par mes oeuvres | car je nay jaimes tache | de vouloir avoir le renon de vous gouverner | ains tant du vivant le feu monseigneur de cherves | que depuis | son trespas | desi en wormes jusques a votre venue pardeca. vous ay persuade et baille les moyens de resoudre les choses de sorte que lon ne puist dire que fussiez gouverne de personne quelconque | Et si pour lauctorite de loffice | lon voulsist dire | que fussiez gouverne | Ce seroit

ung grant abbus tendant a la ruyne de tous voz affaires Et se pourroit dire | que
seroit une maladie generale de tous les roys et princes du monde | puis que tous
chancelliers des roys princes et potentatz ont charge ordinaire que tous les affaires
importans se despechent par leurs mains et ne sensuit pourtant que lesdits roys
et princes ne soient tousiours libres | de donner et disposer a leurs bons plesirs
| de tous offices | et benefices | et autres graces et mercedes encoires que les
despeches et conclusions se resoluent avec les chancelliers et se despechent par leurs
mains | comme se font tous autres affaires dimportance | Et en ce cas seroit plus
suppourtable | et moings preiudiciable a votre auctorite et renommee | que lon deust
dire que faictes les despeches de voz affaires | par advis et conseil de votre
chancellier, et tout le royaulme le prendroit assez mieulx que dire que au desceu
du chancellier et sans quil en sache a parler | faictes conclusions de ce que appertent
a sa charge | avec ung secretaire que commilz dient mande tout le royalume | et
vous induict a faire tout ce quil veult | Si que lon ne peut avoir | ny mercedes |
ny offices ny benefices si ce nest par sa main | et ainsi les tient tous vinclez et obligez
Et en scet bien faire son prouffit | Ayant lui seul la charge de tout ce que tous
autres secretaries souloient avoir Et excerceant par luy et par ses clercs cinq ou
six offices incompatibles contre la forme de ce quavez accourde [19ᵛ/24ᵛ] aux
courtes passees et quilz demandent maintenance estre observe et execute | Et non
lobservant et remediant ne pouvez excuser que pour estre espagne divisee en deux
partialitez et estant ung seul secretaire qui fait tout | lui estant de lune partialite
| ceulx de lautre seront tousiours mal content | et ne pourront bien dire de nulle
chose que se face par ses mains | et le tenant pour contraire ne luy oseront bailler
leurs memoriaulx | ny faire leurs poursuites envers votre maieste | non ayant
ministre duquel ilz se puissent confier | pour consulter | et negocier leurs affaires
dont procede | le mescontentement dune grande partie | du royaulme | Et selon
que jentends lon en parle si publicquement que cest chose assez plus scandaleuse
| que de confirmer lauctorite de mon office | Et ce nest votre service | ny convenable
a votre honneur | ny au myen | Et La tierce obiection je diz que dez le
commencement de mon office jusques au partir de la corogne | je usay de la
preheminence de mondit office | ainsi que mon predecesseur en avoit use Et ne
se despechoit office ny benefice | ny autre mercede que je ny fusse | Et ny avoit
lors secretaire qui est se faire despecher de votre maieste | les provisions | ny les
firmer si elles nestoient premiers signes de moy. Et me tournoy a toutes consultes
| tant de justice que de la chambre | Mais depuis le retour de votre maieste en
espagne | Et depuis ladite maladie que je prins en palence et que me dura si
congreement en valladolid avec la confirmacion | que vous pleut lors faire les choses
furent alterees | et mises en autre trayn. Et combien que depuis ma guerison vous
ayant supple de remede | vous pleut me respondre par escript de votre main | que
entendez que jen usasse comme par avant la maladie | neantmoings pource que
votre maieste ne tarda guieres apres a partie [20/15] de valladolit | pour aller a
burghes | et en chemin me punit la goutte | que me travailla jusques en pampelonne
sans cesse | Et apres me reprint en victoria | et dura jusques a ce que en bourgs
fut parle de mon allee en Rome |. les choses retournerent au mesme desordre de
sorte que jaimes ne se sont remises en bon ordre | Et pource que survivant votre
maladie | de la fievre quarte | pendant laquelle nestoit convenable vous bailler

alteracion dautres choses. Et aussi pour la retiree de votre armee questoit en provence Et la passee du roy de france en italie | avec la surprinse de la cite de millan | et siege de pavye | estoit plus temps de tenir les esperitz esveillez a pourveoir les neccessitez et sercher les remedes pour conduire les affaires de ladite guerre au fin desire que de penser en mes affaires particuliers | lesquelx ay tousiours postpose pour les votredits je me disposay davoir pour lors patience. Et quant votre maieste eust recouvre la faute | et successivement eust la nouvelle de la glorieuse victoire | avec la prison du roy de france | veant qui nestoit plus temps de soutenir audit desordre | et que a demeurer ainsi je recevroye plus de honte | Je vous suppliay avant votre allee a gardeloppes | que pour les alebrices de ladite victoire votre bon plesir fust me donner conge pour aller jusques en ma maison | donner ordre a mes affaires | et neccessitez et attendre illec votre allee en ytalie | et a intencion devicter ce pendant ceste honte | sans vous molester | et neantmoins non laisser de vous servir selon mon pouvoir | quant viendrez en ytalie. Depuis veant que a ma grant honte et confusion me ayant fait signer seul le despeche des deputez de vallence | baillant la commission au licenciado floris pour aller prendre informacion en cas vous eussiez sans men riens dire mande faire autre commission secrete [20^v/15^v] depar linquisiteur | mayeur | Et aussi veant que sans moy aviez faicte la provision des eglises vaccantes | et que a ceulx a qui aviez pourveu | leur aviez fait declairer par bouche dautre en grande diminucion de mon honneur | et contre ce que maviez accourde en bourges | me trouvay si courrousse que je fuz contrainct vous escripre | que si votre maieste ny vouldroit remedier autrement | et pourveoir que lauctorite de mon office me fust garde | et que jen puisse jouir selon les loix despaigne | que je vous suppliaye me vouloir eximer de ceste charge | et la bailler a cuy vous plairoit | Et venu en ceste cite vous ayant supplie deux fois davoir sur ce responce | Et cognoissant tant par voz postes | et par la delay que faisiez a me respondre | que aussi par ce que jen pouvoye savoir daucuns ausquelx parliez plus clerement que a moy | que cest instance ne vous plesoit pour les grans affaires questoient en trayn | nestoye resolu de parachever et que javoye lors par les mains tant des courtes que destat | en intencion toutesfoys de poursuir apres la responce et en avoir votre resolucion soit du remede | ou du conge |. Et estant en ce calme | est survienne nouvelle irritacion | quasi espece de souspecon et diffidence | du couste de votre maieste que de deux choses plus que ordinaires que lon avoit tousiours accoustume despecher sans consulte | questoient une lettre close pour le capitaine de gayette | que puist remplacer son office | en personne habille | et souffisante au contentement du viceroy | Et la confirmacion du privilege du conte de saincte severine | Lequel ayant privilege du feu roy catholique | expressement confirme | et de nouveaul concede par votre maieste | avant que jeusse cest office de pouvoir vincler son estat et en disposer entre deux ses neveurs. Et vous ayant depuis supplie en barcellone estant illec [21/16] le lieutenant de la sommaire | que la faculte quil avoit de disposer | entre lesdits deux neveurs | fut de disposer entre deux de sa maison | telz quil choisiroit | Et ce pour tenir ses neveurs plus en craincte | et quilz ne fussent si asseurez de la succession. votre maieste fit lors despecher instructions au viceroy don raymon de cordona | que a fin que le conte de saincte severine | unist bien au parlement du service droict concede | que lors se devoit demander quil lui deust octroyer ladite faculte | en votre nom | que au lieu des deux neveurs

elle fust simplement de deux de sa maison de curraphe a son choix. Et ainsi ledit
viceroy luy despecha ledit privilege en votre nom en la substance de cellui du feu
roy catholique Lequel quant messire sigismonde de loffred fut despeche par naples
| fut conclud en presence de votre maieste que la confirmacion dudit previlege se
feroit | et maintenant se a faicte ladite confirmacion en restraingnant la substance
du previllege principal plus a votre prouffit surquoy votre maieste monstrant
diffidence et suspicion comme dit est | non seullement resfusa de les signer ou firmer
estant signees de moy | et de messire sigismonde Ains interroga le secretaire comme
telles choses se despechent sans consulte. donnant a entendre que votre maieste
veult que telles choses se consultent que ne peut estre sans sinistre informacion
ou maulvaise presumption et suspicion que en telles choses ne eusse fait mon devoir
ou quil y eust faulte en moy | Et telz preuves oultre la honte que lon me fait |
sont pour plus restraindre lauctorite de loffice et mectre les choses en estat de non
james despecher et destruyre les poursuivans | comme a este fait des memoriaulx
de grace de la coronne darragon que se soulouent tousiours consulter par le chef
| Et vous a pleu les remectre a la consulte du conseil darragon dont votre maieste
en a plus dommage que prouffit | et les poursuyvans [21ᵛ/16ᵛ] en sont se travailliez
que silz obtiennent quelque merced ilz lont despendu avant quilz le puissent
obtenir | et de ce quilz en ont pensent que cellui qui fait la relacion de la consulte
en soit cause | et icellui gaigne honneur et le grey | et quelque fois en ont des presens
quest assez maulvaise introduction | Et la honte en est a moy lostant de ce la
preeminence de loffice |. Et de dire que je doye avoir pacience | jusques a votre
allee en ytalie | ce me seroit honte doublee | et seroit erreur pire que le present
Car je congnois bien la nature des ytaliens qui se reglent aussi bien que ceulx
despardeca | selon lauctorite et faveur que les officiers ont du maistre | Et ny a
office que si les gens ne congnoissent que la maistre le tiengne en la deue auctorite
| et le favorize | qui scent estre bein obey. ny puist bien servyr | Et pource que
comme lon dit a lenfourner lon fait les pains courvus est mestier que avant que
entrer en ytalie | lon sache que loffice soit auctorize et repute | Et que lauctorite
| et preheminence dicellui se doit observer | autrement jaimeroye mieulx dy aller
sans office |. et comme personne privee | que dy entrer ainsi avec desreputacion.
Laquelle se consulteroit pour la desauctorisation precedent | Et quant ores votre
maieste pour reparer lauctorite et preheminence de mon office. et mectre les choses
en trayn. declaireroit que par une provision | quelle entend que aux affaires
despaigne je puisse user de loffice de chancellier conforme aux loix despaigne nest
pourtant dit que les choses importantes a votre estat doyent pource demeurer en
arriere Car je ne suis accoustume les laisser pour affaires de moindre estouffe |
desquelx me souffira que les suppotz entendent que jaye lauctorite de men mesler
| et entretenir quant me plaira |. Car ilz yront plus retenuz aux affaires et ne courront
ainsi a bride lache | craingnants reprehencion [22/17] et congnois bien sire que
les affaires que jay maintenant par les mains | sont assez grans pour mepriser de
travailler en autres | mais sans conserver mon honneur | Et lauctorite de loffice
| je ne vous pourvoye ny sauroye bien servir | ny aux ungs ny aux autres mestres
non ayant ayde quelconque pour me soulaiger delaquelle ay grant mestier en ceste
ma viellesse |. Et a cest effect vous auroye supplie | de mectre en votre conseil
messire jehan bartholome mon cousin qui est desia informer de tous les affaires

secretz | Et estant present a conclure et debaptre les affaires | et estant ordinaire en ma maison que je leusse peu avoir a toutes heures. Il me eust peu myeulx ayder que nul autre a dresser les suyvantes des despeches | sans men travailler tant. Ce ne demandoye pour autre respect quelconque | synon pour votre service | Et ne vous a pleu ladmectre dont ne scay la cause | puis questes content comme mavez et que je luy communique tous les affaires destat Et quil mayde | de quoy me fusse voluntiers contente si par imaginacion il eust peu entendre ce quil auroit a faire pour mayder | sans prendre double travail de linstruire | et apres le corriger | Et pour ces causes sire ay este meu a vous reiterer mes querelles. Et vous declairer que si votre maieste ny mectoit autre remede jestoye constrainct me faire quicter ledit office | pour les causes ja[y] declairees | et que plus amplement declaireroye en presence de votre conseil vous suppliant lors davoir audience | Et ce fut la derniere lettre que eustes de moy pour cest affaire. Et cest sire tout ce que touche au poinct de mon honneur. sans lequel ne vous puis bien servy. Et pource vous supplie | le confermer | et non le souffrir blasser ou dyminuer sans lavoir meriter |

Appendix IV

Gattinara's proposals for
the more effective operation of the Council of State
(HHSA (Belgien), DD 231, fols. 360–61ᵛ)

Pour bien satisfaire a ce que lempereur a ordonne | et mesmes pour pouvoir mieulx entendre et vacquer | a la bonne adresse et conduicte des affaires destat de sa maieste durant lempeschement de sa maladie | Et pour adviser quelque bon ordre en ses finances | en ses gens darmes | et en tous offices et estatz de sa maison | sa maieste a ordonne | et reparty les charges pour evicter confusion et non dylayer les affaires ainsi que sensuit |

Premiers | que monsieur le Marquis de zenette le conte de nassau chef de la maison | le grant chancellier Monsieur le grant maistre | le seigneur de lachaulx | et Messire Jehan Lalemand avec les advis | et informacions quilz vouldront prendre dautres personnes entendues et experimentees prendent le soing | et charge de pourjecter lordre que leur semblera se devoir tenir a dresser | et mectre en bon trayn lestat de la maison | et les offices et estatz dicelle | reduisant tous les livres de la maison. tant de la coronne de Castille que de la coronne darragon | Et de la maison de bourgongne | en ung seul livre | de sorte quilz soient tous paiez par une main Et qui ny ait dyversite de salaires Et que en ce ilz entendent a resequer et restraindre tout ce que serait superflux | et que bonnement et sans esclandre se pourra emender | comme fourriers pourtiers et autres offices de la maison. Et en cas que tous les dessus nommez ny puissent ainsi continuer que du moins les deux deulx ny faillent a entendre et poursuyre ledit pourject pour apres par ensemble le revoir et resouldre tous ensemble soubz le bon plesir de sa maieste. [360ᵛ]

Pour ladresse et conduicte des finances ledit seigneur marquis Et avec luy Don Juan manuel don garcia de padilla don francisco de mendoca Et le secretaire covos appelle avec eulx les personnes experimentees en finances quilz vouldront choisir doivent diligemment senservir a lestat enquoy sont les finances presentement | les debtes que y sont et mesmes celles qui pourtent changes et interetz | Et diviser la forme que lon sen pourra faire quinte sans se laisser manger la layne sur le doz. Se informer et ne que demeurera de cler | les rentes ordinaires | et extraordinaires. Et diviser les moyens comment pourront reduire les frais ordinaires | et quilz ne excedent le cler des rentes ordinaires | Et que les rentes extraordinaires demeurent pour forme aux frais extraordinaires des guerres et autres choses possibles

Deveoir de se informer a tous les moyens possibles pour diminuer les frais tant restant des salaires superflux | limitant daucuns offices de la contadure et des finances et abreviant des comptes et ensembler toutes autres choses que peullent servir au bon ordre desdites finances Et le tout rediger par escript par eulx ou par les deux qui myeulx y pourront entendre pour apres par ensemble veoir de tout comme dessus est dit

Pour ordonner les gens darmes tant des gardes que de accoustamients capitaines coutumes et forteresses et toutes autres choses appertenans a la guerre ledit sieur marquis ayant este capitaine general des pays de pardela bien experimente a la guerre et ayant congneu la facon de la gensdarmerie tant despaigne [361] que de france | flanders | et allemagne aura avec luy le commendador mayor de castille | et cesar farramosce et le secretaire suaçola quest le conseil de guerre Et autres expers en guerre que lui plaira choisir pour assister en cest office et mesmes ceulx de conseil de la guerre quant lon lui semblera. Lesquelz pourront adviser par ensemble Et rediger parescript tous les moyens que lui peuelleront euxmesmes [?] pourbien ordonner ladite gensdarmerie tant du nombre des capitaines et de la forme quilz devront servir et du nombre de gensdarmes | que ung chacun des compagnies devroit avoir | Et des chevaulx et accoustremens que chacun dudit darmes aura et des saleres que lon leur ordonnera Et des consignacions et envies de leurs payements pour les asseurer de sorte qui ny ait faulte. Et de la forme | et temps pour revoir leurs moustres | Et aussi resequer les accoustamients | et coutumes inutilles | et pourveoir que ceulx que lon retiendra facent leurs moustres comme les gens darmes | Et ordonner les frais ordinaires de lartillerie |. faire quelle soit tenue en ordre | et en lieu propre | faire desmolir les chasteaulx inutilles. et les bailler pour maisons playnes pour evicter les frais de la guarde | Et toutes autres choses que leur sembleront convenables a cest effect | Et le tout rediger par ensemble en la maniere dessusdite

Pour ordonner les choses du conseil de justice de la chambre des indes darragon et des autres officiers de justice et aussi pour resequer le nombre superflux des conseillers secretaires alcaydes arqcosez [arqueros?] [361ᵛ] pourteurs et autres officiers supernumeraires desdits conseaulx monsieur le chancelier fera solliciter que le licenciado polanco prende mectre au nect les ordonnances que furent suivies du temps de la feue reyne dona isabel et du roy catholique et de les recouvrer ensemble celles de la maison darragon Et que ledit chancellier prende le soing de veoir per ordonner ce que touchera aufait desdits conseaulx et offices de justice | ayant avec lui le docteur Caravajal | et aucuns des autres conseilleurs plus expers selon les matieres que se devront rediger et ordonner et rediger par ensemble comme dessus.

Pour les choses destat auxquelles doivent entrevenir tous ceulx qui sont du conseil destat | que sont ledit marquis chancellier don Jehan manuel grant maistre commendador mayor Lachaulx | et secretaire Lalemand | Et que pour le repartment des charges particulieres dessus desdites il nest possible desdits pouvoir tous les jours assembler | Et aussi que ledit chancellier a pluseurs autres occupacions | Souffire que le conseil destat se tient trois fois la sepmaine | du matin le mardy jeudy et samedy comme lon avoit a maistiere excepte si savenoit matiere impourtante que requist celerite ou que sa maiste voulsist ouyr la consulte des choses que auroient este advisees audit conseil destat ou quel y eust nouveaul court que faillut veoir les livres promptement que en quelconque ledit cas toutes autres choses delaissees quant plaira a sa maiste ou audit seigneur marquis que ledit conseil destat se assemble a quelcunque paire que sera mande | Et que en tous autres jours chacun prende aux autres charges repartes comme dessus est dit de sorte que quant ung chacun aura fait son poursuit le tout reviengne audit conseil destat pour voir tous ensemble | ce que aura este fait et advise reduire le tout en ung volume bien ordonne par ses rubriques dung chacun office par soy a fin que apres sa maiste bien informee puist au commencement de lan qui vient faire publier ce que aura este advise et par luy approuve | et concluir de ce que peut toucher au conseil des ordres et de la inquisicion lon en laissera a eulx la charge a chacun en son endroit

Fait a valladolid le 19 de Septembre lan xxiiii

Charles

Appendix V

A comparative analysis of the movements of the imperial court and the imperial chancellery 1518–1530

It would be useful to determine more definitely the times of Gattinara's absences from the imperial presence. If one can entertain the assumption that the imperial chancellery pertaining to the empire proper, while outside the confines of the empire, remains with the person of the Grand Chancellor, then by comparing the dates and places of petitions granted by that section of the imperial chancellery receiving petitions, as presented in *Die Reichsregisterbücher Kaiser Karls V*, ed. Lothar Gross (Vienna, Leipzig, 1913/1930), pp. 1–82, with the movements of Charles and his court, as presented in *Collection des Voyages des Souverains des Pays-Bas*, II, 'Itineraire de Charles-Quint', ed. [L. P.] Gachard (Brussels, 1874), pp. 3–50 (see Vandenesse), based on acts in the Archives du Nord, then one might conceivably be able to plot the times at which Gattinara was absent from the emperor. Unfortunately, however, such an assumption is not always supported by the known facts, although in the majority of instances Gattinara's letters will reveal a date and place that corresponds with the time and location of the imperial chancellery. Beyond the obvious extended absences produced by the Calais negotiations from the end of August to early December 1521 and the Italian trip March to September 1527, there exist some other exceptions. Rather than being with the registers of the imperial chancellery at Pamplona until 27 January 1524 Gattinara accompanies the emperor, for he writes on 20 January to Clement VII from Vittoria (Bornate, 'Doc.', p. 437). Another case is that of the chancellery being on 29 April in Valladolid, having been situated up to 18 April at Burgos to which it returns by 2 May. Yet according to a letter of Contarini, Gattinara was at Burgos on 21 April (*Cal. SP Ven.*, III, no. 821), thus leaving him less than eight days to get to Valladolid, if he happened to move with the imperial chancellery. During all of this period Charles remained in the vicinity of Burgos-Lerma. More suggestive is the case of Charles' departure from Granada at the end of 1526. Both Gachard and Salinas agree that it occurred on 10 December; Salinas ('Cartas de Salinas', *43*, 507) goes on to say that the emperor was followed six days later by the chancellor, Lalemand(!), De Praet and himself. But Gattinara would appear to have allowed the imperial chancellery proper to remain longer in Granada, for according to its registers it did not depart until 24 December – eight days after the chancellor's removal.

Beyond these discrepancies that limit the utility of such a comparative analysis there are a few general observations pertaining to the relative movements of chancellery and court that need to be made before one turns to a comparison. First the chancellery lags behind the court; it departs from two to ten days later which likewise affects its arrival. A notable exception to this pattern is the arrival of both court and chancellery on the same day at Worms, 28 November 1520. Another feature particularly evident during Charles' presence in the Netherlands and England 1520–2 is that the chancellery tends to be more stable, situating itself in a city, while the emperor, occupied with hunting or negotiations, moves in a radius of a day's horseback ride from this locus. Finally a further inadequacy in our evidence: the imperial registers indicate lacunae for March 1524 and April 1525.

Allowing for these special peculiarities of the two institutions of court and chancellery, one discovers a general conformity in their locations. One of the periods of greatest conformity is ironically during Gattinara's Italian trip March to September 1527 when the court was relatively stable at Valladolid and Palencia. The following exceptions to this basic conformity are to be noted:

1. While the Court leaves Pamplona for Vittoria on 2 January 1524, the chancellery does not follow until 27 January.
2. While Charles is in the vicinity of Valladolid and Tordesillas, August to October 1524, the chancellery on 29 August to 7 September has moved to Pamplona, rejoining the court at Valladolid by 12 September.
3. While Charles during all of September 1525 is in the vicinity of Madrid-Segovia, the chancellery remains at Toledo.
4. While Charles is at Monzón 31 May–19 July 1528, the chancellery in mid-June 1528 is located at Valencia. Here it is known that Gattinara presided over the cortes at Valencia in May 1528 (Bornate, 'Vita', pp. 362–3) but this body had been prorogued to meet jointly with all the estates of the Crown of Aragon at Monzón on 1 June. (Ricardo García Cárcel, *Las Germanías de Valencia* (Barcelona, 1975), p. 218). Gattinara's return from Monzón, 8 June, to Valencia, 14–15 June, seems improbable for an ailing man.
5. Starting from Toledo on 18 February 1529 the imperial chancellery travels northwest to Valladolid where it remains from 5–15 March rejoining on 28 March at Saragossa the court, which left Toledo on 9 March and travelling northeast reached the capital of Aragon on 23 March.

Lacking supplementary material to corroborate Gattinara's presence with the imperial chancellery, we cannot be certain that the movements of the registers of the imperial chancellery identify the chancellor's own locations. The exceptions are sufficient to invalidate the imperial chancellery's location as a certain indicator of its chancellor's presence. Gattinara's multiple responsibilities help to explain these occasional incoherencies. Furthermore, the Germanic nature of the petitions coming to this section of the imperial chancellery would militate toward his reliance upon the vice-chancellor.

Bibliography

MANUSCRIPT SOURCES

Archives Générales du Royaume de Belgique – Brussels
  Papiers d'État et de l'Audience 1471 (4)
Archivio di Stato di Torino
  Lettere di Cardinale, *mazzo* 1
Archivio di Stato di Vercelli
  Gattinara, *mazzi* 3–10
Archivo de la Corona de Aragón – Barcelona
  Registros de Cancillería

Curiae	R 3896–7
Diversorum	R 3880–90
Itinerum	R 3911–13
Officialium	R 3877–9
Partium	R 3954–5
Privilegiorum	R 3931–8
Secretorum	R 3950
Sententiarum	R 3907
Varia	R 3973

Archivo General de Simancas
  Aragón: 267–8
  Estado: 17–20, 77, 635, 848–50, 1005 (Naples), 1454 (Milan), 1551–5
  Patronato Real: 1, 16, 28, 45, 56, 60, 62, 70
Biblioteca Nacional de Madrid
  Manuscritos: nos. 1010 fols. 31–150, 1778 fols. 172^v–90^v
  Estado: 50
Biblioteca Reale di Torino
  Miscellanea politica del secolo XVI, St. d'It. 75
Bibliothèque Municipale de Besançon
  Collection Chifflet, CLXXXVII, fols. 116–34
Haus-, Hof-und Staatsarchiv – Vienna
  Belgien (PA): 1, 2 (konv. 2), 13 (alt 14–15), 18 (alt 21), 21 (alt 24), 91–6
  Belgien (PC): 3, 4, 68, 72
  Belgien (DD): 231, fols. 360–61^v
Real Academia de la Historia – Madrid
  Colección Muñoz: 56

Bibliography

Colección Salazar (A): 18, 20, 22–3, 26, 28–34, 39–42, 45
Colección Salazar (G): 2, 23
Colección Salazar (K): 47

PRIMARY PRINTED SOURCES

Acta Tomiciana, eds. W. Ketrzyński and Z. Celichowski (Posnan, 1852–60, 1876–1915).

Agrippa of Nettesheim, *Opera*, 2 vols. (Lyons, n.d.).

Aktenstücke und Briefe zur Geschichte Kaiser Karl V, ed. Karl Lanz, Monumenta Habsburgica, II, (Vienna, 1853).

Albèri, Eugenio, ed., *Relazioni degli ambasciatori veneti al senato*, 1st Series, II (Florence, 1840).

Allen, P. S. *et al.*, eds., *Opus epistolarum Des. Erasmi Roterodami* (Oxford, 1906–58).

Die Amerbachkorrespondenz, ed. A. Hartmann (Basel, 1942–).

Anales de Aragón:
...*desde el año MDXVI [hasta el de MDXX]*. By Bartolomé Juan Leonardo y Argensola (Saragossa, 1630).
...*desde el año de MDXX...hasta el de MDXXV*. By Francisco Diego de Sayas Rabanera y Ortubia (Saragossa, 1666).
...*desde el año MDXXV...hasta el de MDXL*. By Diego José Dormer (Saragossa, 1697).

Apologia Altera Refutatoria Illius Quae est pacti Madriciae conventionis dissuasoria. Apologia Madriciae Conventionis inter Francorum Regem, & Carolem Imperatorem, dissuasoria [Rome, 1528].

Balan, Petrus, ed., *Monumenta reformationis Lutheranae 1521–25* (Ratisbon, 1884).

Baldus de Ubaldis, *Opus aureum iuris utriusque luminis domini Baldi de perusio super feudis* ([Lyons, Caspar Trechsel], 1545).

Bartel, Hilarius, ed., *Epitaphia epigrammata et eligiae aliquot illustrium virorum in funere Mercurini cardinalis, marchionis Gattinariae, caesaris Caroli Quinti augusti supremi cancellarii* (Antwerp, Joannes Grapheus, 1531).

Bauer, Wilhelm, ed., *Die Korrespondenz Ferdinands I*, Veröffentlichungen der Kommission für Neure Geschichte Österreichs, II (Vienna, 1912–38).

Beale, Robert, *Treatise of the office of a Councillor and Secretary to Her Majesty* (n.p., 1592).

Bermúdez de Pedraza, Francisco, *El secretario del rey* ([Madrid, 1620] 2nd edn Granada, 1637).

Boehmer, E. B., 'A. Valdesii Litterae XL', *Homenaje a Menéndez y Pelayo* (Madrid, 1875).

Bonilla [y San Martín, Adolfo] 'Clarorum Hispaniensium epistolae ineditae', *Revue Hispanique*, 7 (1901).

Bornate, Carlo, 'Historia vite et gestorum per dominum magnum cancellarium Mercurino Arborio di Gattinara, con note, aggiunte e documenti', *Miscellanea de Storia Italiana*, 48 (Turin, 1915), 233–568.

— ed., 'Mémoire du chancelier de Gattinara sur les droits de Charles-Quint au duché de Bourgogne', *Bulletin de la Commission Royale d'Histoire*, 67 (1907), 391–533.

Bibliography

Brandi, Karl, 'Aus den Kabinettsakten des Kaiser', Berichte und Studien zur Geschichte Karls V, XIX, *Nachrichten von der Akademie der Wissenschaften zu Göttingen*, Philologisch-Historische Klasse (1941).

'Nach Pavia. Pescara und die italienischen Staaten, Sommer und Herbst 1525', Berichte und Studien zur Geschichte Karls V, XVII, *Nachrichten von der Gesellschaft der Wissenschaften zu Göttingen*, Philologisch-Historische Klasse (1939).

Brown, Edward, *Fasciculus rerum expetendarum & fugiendarum* (London, 1690).

Calendar of Letters, Despatches, and State Papers relating to the Negotiations between England and Spain preserved in archives of Simancas and elsewhere, eds. G. A. Bergenroth, Pascual de Gayangos *et al.* (London, 1862–1954).

Calendar of State Papers and Manuscripts existing in the Archives and Collections of Venice, ed. Rawdon Brown (London, 1864–73).

Capella, Galeazzo, *Geleatii Capellae De rebus nuper in Italia gestis libri octo* (Antwerp, Martin de Keyser, 1533).

Castiglione, Baldassar, *Lettere inedite e rare*, ed. Guglielmo Gorni (Milan, Naples, 1969).

Chagny, André, ed., *Correspondance politique et administrative de Laurent de Gorrevod*, I (Mâcon, 1913).

Champollion-Figeac, Aumé, ed., *Captivité du Roi Francois Ier* (Paris, 1847).

Charles V, Holy Roman Emperor, *Caroli Ro[manorum] Regis Recessuri Adlocutio in Conventu Hispaniarum* [Rome, Jacobus Mazochius, 1520].

Pro divo Carolo eius nominis quinto Romanorum Imperatore Invictissimo, pio, felice, semper Augusto, Patrepatriae, in satisfactionem quidem sine talione eorum quae in illum scripta, ac pleraque etiam in vulgum aedita fuere, Apologetici libri duo nuper ex Hispanis allati cum alijs nonnullis, quorum catalogus ante cuiusque exordium reperies (Mainz, Joannes Schoeffer, 1527).

Chytraeus, David, *Historia Augustanae Confessionis* (Frankfurt am Main, 1578).

Ciaconius, Alphonsus, *Vitae et res gestae pontificum Romanorum et S.R.E. cardinalium ab initio nascentis Ecclesiae usque ad Clementem IX. P.O.M.* (Rome, 1677).

Claretta, Gaudenzio, ed., 'Notice pour servir à la vie de Mercurin de Gattinara Grand Chancelier de Charles-Quint d'après des documents originaux', *Mémoires et Documents Publiés par la Société Savoisienne d'Histoire et d'Archéologie*, 2nd Series, *12* (1898), 245–344.

Coelestinus, Georgius, *Historia comitiorum anno M.D. XXX Augustae celebratorum...*(Frankfurt, 1577).

Contelorius, Felix, *Pars altera elenchi S.R.E. cardinalium ab anno 1430 ad annum 1549 ex bibliotheca eminentissimi Francisci Cardinalis Barbarini...*(Rome, 1659).

Corpus Documental de Carlos V, ed. Manuel Fernández Alvarez, I (Salamanca, 1973).

Cortes de los antiguos reinos de León y de Castilla, La Real Academia de la Historia, IV (Madrid, 1882).

Crespí de Valldaura, Cristóbal, *Observationes illustratae decisionibus Sacri Supremi*

Bibliography

regii Aragonum consilii, Supremi consilii s. cruciatae, et Regiae Audientiae Valentinae (Lyons, 1677).

Danvila, Manuel, *Historia crítica y documentada de las comunidades de Castilla*, 5 vols., La Real Academia de la Historia (Madrid, 1897–9).

Deutsche Reichstagsakten unter Kaiser Karl V, Jüngere Reihe, eds. A. Wrede *et al.* (Gotha, 1893–   ).

Dormer, Diego José, *Anales de Aragón desde el año MDXXV del nacimiento de nuestro redemptor hasta el de MDXL* (Saragossa, 1697).

Duchesne, François, *Histoire des chanceliers et gardes des sceaux de France* (Paris, 1680).

Dumont Jean, ed., *Corps universel diplomatique du droit des gens*, IV (Amsterdam, The Hague, 1726–31/1739).

Encyclopédie Méthodique, Jurisprudence II (Paris, Liége, 1783).

Erasmus, *The Education of a Christian Prince*, ed. Lester K. Born (New York, 1936).

Förstemann, Karl Edward, ed., *Urkundenbuch zu der Geschichte des Reichstages zu Augsburg im Jahre 1530* (Osnabrück, 1966/1833).

Francis I, *Oratio ad proceres Germaniae in conventu Ratisponensi habita per legatum Regis Galliae* (n.p., 1527).

Freccia, Marino, *De subfuedis baronum, & investituris feudorum quibus accesserunt nonnulli Tractatus aurei* (Naples, Matthias Cancer, 1554).

Furio Ceriol, Frederic, *El concejo i consejeros del príncipe* (Antwerp, 1559).

Godefroy, Denis, *Praxis civilis ex antiquis et recentioribus authoribus* (Frankfurt am Main, 1591).

Goldast, Melchior, ed., *Collectio constitutionum imperialium* (Frankfurt am Main, 1613). *Politica imperialia* (Frankfurt am Main, 1614).

Gómara, Francesco López de, *Annals of Emperor Charles V*, ed. R. B. Merriman (Oxford, 1912).

Guicciardini, Francesco, *Storia d'Italia*, ed. Silvano Seidel Menchi (Turin, 1971).

Hane, P. F., *Historia sacrorum* (Leipzig, 1729).

Hasenclever, Adolf, 'Eine Kanzleiordnung Gattinaras vom Jahre 1524', *Archiv für Urkundenforschung*, 7 (1921), 47–52.

Hortleder, Friederich, *Der Römischen Keyser und Koniglichen Maisteten Auch dess Heiligen Romeschen Reichs* (Gotha, 1645).

Journal d'un bourgeois de Paris sous le règne de François premier (1515–36), ed. Ludovic Lalanne (Paris, 1854).

Journal de Jean Barrillon, Secrétaire du Chancelier Duprat, 1515–1521, ed. Pierre de Vaissière (Paris, 1897–9).

Kawerau, Gustav, ed., *Der Briefwechsel des Justus Jonas* (Hildesheim, 1964).

Las Casas, Bartolomé de, *Historia de las Indias*, eds. Agustín Millares Carlo and Lewis Hanke (Buenos Aires, 1951).

Le Glay, André, ed., *Correspondance de l'empereur Maximilien I et de Marguerite d'Autriche...1507–1519*, 2 vols. (Paris, 1839).

ed., *Négociations diplomatiques entre la France et l'Autriche durant les trente premières années du XVIe siècle*, 2 vols. (Paris, 1845).

Le Plat, J., ed., *Monumentorum ad historiam Concilii Tridentini...collectio*, II (Louvain, 1782).

Bibliography

Letters and Papers, Foreign and Domestic, on the Reign of Henry VIII, eds. J. S. Brewer, James Gairdner, and R. H. Browdie (London, 1862–1932).

Lettres du roy Louis XII et du cardinal Georges d'Amboise, ed. Jean Godefroy, 4 vols. (Brussels, 1712).

Lünig, Johannus Christianus, *Codex Germanicae diplomaticus* (Leipzig, 1732–3).

[Luther] D. *Martin Luthers Briefwechsel*, V (Weimar, 1934).

Marongiu, Antonio, *Lo stato moderno: Documenti e testimonianze del secolo XVI* (Rome, 1973).

Marsilius of Padua, *Opus insigne cui titulum fecit autor defensorem pacis...* (Basel, 1522).

Martyr, Peter (of Anghiera), *Opus epistolarum Petri Martyris Mediolanensis* (Alcalá, 1530).

Mexía, Pedro, 'Historia de Carlos Quinto', ed. J. Deloffre, *Revue Hispanique, 44* (1918).

[Munich] Münchner Universitätsbibliothek – Pamphlets, 4° Hist. 2973, Hist. 591/74.

Nijhoff, Wouter and Kronenberg, M. E., *Nederlandsche Bibliographie van 1500 tot 1540* (S-Gravenhage, 1923–).

Opera omnia Desiderii Erasmi Roterodami, I/3 and IV/2 (Amsterdam, Oxford, 1972 | 1977).

Ordonnances des rois de France, Règne de François I, Académie des sciences morales et politiques, IV (1524–6) (Paris, 1933).

Palau y Dulcet, Antonio, *Manuel del librero Hispanoamericano* (Oxford, Madrid, Barcelona, 1950).

Papon, Jean, *Instrument du premier notaire* (Lyon, Jean de Tournes, 1576).

Recueil d'Arrestz notables des courts souveraines de France (Paris, Jaques Mace, 1566).

Secrets du troisième et dernier notaire (Lyon, Jean de Tournes, 1583).

Konrad Peutingers Briefwechsel, ed. Erich König (Munich, 1923).

Piot, Charles, ed., 'Correspondance politique entre Charles Quint et le Portugal de 1521 à 1522: Gattinara et Barroso', *Bulletin de la Commission Royale d'Histoire*, 4th Series, 7 (1879).

Privilegios otorgados por el Emperador Carlos V en el Reino de Nápoles, ed. J. Ernesto Martínez Ferrando (Barcelona, 1943).

Promis, Vincenzo, 'Il testamento di Mercurino Arborio di Gattinara, gran cancelliere di Carlo V', *Miscellanea di Storia Italiana, 18* (Turin, 1879), 61–147.

Die Reichsregisterbücher Kaiser Karls V, ed. Lothar Gross (Vienna, Leipzig, 1913/1930).

Regesto della cancelleria aragonese di Napoli, ed. Jole Mazzoleni (Naples, 1951).

Registro general del sello, ed. María Asunción de Mendoza Lassalle (Valladolid, 1950).

Raynaldus, O, *Annales ecclesiastici* (Rome, 1646–).

Rodríguez Villa, A., ed., 'El emperador Carlos V y su Corte. Cartas de D. Martin de Salinas', *Boletín de la Real Academia de la Historia, 43* (1903), 5–240, *44* (1904), 5–36, 142–78, 197–246, 285–333, 366–414, 465–505.

Bibliography

Sandoval, Prudencio, *Historia de la vida y hechos del emperador Carlos V* (Barcelona, Sebastián de Cormellas, 1625).

Santa Cruz, Alonso de, *Crónica del Emperador Carlos V*, eds. D. Ricardo Beltrán y Rózpide and Antonio Blázquez y Delgado Aguilera, 5 vols., La Real Academia de la Historia (Madrid, 1920–5).

Sarpi, Fra Paolo, *Istoria del Concilio Tridentino*, ed. Giovani Gambarin, 3 vols. (Bari, 1935).

Sayas Rabanera y Ortubia, Don Francisco Diego de, *Anales de Aragón desde el año de MDXX del nacimiento de nuestro redemptor hasta el de MDXXV* (Saragossa, 1666).

Schard, Simon, *De jurisdictione, autoritate, et praeeminentia imperiali, ac potestate ecclesiastica* (Basel, Oporinus, 1566).

Scheurl, Christoph, *Briefbuch*, eds. Franz Freiherr von Soden and J. K. T. Knaake (Aalen, 1962).

Schottenloher, Karl, *Bibliographie zur deutschen Geschichte im Zeitalter der Glaubensspaltung*, 6 vols. (Leipzig, 1933–40).

Seckendorf, Veit Ludwig von, *Commentarius historicus et apologeticus de Lutheranismo* (Frankfurt, J. F. Gleditsch, 1692).

Sepúlveda, J. G., *De rebus gestis Caroli Quinti Imperatoris et Regis Hispaniae* (Madrid, 1780).

'Ad Carolum V. Imperatorem invictissimum ut facta cum omnibus Christianis pace bellum suscipiat in Turcas, Cohortatio', *Opera, cum edita, tum inedita*, IV (Madrid, 1780).

Serassi, P. A., ed., *Lettere del conte Baldassare Castiglione* (Padua, 1769/71).

Sigonius, Carolus, *Opera Omnia*, III (Milan, 1733).

Sleidanus, Joannes, *De statu religionis et reipublicae Carolo Quinto Caesare commentarii* (Kaufburen, 1785).

Solis, Antonio de, *Istoria della conquista del Messico* (Venice, 1715).

Spont, Alfred, *De cancellariae regum Franciae officiariis et emolumento 1440–1523* (Besançon, 1894).

Tasso, Torquato, *Il secretario et il primo volume delle lettere familiari* (Venice, Lucio Spineda, 1605).

Tractatus universi iuris, duce & auspice Gregorio XIII..., XVI (Venice, Franciscus Zilettus, 1584).

Ulzurrun, Miguel de, *Catholicum opus imperiale regiminis mundi* (Saragossa?, Geo. Coci?, 1525).

Valdés, Alfonso de, *Diálogo de las cosas ocurridas en Roma*, ed. José F. Montesinos (Madrid, 1969).

Diálogo de Mercurio y Caron, ed. José F. Montesinos (Madrid, 1971).

Vandenesse, Jean de, *Journal des voyages de Charles-Quint de 1514 à 1551*, II, *Collection des voyages des souverains des Pays-Bas*, ed. [L.P.] Gachard (Brussels, 1874).

Varchi, Benedetto, *Storia fiorentina* (Cologne, 1721).

Vives, Juan Luis, *Opera omnia*, V (Valencia, 1784).

Vocht, Henry de. *Literae virorum eruditorum ad Franciscum Craneveldium 1522–1528* (Louvain, 1928).

Bibliography

Walser, Fritz. 'Spanien und Karl V: Fünf spanische Denkschriften an den Kaiser', Berichte und Studien zur Geschichte Karls V, VI, *Nachrichten von der Gesellschaft der Wissenschaften zu Göttingen*, Philologisch-Historische Klasse (Berlin, 1932, Göttingen, 1935). Fasc. 2, pp. 120–81.

Walther, Andreas, 'Kanzleiordnungen Maximilians I, Karls V und Ferdinands I', *Archiv für Urkundenforschung*, 2 (1909).

Weiss, Charles, ed., *Papiers d'État du Cardinal de Granvelle*, I (Paris, 1841).

Wencker, Jacob, *Collectio Archivi et Cancellariae Jura, quibus accedunt. De Archicancellariis, Commentationes* (Strasburg, 1715).

Zedler, Johann Heinrich, *Grosses Vollständiges Universal–Lexicon* (Halle, Leipzig, 1735).

SECONDARY PRINTED SOURCES

Abellón, José Luis, *El erasmismo español: una historia de la otra España* (Madrid, 1976).

Arribas Arránz, Filemon, 'Los registros de cancillería de Castilla', *Boletín de la Real Academia de Historia*, *162* (1968), 171–200, *163* (1969), 143–62.

'La organización de la cancillería y el despacho de documentos durante los comunidades de Castilla', *Hispania: Revista Española de Historia*, *10* (1950), 61–84.

Ascarelli, Fernanda, *Le cinquecentine Romane. 'Censimento delle edizioni romane del XVI secolo possedute dalle biblioteche di Roma'* (Milan, 1972).

Avonto Luigi, *Mercurino Arborio di Gattinara e l'America*, Biblioteca della Società Storica Vercellese (Vercelli, 1981).

Bagnatori, Giuseppe, 'Cartas inéditas de Alfonso de Valdés sobre la Dieta de Augsburgo'. *Bulletin Hispanique*, *57* (1955), 353–74.

Barbero, Giovanni, 'A proposito del giudizio del Guicciardini su Gattinara, Gran Cancelliere di Carlo V', *Bollettino storico per la Provincia di Novara*, *61* (1970), 21–8.

'Idealismo e realismo nella politica del Gattinara, Gran Cancelliere di Carlo V', *Bollettino Storico per la Provincia di Novara*, *58* (1967), 3–18.

Bataillon, Marcel, 'Alonso de Valdés, auteur du "Diálogo de Mercurio y Caron"', *Homenaje ofrecido a Menéndez Pidal*, I (Madrid, 1925), 403–15.

'Charles-Quint, "Bon Pasteur" selon Cipriano de Huerga', *Bulletin Hispanique*, *50* (1948), 398–406.

'Le "Clerigo Casas" ci-devant Colon, réformateur de la colonisation', *Bulletin Hispanique*, *54* (1952), 276–369.

'Erasme et la chancellerie impériale'. *Bulletin Hispanique*, *26* (1924), 27–34.

Érasme et l'Espagne (Paris, 1937).

'Erasmo y España (Buenos Aires, 1966).

'Du nouveau sur J. L. Vives', *Bulletin Hispanique*, *32* (1930), 97–113.

'Plus oultre: la cour découvre les Indes', *Études sur Bartolomé de Las Cases* (Paris, 1965), pp. 95–115.

'Les sources espagnoles de "L'Opus epistolarum Erasmi"', *Bulletin Hispanique*, *31* (1929), 181–203.

Baumgarten, Hermann, *Geschichte Karls V* (Stuttgart, 1885–92).

Bibliography

Beaune, Henri et d'Arbaumont, *Universités de Franche-Comté* (*Gray, Dole, Besançon*) (Dijon, 1870).

Bierlaire, Franz, *La familia d'Erasme* (Paris, 1968).

Boehmer, Edward, *Spanish reformers of two centuries* (Biblioteca Wiffenia) [Strassburg, 1874, repr. New York].

Bornate, Carlo, 'L'apogeo della Casa di Absburgo e l'opera politica di un Gran Cancelliere di Carlo V', *Nuova Rivista Storica, 3* (1919), 396–439.

Ricerche intorno alla vita di Mercurino Gattinara, gran cancelliere di Carlo V (Novara, 1899).

Brandi, Karl, 'Eigenhändige Aufzeichnungen Karls V aus dem Jahre 1525. Der Kaiser und sein Kanzler', Berichte und Studien zur Geschichte Karls V, IX, *Nachrichten von der Gesellschaft der Wissenschaften zu Göttingen*, Philologisch – Historische Klasse (1933), pp. 219–60.

The Emperor Charles V, tr. C. V. Wedgwood (London, 1954).

Kaiser Karl V, II, *Quellen und Erörterungen* (Darmstadt, 1967).

'Nach Pavia. Pescara und die italienischen Staaten, Sommer und Herbst 1525'. Berichte und Studien zur Geschichte Karls V, XVII, *Nachrichten von der Gesellschaft der Wissenschaften zu Göttingen*, Philologisch-Historische Klasse (1939).

'Die politische Korrespondenz Karls V. Alte und neue Editionspläne. Die politische Testamente Karls V', Berichte und Studien zur Geschichte Karls V, *Nachrichten von der Gesellschaft der Wissenschaften zu Göttingen*, Philologisch-Historische Klasse (Berlin, 1930), pp. 250–93.

'Die Überlieferung des Akten Karls V im Haus-, Hof-und Staatsarchiv Wien', Berichte und Studien zur Geschichte Karls V, V, *Nachrichten von der Gesellschaft der Wissenschaften zu Göttingen*, Philologisch-Historische Klasse (Berlin, 1932), pp. 18–51.

Braudel, Fernand, *The Mediterranean and the Mediterranean world in the age of Philip II*, 2 vols. (New York, 1973).

Bruchet, Max, *Marguerite d'Autriche, Duchesse de Savoie* (Lille, 1927).

Buisson, Albert, *Le chancelier Antoine Du Prat* (Paris, 1935).

Buraggi, Carlo, 'Jacques Cujas, professeur à l'université de Turin', *Nouvelle Revue Historique de Droit Français et Étranger, 32* (1908), 578–83.

Caballero, Don Fermín, *Alonso y Juan de Valdés*, Conquénses ilustres, IV (Madrid, 1875).

Cantimori, Delio, 'L'influence du manifeste de Charles-Quint contre Clément VII (1526) et de quelques documents similaires de la littérature philoprotestante et anticuriale d'Italie', *Charles-Quint et son temps*, Colloques Internationaux du Centre National de la Recherche Scientifique (Paris, 1959).

Carande, Ramón, *Carlos V y sus Banqueros*, 3 vols. (Madrid, 1949–69).

'El Imperio de Carlos V. (Comentarios a P. Rassow)', *Boletín Bibliográfico del Instituto Alemán de Cultura de Madrid, 12* (1944), 1–13.

Castro, Américo, 'Antonio de Guevara. Un hombre y un estilo del siglo XVI', *Boletín del Instituto Caro y Cuervo* (Colombia), 1 (1945), 46–67.

Cereceda, F., S. J., 'El diálogo Menéndez Pidal-Brandi-Rassow, sobre la idea imperiale de Carlos V', *Razón y Fe, 134* (1946), 411–27.

Chabod, Federico, 'Carlo V nell'opera del Brandi', *Studi Germanici, 5* (1940).

Bibliography

'Milan o los Países Bajos? Las discusiones en España sobre la "alternativa" de 1544', *Carlos V* (*1500–1558*). *Homenaje de la Universidad de Granada* (Granada, 1955).

Storia di Milano nell'epoca di Carlo V (Turin, 1971).

'Venezia nella politica italiana ed europea del Cinquecento', *La civiltà veneziana del Rinascimento*, ed. Fondazione Cini (Florence, 1958).

Chagny, A. and Gisard, F., *Marguerite d'Autriche-Bourgogne. Fondatrice de léglise de Brou* (*1480–1530*) (Chambéry, 1929).

Cian, Vittorio, *Un illustre nunzio pontificio del Rinascimento, Baldassar Castiglione*, Studies and Texts, no. 156 (Città del Vaticano, 1951).

Cicogna, Emmanuele Antonio, *Delle inscrizioni veneziane*, VI, (Venice, 1824–53, repr. 1969).

Claretta, Gaudenzio, 'Notice pour servir à la vie de Mercurin de Gattinara, Grand Chancelier de Charles-Quint d'après des documents originaux', *Mémoires et Documents Publiés par la Société Savoisienne d'Histoire et d'Archéologie*, 2nd Series, *12* (1898), 245–344.

'Notizie per servire alla vita del Gran Cancelliere di Carlo V, Mercurino di Gattinara', *Memorie della Reale Accademia delle Scienze di Torino*, 2nd Series (Scienze morali, storiche e filologiche), *47* (1897), 67–147.

Clavería, Carlos, *Le Chevalier Délibéré de Olivier de la Marche y sus versiones españolas del siglo XVI*, (Saragossa, n.d.).

Clement-Simon, G., 'Jean de Selve, négotiateur du traité de Madrid', *Revue des Questions Historiques*, *73* (1903), 45–120.

Clerc, Edouard, *Histoire des États Généraux et des libertés publiques en Franche-Comté* (Besançon, 1876).

Coniglio, Giuseppe, *Il regno di Napoli al tempo di Carlo V* (Naples, 1951).

Contreras, Luis Núñez, *Un registro de cancillería de Carlos V. El MS 917 de la biblioteca nacional de Madrid* (Madrid, 1965).

Coroleu e Ynglada, José y Pella y Forgas, José, *Las Córtes Catalanas: Estudio jurídico y comparativo* (Barcelona, 1876).

Costes, René, 'Antonio de Guevara. Sa vie', *Bulletin Hispanique*, *25* (1923), 305–60, *26* (1924), 193–208.

'Pedro Mexia, chroniste de Charles Quint', *Bulletin Hispanique*, *22* (1920), 1–36, *23* (1921), 95–110.

Crespo, Lucio Andrés, 'Influencia de las cortes particulares del año 1528 sobre las instituciones aragonesas en esa epoca', *Jerónimo Zurita Cuadernos de Historia*, nos. 19–20 (1966–7), 157–82.

Cuesta, Luisa, 'Lo que no conocemos de Carlos V', *Revista de Archivos, Bibliotecas y Museos*, *68* (1960), 29–79.

Cuesta, Luisa y Florentinio Zamora Lucas, 'Los secretarios de Carlos V', *Revista de Archivos, Bibliotecas y Museos*, *64* (1958), 415–46.

Cuesta Gutierrez, Luisa, 'Tres Hijos de madrileños Tesoreros del Emperador Carlos V', *Madrid en el siglo XVI* (Madrid, 1962), pp. 69–99.

Dansaert, Georges, *Guillaume de Croy-Chièvres* (Paris, Courtrai, Brussels, 1942).

Danvila y Collado, Manuel, 'Mercurino de Gattinara, gran canciller de España', *Boletín de la Real Academia de la Historia*, *35* (1899).

Bibliography

Dawson, John P., *Oracles of the Law* (Ann Arbor, 1968).

De Caprariis, Vittorino, 'Il "Panegyricus" di Erasmo a Felippo di Borgogna', *Rivista Storica Italiana*, *65* (1953), 199–221.

Denina, Carlo, *Elogio storico di Mercurino di Gattinara Gran Cancelliere dell' imperadore Carlo V e cardinale di S. Chiesa*, Piemontesi Illustri, III (Turin, 1783).

Di Meglio, Giovannangelo, *Carlo V e Clemente VII. Dal carteggio diplomatico* (Milan, 1970).

Doucet, Roger, *Étude sur le gouvernement de François Ier* (Paris, 1921).

Les institutions de la France au XVIe siècle, 2 vols. (Paris, 1948).

Drion du Chapois, François, *Charles Quint et l'Europe* (Brussels, 1962).

Elias de Tejada, Francisco, *El pensamiento político del Franco Condado di Borgoña* (Seville, 1966).

Elton, G. R., *The Tudor revolution in Government* (Cambridge, 1962).

Engelhardt, Adolf, 'Eine missglückte Gesandtschaft unter Nürnbergs Führung', *Mitteilungen des Vereins für Geschichte des Stadt Nürnberg*, *32* (1934), 79–98.

Escudero, José Antonio, 'Orígenes de la administración central austro-alemana: las reformas de Maximiliano a finales del siglo XV', *Anuario de Historia del Derecho Español*, *36* (1966), 255–99.

Los secretarios de estado y del despacho 1474–1724, 4 vols. (Madrid, 1969).

Faunt, Nicholas, 'Discourse touching the Office of the Principal Secretary of Estate' (MS., April 1592), *English Historical Review*, *20* (1905), 499–508.

Febvre, Lucien, *Philippe II et la Franche-Comté* (Paris, 1912 [1970]).

Fellner, Thomas and Kretschmayr, Heinrich, *Die österreichische Zentralverwaltung*, I (Vienna, 1907).

Fernández Alvarez, Manuel, *La España del Emperador Carlos V, Historia de España*, ed. Ramón Menéndez Pidal, XVIII (Madrid, 1966).

Ferrara, O., *Gasparo Contarini et ses missions* (Paris, 1958).

Fichtner, Paula Sutter, 'The politics of honor: Renaissance chivalry and Habsburg dynasticism', *Bibliothèque d'Humanisme et Renaissance*, *29* (1967), 567–80.

Fisher, John L., 'Chancery and the emergence of standard written English in the fifteenth century', *Speculum*, *52* (1977), 870–99.

Fletcher, Jefferson B., 'Dante's School of the Eagle', *Romanic Review*, *22* (1931), 191–209.

Foronda y Aguilera, Manuel de, *Estancias y viajes del Emperador Carlos V* (Madrid, 1914).

Forsslund, Jacobus, *Dissertatio academica de Mercurino Gattinara, doctrinae per Lutherum repurgandae faventissimo* (Upsala, 1761).

Frappier, Jean, 'L'Humanisme de Jean Lemaire de Belge', *Bibliothèque d'Humanisme et Renaissance*, *25* (1963), 289–306.

Gachard, L. P., *La captivité de François Ier et la traité de Madrid* (Brussels, 1860).

ed., *Correspondance de Charles-Quint et d'Adrian VI* (Brussels, Gand, Leipzig, 1859).

Gaillard, A., *Inventaire des mémoriaux du grand conseil de Malines*, I (Brussels, 1900).

Galasso, Giuseppe, *Mezzogiorno medievale e moderno* (Turin, 1965).

Bibliography

'L'opera del Brandi e alcuni studi recenti su Carlo V', *Rivista Storica Italiana*, *74* (1962), 93–119.

Gauthier, Jules, 'Du degré de confiance que méritent les généalogies historiques', *Société d'Émulation de Doubs*, 7 (1902), 186–201.

Geldner, Ferdinand, *Die Staatsauffassung und Fürstenlehre des Erasmus von Rotterdam*, Historische Studien (Berlin, 1930).

Giannone, Pietro, *Istoria civile del regno di Napoli*, ed., Antonio Marongiu (Milan, 1970).

Istoria civile del regno di Napoli, III (The Hague, 1753).

Gilbert, Felix, 'Venetian diplomacy before Pavia: from reality to myth', *The diversity of history: essays in honor of Sir Herbert Butterfield*, eds. J. H. Elliott and H. G. Koenigsberger (Ithaca, 1970).

Giménez Fernández, Manuel, *Bartolomé de las Casas*, II (Seville, 1960).

'Política indiana del Canciller Jean Le Sauvage', *Anuario de Estudios Americanos*, *12* (1955), 131–218.

Girard, F., 'Un diplomate franc-comtois sous Marguerite d'Autriche', *Mémoires de la Société d'Émulation du Jura* (1871), 159–89.

Goni Gaztombide, José, 'El impresor Miguel de Eguía procesado por la Inquisición (c. 1495–1546)', *Hispania Sacra*, *1* (1948), 35–88.

Gossart, Ernest, *Espagnols et Flamands au XVIe siècle: Charles-Quint roi d'Espagne. Suivi d'une étude sur l'apprentissage politique de l'empereur* (Brussels, 1910).

Grand, Georges, 'Complément à mon étude sur Mercurin Arborio de Gattinara lue dans la séance du 28 avril 1958', *Académie des Sciences, Belles-Lettres et Arts de Besançon. Procès-Verbaux et Mémoires*, *175* (1962–3), 79–84.

Gross, Lothar, *Die Geschichte der deutschen Reichshofkanzlei von 1559 bis 1806* (Vienna, 1933).

Haffner, Franz, 'Die Konzilsfrage auf dem Reichstag zu Speyer 1526 im Spiegel des damaligen aussen-und innerpolitischen Situation', *Blätter für pfalzische Kirchengeschichte*, *37/8* (1970/1), 59–201.

Halkin, Léon E., and Dansaert, Georges, *Charles de Lannoy, viceroi de Naples* (Brussels, 1934).

Hanke, Lewis y Manuel Giménez Fernández, *Bartolomé de las Casas 1474–1566. Bibliografía crítica* (Santiago de Chile, 1954).

Hartung, Fritz, 'Der französisch-burgundische Einfluss auf die Entwicklung der deutschen Behördenverfassung', *Historische Zeitschrift*, *167* (1943), 3–12.

Hasenclever, Adolf, 'Kritische Bemerkungen zu Melanchthons "Oratio de congressu Bononiensi Caroli Imperatoris et Clementis Pontificis" [CR XII, 307–17]', *Zeitschrift für Kirchengeschichte*, 29 (1908), 154–73.

'Balthasar Merklin, Propst von Waltkirch, Reichsvizekanzler unter Kaiser Karl V', *Zeitschrift für die Geschichte des Oberrheins*, New Series, 34 (1919), 485–502, *35* (1920), 36–80.

Hauser, H., *Le traité de Madrid et la cession de la Bourgogne à Charles-Quint: étude sur le sentiment national bourgignon en 1525–1526* (Dijon, Paris, 1912).

Headley, John, M., 'The conflict between nobles and magistrates in Franche-Comté, 1508–1518', *Journal of Medieval and Renaissance Studies*, 9 (1979), 49–80.

Bibliography

'Gattinara, Erasmus and the imperial configurations of Humanism', *Archiv für Reformationsgeschichte, 71* (1980), 64–98.

'The Habsburg world empire and the revival of Ghibellinism', *Medieval and Renaissance Studies, 7*, ed. Siegfried Wenzel (Chapel Hill, 1978), pp. 93–127.

'Toward the historical recovery of Charles V's Grand Chancellor: problems, progress, prospects', *Atti del Convegno di Studi Storici su Mercurino Arborio di Gattinara nel 450° anniversario della morte*, Gattinara, 4–5 October 1980 (Vercelli, 1982).

Heidenheimer, Heinrich, *Petrus Martyr Anglerius und sein Opus Epistolarum* (Berlin, 1881).

Higham, Florence, M. G., 'A note on the pre-Tudor Secretary', *Essays in Medieval History presented to Thomas Frederick Tout*, eds. A. G. Little and F. M. Powicke (Freeport, N.Y., 1967), pp. 361–6.

Hintze, Otto, *Staat und Verfassung* (Göttingen, 1970).

Hook, Judith, *The Sack of Rome* (London, 1972).

Hornedo, Rafael Maria de, S.J., 'Carlos V y Erasmo', *Miscellanea Comillas, 30* (1957), 201–47.

Huart, M., *Le Cardinal Arborio de Gattinara Président du Parlement de Dole et chancellier de Charles-Quint* (Besançon, 1876).

Ibáñez de Ibero, Carlos, *Carlos V y su política mediterránea* (Madrid, 1962).

Jedin, Hubert, *A history of the Council of Trent*, I (London, 1957).

'Die Päpste und das Konzil in der Politik Karls V'. *Karl V: Der Kaiser und Seine Zeit*, Kölner Colloquium 26–29 Nov. 1958 (Köln, 1960), pp. 104–17.

Kalkoff, Paul, *Die Depeschen des Nuntius Aleander vom Wormser Reichstage 1521* (Halle a. s., 1897).

Keniston, Hayward, *Francisco de los Cobos: Secretary of the Emperor Charles V* (Pittsburgh, n.d.).

Kierstead, Raymond F., *Pomponne de Bellièvre. A study of king's men in the age of Henry IV*, Northwestern University Press (n.p., 1968).

Kipling, Gordon, 'John Skelton and Burgundian letters', *Ten Studies in Anglo-Dutch Relations*, ed. Jan Van Dorsten (Oxford, 1974), pp. 1–29.

Klewitz, Hans-Walter, 'Cancelleria. Ein Beitrag zur Geschichte des geistlichen Hofdienstes', *Deutsches Archiv für Geschichte des Mittelalters, 1* (1937), 44–79.

Koenigsberger, H. G., *Estates and revolutions: essays in early modern European history* (Ithaca, London, 1971).

Konetzke, Richard, 'Die Aussenpolitik König Ferdinands des Katholischen von Spanien', *Historische Zeitschrift, 175* (1953), 463–82.

Kooperberg, L. M. G., *Margaretha von Oostenrijk, Landvoogdes der Nederlanden, tot den vrede van Kamerijk* (Amsterdam, 1908).

Kraus, Andreas, 'Secretarius und Sekretariat', *Römische Quartalschrift, 55* (1960), 43–84.

'Die Sekretäre Pius' II – ein Beitrag zur Entwicklungsgeschichte des päpstlichen Staatssekretariat', *Römische Quartalschrift, 53* (1958), 25–80.

Labande, L. H., *Recueil de lettres de Charles-Quint, conservées dans les archives du palais de Monaco* (Paris, 1900, Monaco, 1910).

Laiglesia, F. de, *Estudios históricos 1515–55*, 3 vols. (Madrid, 1918).

Bibliography

Lalinde Abadía, Jesús, 'El Vicecanciller y la Presidencia del Consejo de Aragón', *Anuario de Historia del Derecho Español, 35* (1965), 175–248.

Lambert, Maurice, 'L'enseignement du droit en Franche-Comté', *Les Annales Franc-comtoises*, New Series, *3* (Besançon, 1891), 116–35.

Lapeyre, Henri, 'Economía y sociedad en los países de la corona de Aragón durante el siglo XVI', *VIII Congreso de Historia de la Corona de Aragón* (Valencia, 1973), pp. 9–34.

Laubach, Ernst, 'Wahlpropaganda im Wahlkampf um die deutsche Königswürde 1519', *Archiv für Kulturgeschichte, 53* (1971), 208–48.

Le Glay, André, 'Études biographiques sur Mercurino Arborio di Gattinara'. *Société Royale des Sciences, de l'Agriculture, et des Arts de Lille. Mémoires, 31* (1847), 183–260.

Lerner, Robert E., 'Medieval prophecy and religious dissent', *Past and Present*, no. 72 (Aug. 1976), 3–24.

Lhotsky, Alphons, *Das Zeitalter des Hauses Österreich: die ersten Jahre der Regierung Ferdinands I in Österreich (1520–1527)*, Österreichische Akademie der Wissenschaften, Veröffentlichungen der Kommission für Geschichte Osterreichs no. 4 (Vienna, 1971).

Longhurst, John E., *Alfonso de Valdés and the Sack of Rome: Dialogue of Lactancio and an Archdeacon* (Albuquerque, N.M., 1952).

Looz-Corswaren, Otto Graf von, *Kaiser und Reich unter Kaiser Karl V. Urkunden und Akten im Staatsarchiv Koblenz* (Koblenz, 1964).

López De Meneses, Amada, 'Carlos de Borbón-Montpensier, Duque de Borbón, Condestable de Francia, su viaje a España (1525–26)', *Hispania: Revista Española de Historia, 18* (1958), 573–650.

Ludolphy, Ingetrout, *Die Voraussetzungen der Religionspolitik Karls V* (Stuttgart, 1965).

Lynch, John, *Spain under the Habsburgs. Empire and Absolutism*, 1 (New York, 1964).

Maravall, J. A., *Carlos V y el pensamiento político del renacimiento* (Madrid, 1960).
'El pensamiento político de Fernando el Católico', *V Congreso de Historia de la Corona de Aragón* (Saragossa, 1956), pp. 9–24.

Martín Postigo, M. S., 'La cancillería castellana en la primera mitad del siglo XVI', *Hispania: Revista Española de Historia, 24* (1964), 348–67, 509–51.
La cancillería castellana de los reyes católicos (Valladolid, 1959).
'Registrador mayor y chanciller del sello mayor en la Cancillería Castellana de la segunda mitad del siglo XVI', *Homenaje al Excmo Sr Dr D. Emilio Alarcos García* (Valladolid, 1965–7).

Martínez Ferrando, J. Ernesto, 'Aportación de datos acerca del archivo real de Barcelona y de sus archiveros durante los reinados de Juan II y Fernando el Católico', *V Congreso de Historia de la Corona de Aragón* (Saragossa, 1961), pp. 77–109.

Mattingly, Garrett, 'Eustache Chapuys and Spanish diplomacy in England (1488–1536). A study in the development of resident embassies' (unpublished Harvard dissertation, February, 1935).

Bibliography

McNeil, David O., *Guillaume Budé and Humanism in the reign of Francis I*, Travaux d'Humanisme et Renaissance, CXLII (Geneva, 1975).

Mesnard, Pierre, 'L'expérience politique de Charles Quint et les enseignements d'Érasme', *Fêtes et Cérémonies au temps de Charles Quint*, Ier Congrès de l'Association Internationale des Historiens de la Renaissance (Paris, 1960), pp. 46–56.

Michaud, Hélène, *La grande chancellerie et les écritures royales au seizième siècle, 1515–89* (Paris, 1967).

Moglia, Girolamo, *Il borgo di Gattinara. Memorie storiche* (Vercelli, 1886).

Morel-Fatio, Alfred, *Historiographie de Charles-Quint* (Paris, 1913).

Morrison, Karl F., 'History malgrè lui: a neglected Bolognese account of Charles V's coronation in Aachen 1520', *Studia Gratiana XV. Post Scripta.* (Rome, 1972), pp. 675–98.

Müller, Gerhard, 'Franz Lambert von Avignon und die Reformation in Hessen', *Veröffentlichungen der historischen Kommission für Hessen und Waldeck* XXIV (Marburg, 1958).

Die römische Kurie und die Reformation 1523–1534. Kirche und Politik während des Pontifikates Clemens' VII (Gütersloh, 1969).

'Zur Vorgeschichte des Tridentinums. Karl V und das Konzil während des Pontifikates Clemens' VII', *Zeitschrift für Kirchengeschichte, 74* (1963), 83–108.

Müller, Johannes, 'Nürnbergs Botschaft nach Spanien zu Kaiser Karl V im Jahre 1519', *Historische Zeitschrift, 98* (1907), 303–28.

Müller-Blessing, Inge Brigitte, 'Johannes Dantiscus von Höfen. Ein Diplomat und Bischof zwischen Humanismus und Reformation (1485–1548)', *Sonderdruck aus Zeitschrift für Geschichte und Altertumskunde Ermlands* (Osnabrück, 1968).

Nada, Narciso, *Stato e società nel regno di Napoli dalla dominazione spagnuola all' unità d'Italia* (Turin, 1972).

Nitti, Francesco, *Leone X e la sua politica* (Florence, 1892).

Otway-Ruthven, Annette Jocelyn, *The King's Secretary and the Signet Office in the XV Century* (Cambridge, 1939).

Paquier, Jules, *Jérôme Aléandre. De sa naissance à la fin de son séjour à Brindes 1480–1529* (Paris, 1900).

Penna, Don Mario, 'Las ideas imperiales de Carlos V y de su Gran Canciller Gattinara', *Estudios Carolinos*, Quarto Centenario del Emperador Carlos V, Curso de Conferencias Oct.–Dec. 1958, Universidad de Barcelona (1959).

'Mercurino Arborio de Gattinara, Gran Canciller del Cesar', Congreso de Cooperación Intelectual (Madrid, 1958).

Perena, Vicente L., 'Miguel de Ulcurrun. El Emperador, organo y garantía del derecho de gentes positivo', *Revista Española de Derecho Internacional, 6* (1953), 313–23.

Pezzella, Sosio, 'Alfonso de Valdés e la politica religiosa di Carlo V', *Studi e Materiali di Storia delle Religioni, 36* (1965), 211–68.

Piaia, Gregorio, *Marsilio da Padova nella riforma e nella controriforma* (Padua, 1977).

Bibliography

Pirenne, Henri, *Histoire de Belgique*, II (Paris, 1922), III (Brussels, 1923).

Post, Gaines, *Studies in medieval legal thought* (Princeton, 1964).

Prezzolini, Giuseppe, 'Castiglione and Alfonso de Valdés', *Romanic Review 29* (1938), 26–36.

Prosperi, Adriano, *Tra Evangelismo e controriforma: G. M. Giberti (1495–1543)* (Rome, 1969).

Rassow, Peter, *Die Kaiser-Idee Karls V dargestellt an der Politik der Jahre 1528–1540* (Berlin, 1932).

Redondo, Augustin, *Antonio de Guevara (1480?–1545) et l'Espagne de son temps* (Geneva, 1976).

Reglá Campistol, Juan, 'La corona de Aragón dentro de la monarquía hispánica de los Habsburgo', *VIII Congreso de Historia de la Corona de Aragón*, III/2 (Valencia, 1973), pp. 129–64.

Introducció a la historia de la corona d'Aragó. Dels origens a la nova planta (Palma de Mallorca, 1969).

'Política de Carlos V en Cataluña', *Carlos V 1500–1558. Homenaje de la Universidad de Granada* (Granada, 1958), pp. 257–70.

Repgen, Konrad, *Die römische Kurie und der Westfälische Friede*, I, *Papst, Kaiser und Reich* (Tübingen, 1962).

Reuter, Fritz, ed., *Der Reichstag zu Worms von 1521: Reichspolitik und Luthersache* (Worms, 1971).

Roersch, Alphonse, *L'humanisme belge à l'époque de la Renaissance* (Louvain, 1933).

L'humanisme belge à l'époque de la Renaissance. Études et portraits (Brussels, 1910).

Rosenthal, Earl E., 'The invention of the columnar device of Emperor Charles V at the Court of Burgundy in Flanders in 1516', *Journal of the Warburg and Courtauld Institutes, 36* (1973), 198–230.

Roth, F. W. E., 'Die Mainzer Buchdruckerfamilie Schoeffer', *Beihefte zum Centralblatt für Bibliothekswesen, 9* (Leipzig, 1892), 3–11.

Rubinstein, Nicolai, 'Italian reactions to Terraferma expansion in the fifteenth century', *Renaissance Venice*, ed. J. R. Hale (London, 1973), pp. 197–217.

'Political rhetoric in the imperial chancery', *Medium Aevum, 14* (1945), 21–43.

Russell, Joycelyne G., 'The search for universal peace: the conference at Calais and Bruges in 1521', *Bulletin of the Institute of Historical Research, 44* (1971), 162–93.

Ryder, Alan Frederick Charles, *The Kingdom of Naples under Alfonso the Magnanimous* (Oxford, 1976).

Schäfer, Ernesto, *El Consejo real y supremo de las Indias* (Seville, 1935).

Schubert, Ernst, *König und Reich: Studien zur spätmittelalterlichen deutschen Verfassungsgeschichte* (Göttingen, 1979).

Schmid, Oskar, *Belgien. Gesamtinventar des Haus-, Hof- und Staatsarchivs* (Vienna, 1938).

Sevillano Colom, Francisco, 'Cancillerías de Fernando I de Antequera y de Alfonso V el Magnánimo', *Anuario de Historia del Derecho Español, 35* (1965), 169–216.

'La cancillería de Fernando el Católico', *V Congreso de Historia de la Corona de Aragón* (Saragossa, 1955), pp. 215–53.

Bibliography

Solano Costa, Fernando, 'Introducción a la historia de Aragón en el siglo XVI', *Libre Homenaje a Pardo de Santayana* (Saragossa, 1966).

Steglich, Wolfgang, 'Die Stellung der evangelischen Reichsstände und Reichsstädte zu Karl V zwischen Protestation und Konfession 1529/30', *Archiv für Reformationsgeschichte, 62* (1971), 161–92.

Strelka, Josef, *Der burgundische Renaissancehof Margarethes von Österreich und seine literarhistorische Bedeutung* (Vienna, 1957).

Terlinden, le Vicomte, 'La politique italienne de Charles Quint et le triomphe de Bologne', *Fêtes et cérémonies au temps de Charles Quint* (Paris, 1960), pp. 29–43.

Toro, José López de, 'Pedro Martir de Angleria, Cronista íntimo del emperador', *Hispania: Revista Española de Historia, 18* (1958), 469–504.

Tout, T. F., *Chapters in the administrative history of medieval England*, 6 vols. (London, 1930, repr. 1967).

Tracy, James D., *The politics of Erasmus. A pacifist intellectual and his political milieu* (Toronto, 1978).

Vander Linden, Herman, 'Articles soumis à Charles-Quint par son chancelier Gattinara concernant l'office de la chancellerie en 1528', *Bulletin de la Commission Royale d'Histoire, Académie Royale de Belgique, 100* (1936), 265–80.

'Le chancelier Gattinara et la politique méditerranéene de Charles-Quint', *Bulletin de la Classe des Lettres*, 5th Series, Académie Royale de Belgique, *22* (1936), 361–72.

'La politique méditerranéene de Charles-Quint', *Bulletin de la Classe des Lettres*, 5th Series, Académie Royale de Belgique, *14* (1928), 11–23.

'La souscription des actes de Charles-Quint expédiés dans les Pays Bas', *Bulletin de la Commission Royale d'histoire, 92* (1928), 165–72.

Van Durme, M., *El Cardinal Granvela 1517–1586. Imperio y revolución bajo Carlos V y Felipe II* (Barcelona, 1957).

'À propos du quatrième centenaire de la mort de Nicolas Perrenot de Granvelle', *Bibliothèque d'Humanisme et Renaissance, 13* (1951), 271–94.

Vilanova, Ramón de Vilanova de Rosselló, Conde de, *Capítulo del Toisón de Oro celebrado en Barcelona el año 1519*, I (Barcelona, 1930).

Vilar-Berrogain, Gabrielle, 'Trois documents pour l'étude de l'administration intérieure du royaume d'Aragon', *Bulletin Hispanique, 37* (1935), 309–28.

Vocht, Henry de, *John Dantiscus and his Netherlandish friends as revealed by their correspondence 1522–46*, Humanistica Lovaniensia, XVI (Louvain, 1961).

History of the Foundation and Rise of the Collegium Trilingue Lovaniense 1517–50 (Louvain, 1953).

Voltes Bou, Pedro, *Carlos V y Barcelona* (Barcelona, 1958).

Walser, Fritz, *Die spanischen Zentralbehörden und der Staatsrat Karls V. Grundlagen und Aufbau bis zum Tode Gattinaras*, revised, supplemented and edited by Rainer Wohlfeil, Abhandlungen der Akademie der Wissenschaften in Göttingen, Phil. Hist. Klasse, 3rd Series, no. 43 (Göttingen, 1959).

'Die Überlieferung der Akten der kastilisch-spanischen Zentralbehörden unter Karl V: Geschichte und allgemeine Grundzüge', *Berichte und Studien zur Geschichte Karls V*, VIII, *Nachrichten von der Gesellschaft der Wissenschaften zu Göttingen*, Philologisch-Historische Klasse (1933), pp. 94–138.

Bibliography

Walther, Andreas, *Die Anfänge Karls V* (Leipzig, 1911).
Die burgundischen Zentralbehörden unter Maximilian I und Karl V (Leipzig, 1909).
Wegg, Jervis, *Richard Pace* (London, 1932).
Wernham, R. B., *Before the Armada* (London, 1966).
Wiesflecker, Hermann, *Kaiser Maximilian I*, 1 (Vienna, 1971).

Index

Index

Index

Index

Index

Olivier, François, 15
Orange, *see* Philibert of Chalon, Prince of Orange
Order of the Golden Fleece, 55
Ordo consilii, 84–5
Orihuela, Sánchez de, 8on
Osnabrück, Jordanes of, 112n

Padilla, García de, 161
Parlement at Dole, 5, 7–10, 20, 35, 134
Pastor, Ludwig von, 110n
Paul IV, Pope, 112n
Pavia, imperial victory, 55, 82, 85–6, 91, 93, 114, 158
Pedro III, King of Aragon, 149
Perez, Antonio, 130
Perez, Juan, 96n, 106, 110
Péronne, treaty of, 103
Perrenin, Antoine, 121–2, 125, 128, 142n
Perrenot, Nicholas de, Lord of Granvelle, 25, 81, 83–4, 112n, 120, 123, 127, 128n, 134–8, 142
Per Venerabilem, 103–4
Pescara, Davalos d'Aquino, Hernando, Marquis of, 97–8
Peter of Belluga, 10
Pharamond, 103
Philibert of Chalon, Prince of Orange, 136
Philip II of Spain, 130
Philip IV of Spain, 130n
Philip V of Spain, 60
Philip Augustus, King of France, 142
Philip, Landgrave of Hesse, 136
Philip the Good (of Burgundy), 21n
Pistophilus, Nicetes, 112
Plutarch, 102
Polanco, *licenciado,* 162
Poligny, Dean of, 126
Post-Glossators, 12
praefectus praetorio, 8
Prantner, Wolfgang, 62, 70–1
printing, 87–8, 91, 93n, 96–7, 104–13, 134
Priuli, Lorenzo, 46
Protestants at Piacenza, 71, 136
protonotary, 21, 25, 27–8, 62, 75, 150
Provence, Dolza of, 103n

Quentell, Peter, 106

Ranzo, Hieronymus, 32, 69, 71
Raphael, Juan, 78
Raymond, Count of Barcelona, 103

referendarius, 17
reggenti (Naples), 16, 74–5
Regulus, 102
Reich, 30, 66, 136
Reichskammergericht, 16, 69
Reichsregiment, 69
Rhenanus, Beatus, 99, 105n
Robertet, Florimond, 15, 6on
Roes, Alexander von, 112n
Rolin, Nicolas, chancellor, 21n
Roman Empire, 8, 11–12
Roman law, 8, 11–12
Rome, 96n; sack of 6, 7, 110–13, 118, 122–3
Rothfels, Hans, 18n

Sadoleto, Jacopo, 14
Saint-Pol, Count of, 9n
Salamanca, Gabriel, Count of Ortenburg, 129
Salazar Colección (RAH), 61n
Salinas, Martin de, 38, 40, 45, 48n, 58, 93, 108, 115, 118, 121, 124, 130, 164
Salisbury, John of, 102
Sallust, 5
Salutati, Coluccio, 86
Sampson, Richard, 46
Sancho IV of Castile, 23
Sandoval, Prudencio, 104–5
Santa Cruz, Alonso de, 132
Santiago, Archbishop of, *see* Tavera, Juan Pardo de
Sarpi, Paolo, 100
Scepperus, Cornelius (de Schepper), 71–2, 81–2, 93n, 139
Scheurl, Christopher, 79–80
Schoeffer, Joannes, 105, 107–8, 110
Schomberg, Nicholas von, Archbishop of Capua, 46, 90
Schweis, Alexander, 62–3, 70–1, 94, 136
seals, 29–30, 34, 43, 54, 59, 61, 67, 72, 75–6, 82
secretaries, 16, 36, 46–55, 58–60, 67, 141–3, 154–60; Aragonese, 23–5, 27–9, 141, 148–50; Burgundian, 27n, 36, 85; Castilian, 22–4, 141; French, 6on; Holy Roman Empire, 29; imperial chancellery, 32–3; *secrétaire de l'empereur,* 83; secretary of state, 15–16, 17–19, 38, 44–5, 121, 123, 135, 141–3
Servius (Marius Servius Honoratus), 104, 105n

187

Index